Garfield
eats his heart out

BY JIM DAVIS

Ballantine Books • **New York**

A Ballantine Book
Published by The Random House Publishing Group
Copyright © 1983, 2004 by PAWS, Inc. All Rights Reserved.

Published in the United States by Ballantine Books, an imprint of The Random House Publishing Group, a division of Random House, Inc., New York, and simultaneously in Canada by Random House of Canada Limited, Toronto. Originally published in slightly different form by The Random House Publishing Group, a division of Random House, Inc., in 1983.

Ballantine and colophon are registered trademarks of Random House, Inc.

"GARFIELD" and the GARFIELD characters are registered and unregistered trademarks of PAWS, Inc.

www.ballantinebooks.com

Library of Congress Control Number: 2003095696

ISBN 0-345-46459-1

Manufactured in China

First Colorized Edition: January 2004

9 8 7 6 5 4

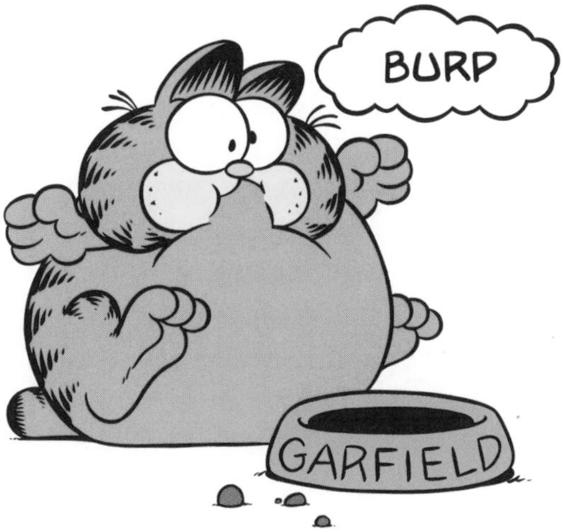
BURP
GARFIELD

GARFIELD DIET TIPS

1. Never go back for seconds—get it all the first time.
2. Set your scale back five pounds.
3. Never accept a candygram.
4. Don't date Sara Lee.
5. Vegetables are a must on a diet. I suggest carrot cake, zucchini bread, and pumpkin pie.
6. Never start a diet cold turkey (maybe cold roast beef, cold lasagna . . .).
7. Try to cut back. Leave the cherry off your ice cream sundae.
8. Hang around people fatter than you.

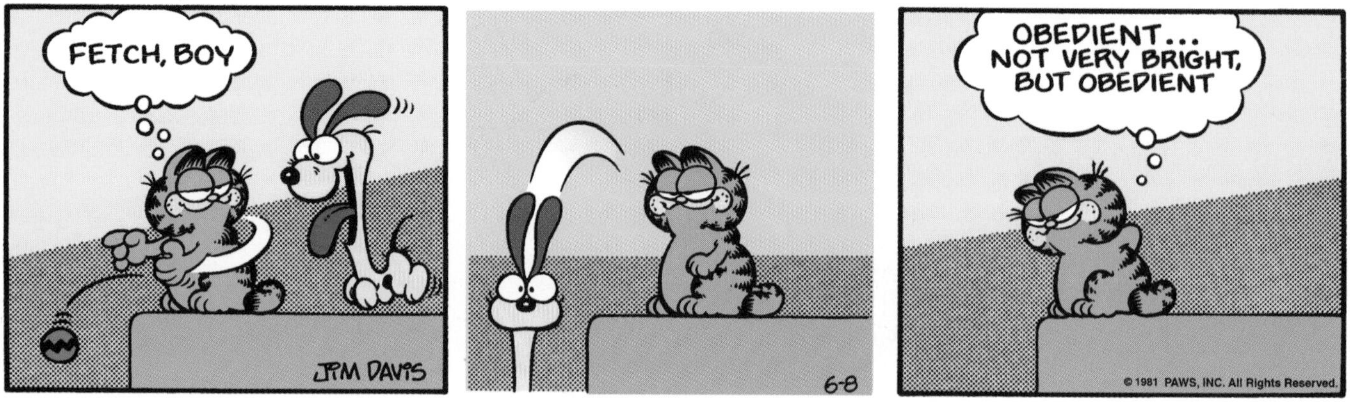
FETCH, BOY
JIM DAVIS
6-8
OBEDIENT... NOT VERY BRIGHT, BUT OBEDIENT
© 1981 PAWS, INC. All Rights Reserved.

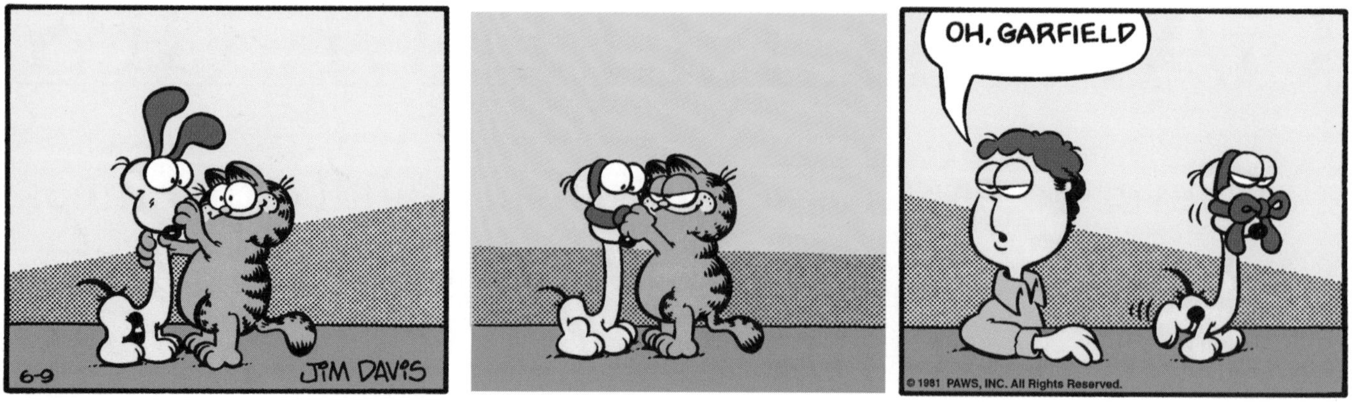
6-9
JIM DAVIS
OH, GARFIELD
© 1981 PAWS, INC. All Rights Reserved.

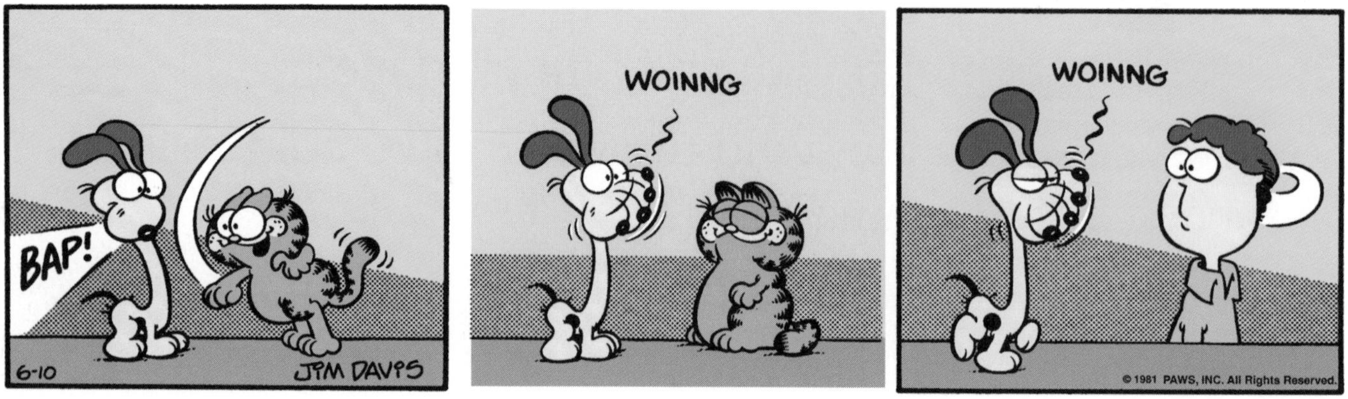
BAP!
6-10
JIM DAVIS
WOINNG
WOINNG
© 1981 PAWS, INC. All Rights Reserved.

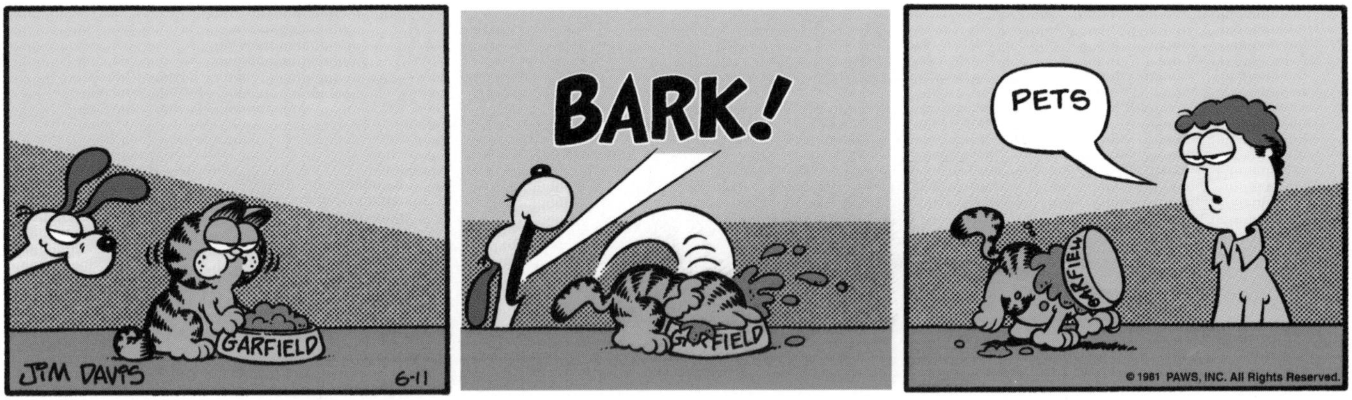
JIM DAVIS
GARFIELD
6-11
BARK!
GARFIELD
PETS
GARFIELD
© 1981 PAWS, INC. All Rights Reserved.

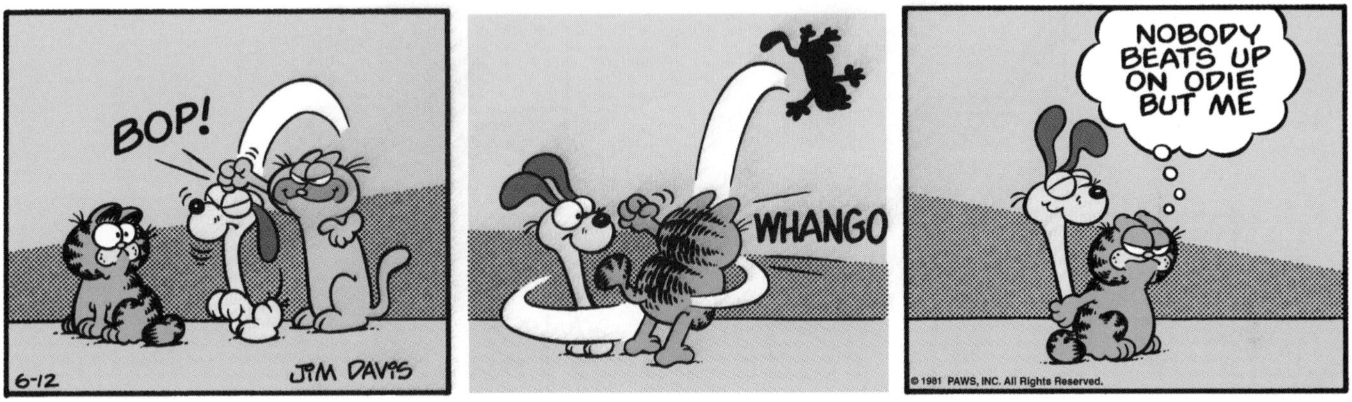
BOP!
6-12
JIM DAVIS
WHANGO
NOBODY BEATS UP ON ODIE BUT ME
© 1981 PAWS, INC. All Rights Reserved.

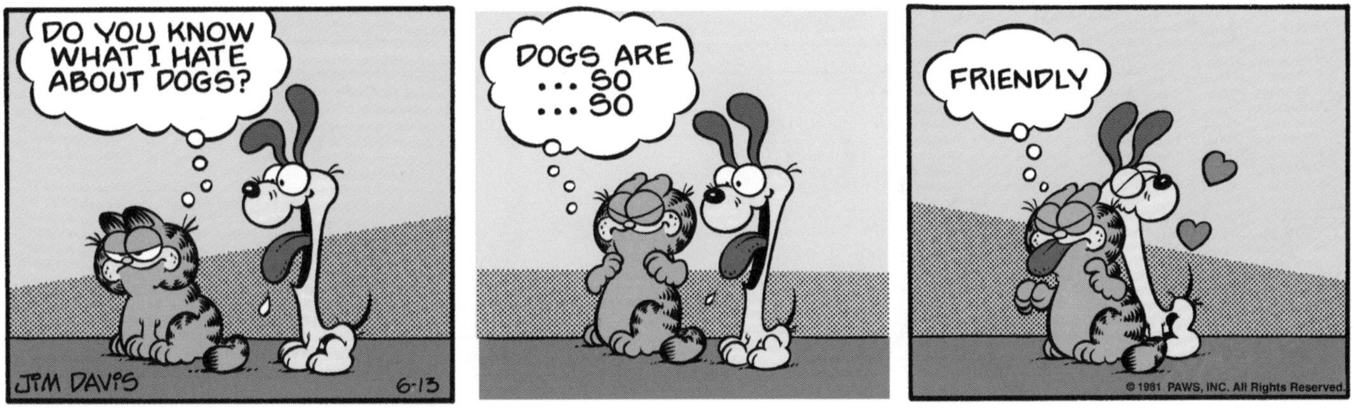
DO YOU KNOW WHAT I HATE ABOUT DOGS?
JIM DAVIS
6-13
DOGS ARE ... SO ... SO
FRIENDLY
© 1981 PAWS, INC. All Rights Reserved.

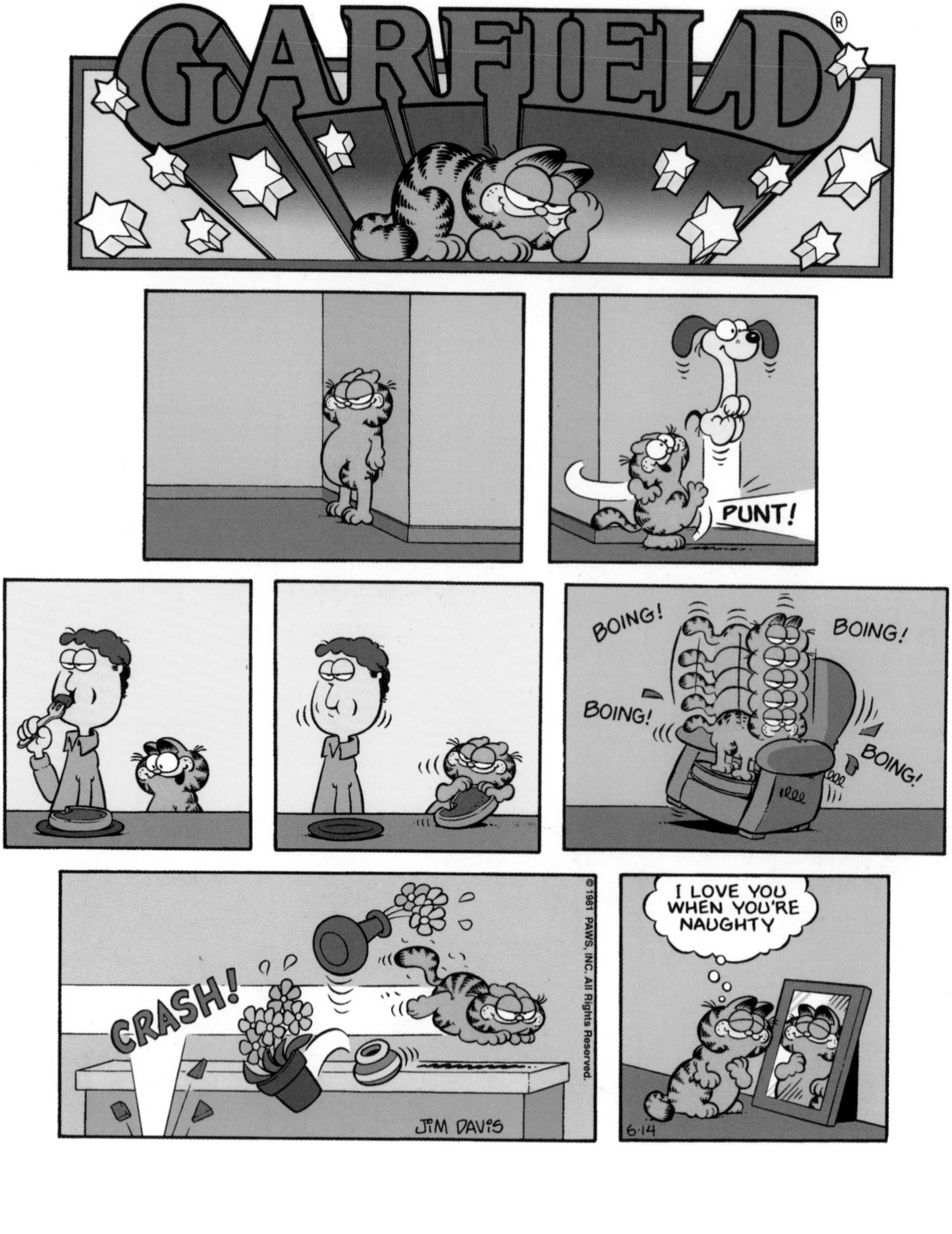
GARFIELD®
PUNT!
BOING!
BOING!
BOING!
BOING!
CRASH!
© 1981 PAWS, INC. All Rights Reserved.
JIM DAVIS
I LOVE YOU WHEN YOU'RE NAUGHTY
6·14

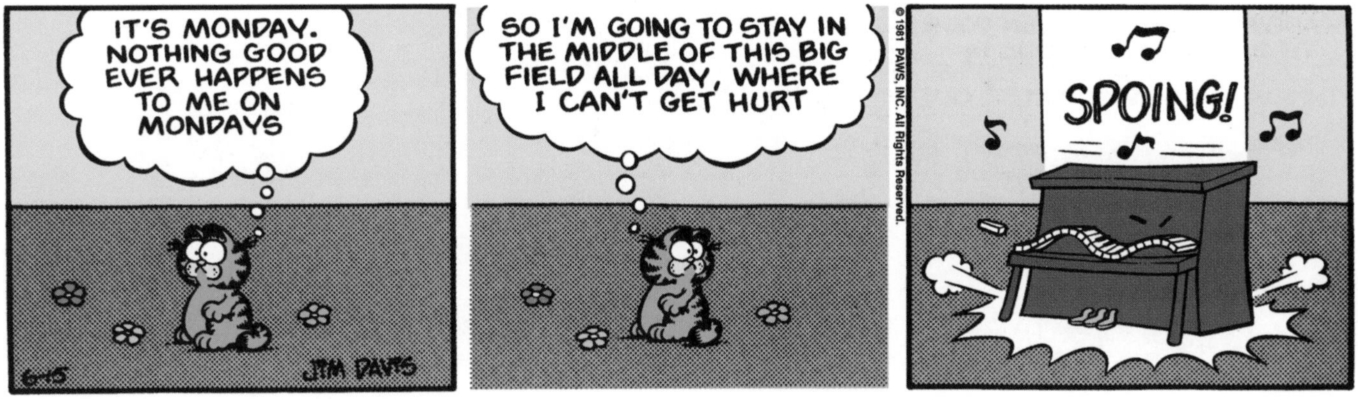
IT'S MONDAY. NOTHING GOOD EVER HAPPENS TO ME ON MONDAYS
SO I'M GOING TO STAY IN THE MIDDLE OF THIS BIG FIELD ALL DAY, WHERE I CAN'T GET HURT
SPOING!
JIM DAVIS
6-15
© 1981 PAWS, INC. All Rights Reserved.

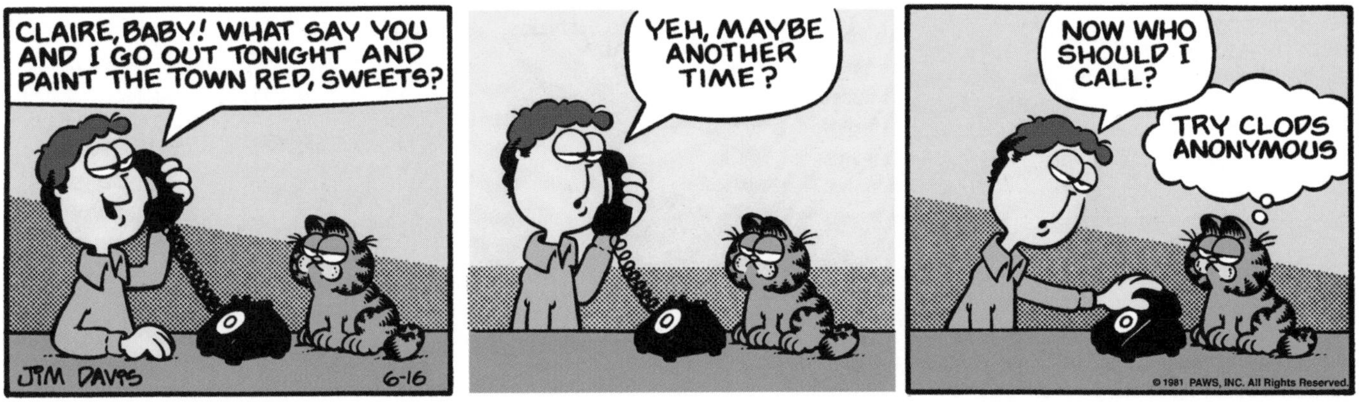
CLAIRE, BABY! WHAT SAY YOU AND I GO OUT TONIGHT AND PAINT THE TOWN RED, SWEETS?
YEH, MAYBE ANOTHER TIME?
NOW WHO SHOULD I CALL?
TRY CLODS ANONYMOUS
JIM DAVIS
6-16
© 1981 PAWS, INC. All Rights Reserved.

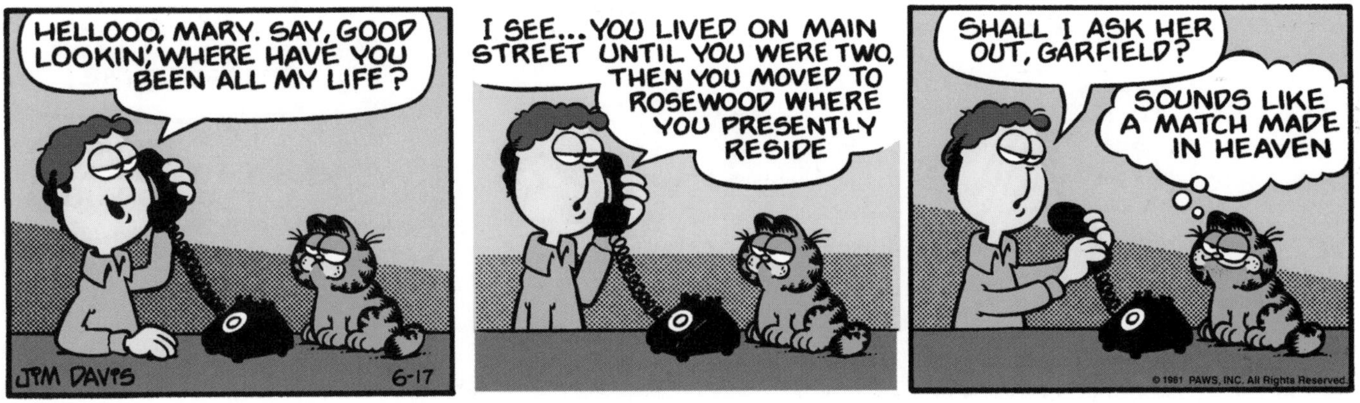
HELLOOO, MARY. SAY, GOOD LOOKIN', WHERE HAVE YOU BEEN ALL MY LIFE?
I SEE... YOU LIVED ON MAIN STREET UNTIL YOU WERE TWO, THEN YOU MOVED TO ROSEWOOD WHERE YOU PRESENTLY RESIDE
SHALL I ASK HER OUT, GARFIELD?
SOUNDS LIKE A MATCH MADE IN HEAVEN
JIM DAVIS
6-17
© 1981 PAWS, INC. All Rights Reserved.

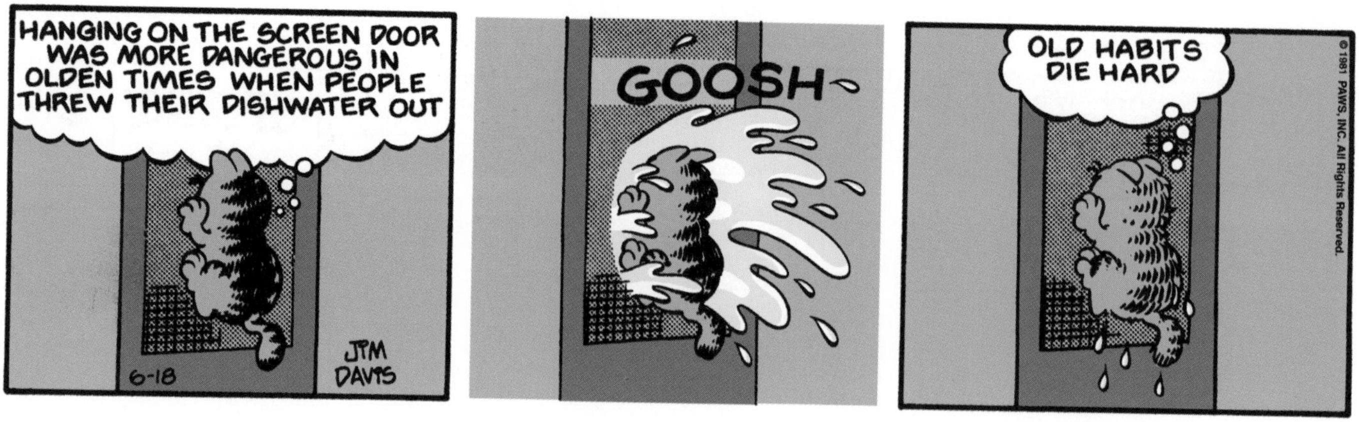
HANGING ON THE SCREEN DOOR WAS MORE DANGEROUS IN OLDEN TIMES WHEN PEOPLE THREW THEIR DISHWATER OUT
6-18
JIM DAVIS
GOOSH
OLD HABITS DIE HARD
© 1981 PAWS, INC. All Rights Reserved.

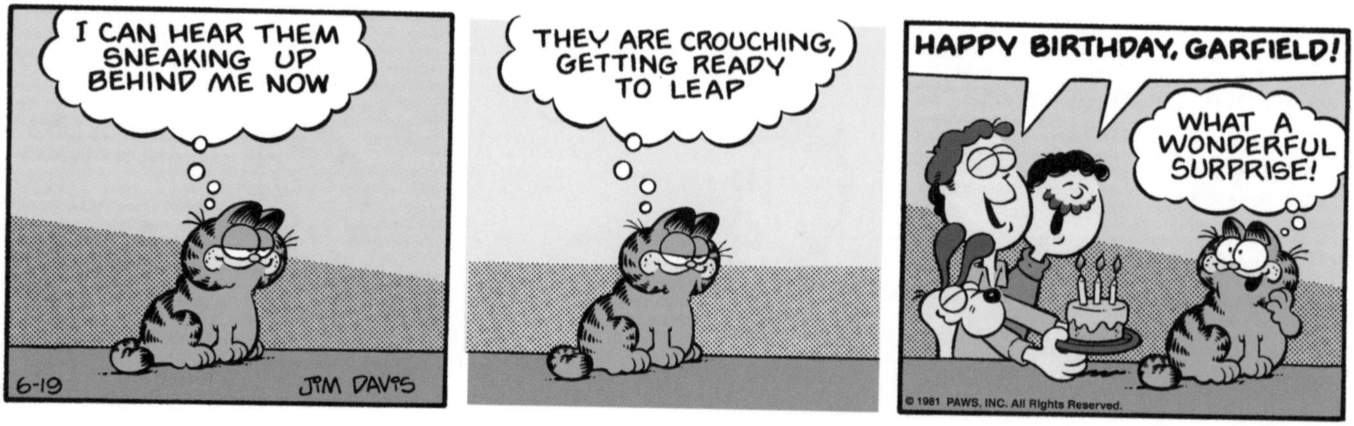
I CAN HEAR THEM SNEAKING UP BEHIND ME NOW
6-19
JIM DAVIS
THEY ARE CROUCHING, GETTING READY TO LEAP
HAPPY BIRTHDAY, GARFIELD!
WHAT A WONDERFUL SURPRISE!
© 1981 PAWS, INC. All Rights Reserved.

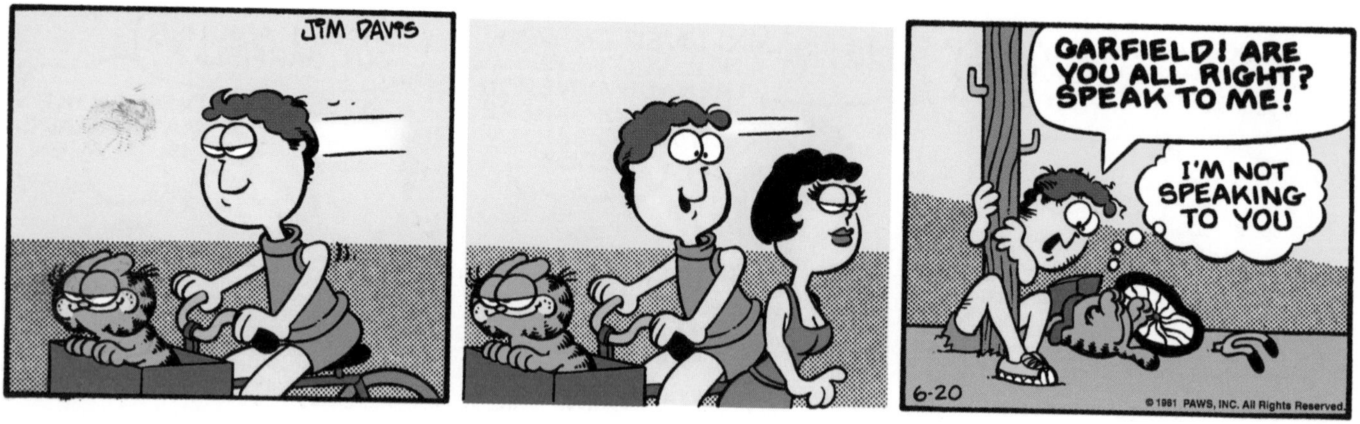
JIM DAVIS
GARFIELD! ARE YOU ALL RIGHT? SPEAK TO ME!
I'M NOT SPEAKING TO YOU
6-20
© 1981 PAWS, INC. All Rights Reserved.

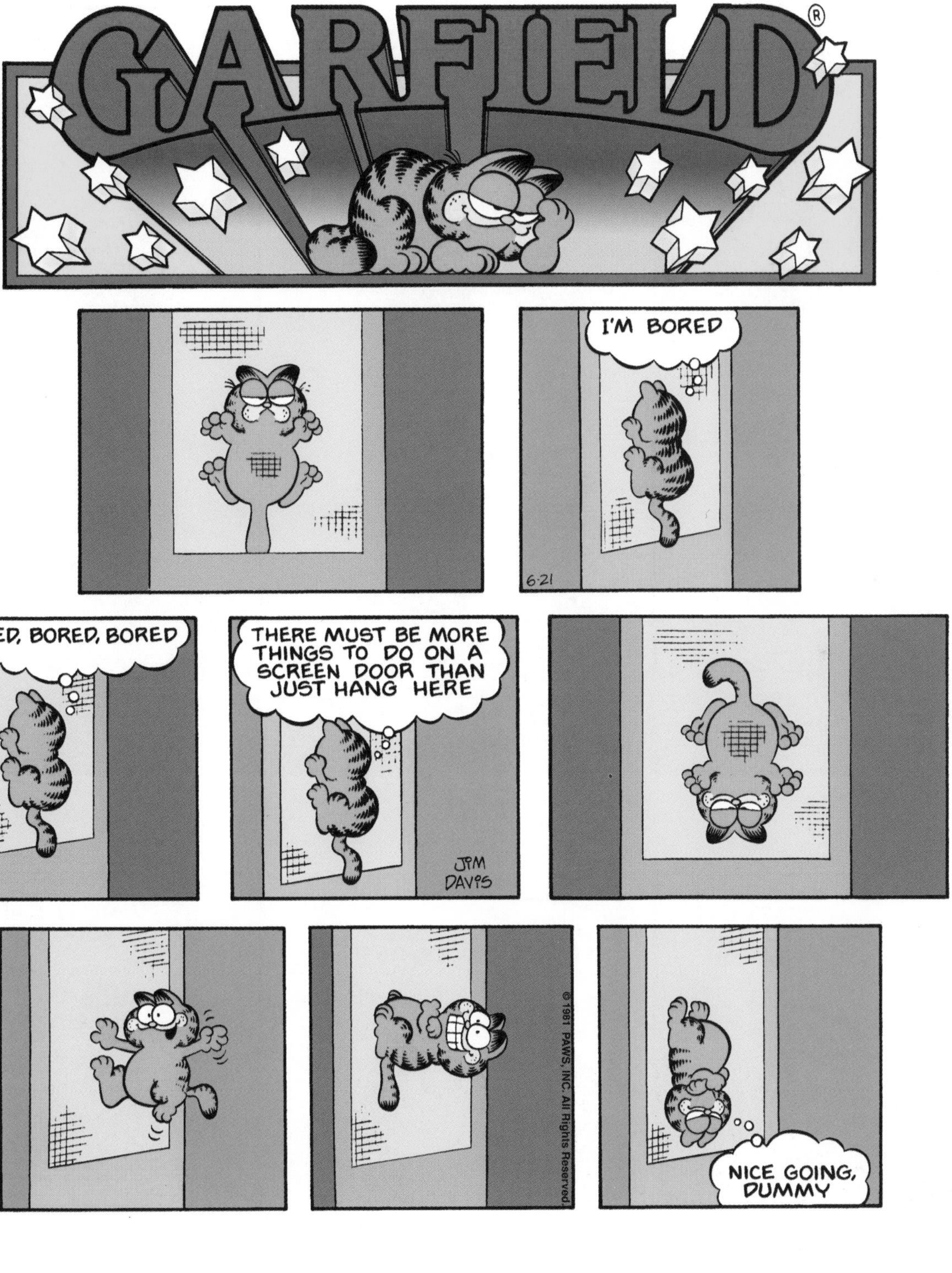
GARFIELD®
I'M BORED
6·21
BORED, BORED, BORED
THERE MUST BE MORE THINGS TO DO ON A SCREEN DOOR THAN JUST HANG HERE
JIM DAVIS
© 1981 PAWS, INC. All Rights Reserved.
NICE GOING, DUMMY

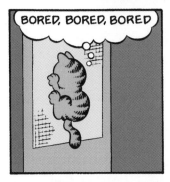

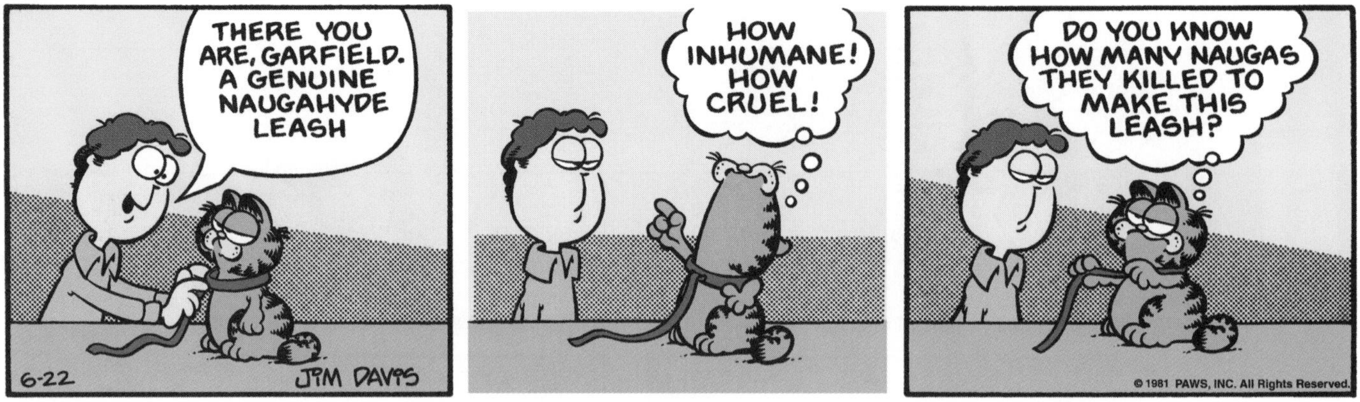
THERE YOU ARE, GARFIELD. A GENUINE NAUGAHYDE LEASH
6-22
JIM DAVIS
HOW INHUMANE! HOW CRUEL!
DO YOU KNOW HOW MANY NAUGAS THEY KILLED TO MAKE THIS LEASH?
© 1981 PAWS, INC. All Rights Reserved.

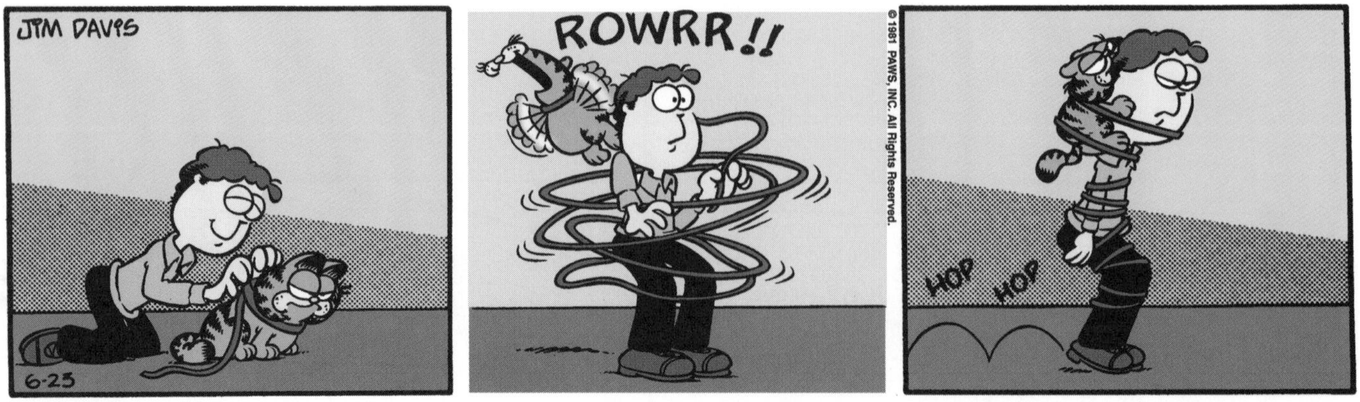
JIM DAVIS
6-23
ROWRR!!
© 1981 PAWS, INC. All Rights Reserved.
HOP
HOP

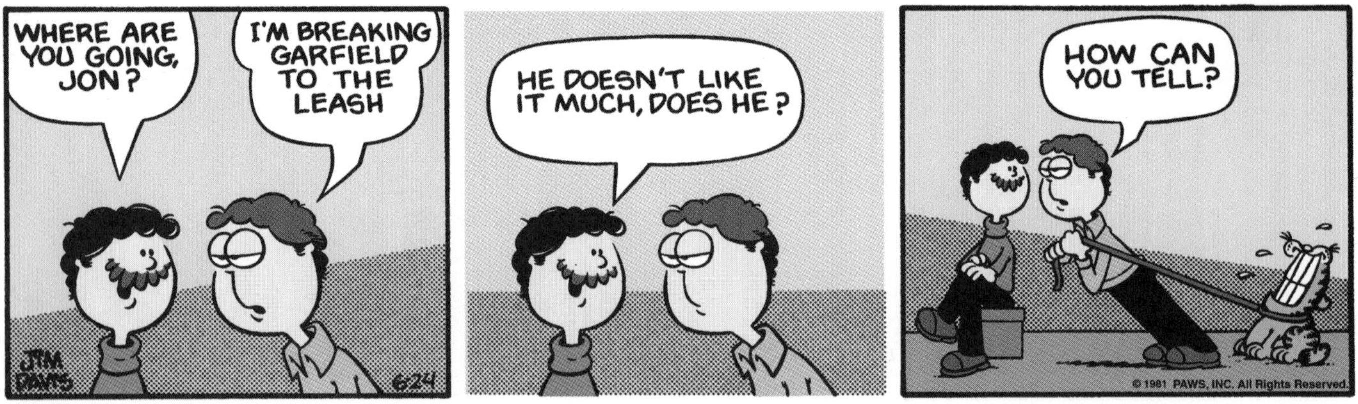
WHERE ARE YOU GOING, JON?
I'M BREAKING GARFIELD TO THE LEASH
JIM DAVIS
6-24
HE DOESN'T LIKE IT MUCH, DOES HE?
HOW CAN YOU TELL?
© 1981 PAWS, INC. All Rights Reserved.

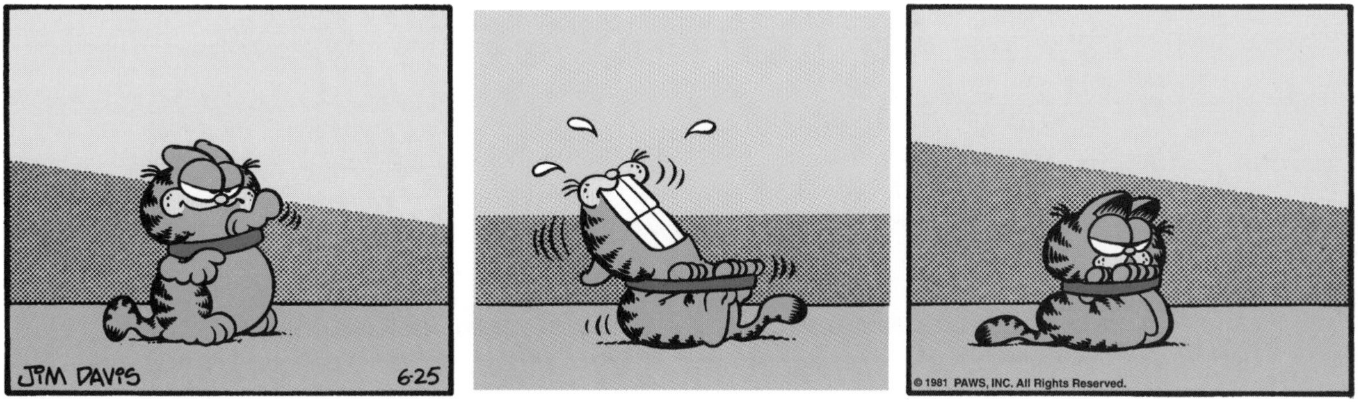
JIM DAVIS
6-25
© 1981 PAWS, INC. All Rights Reserved.

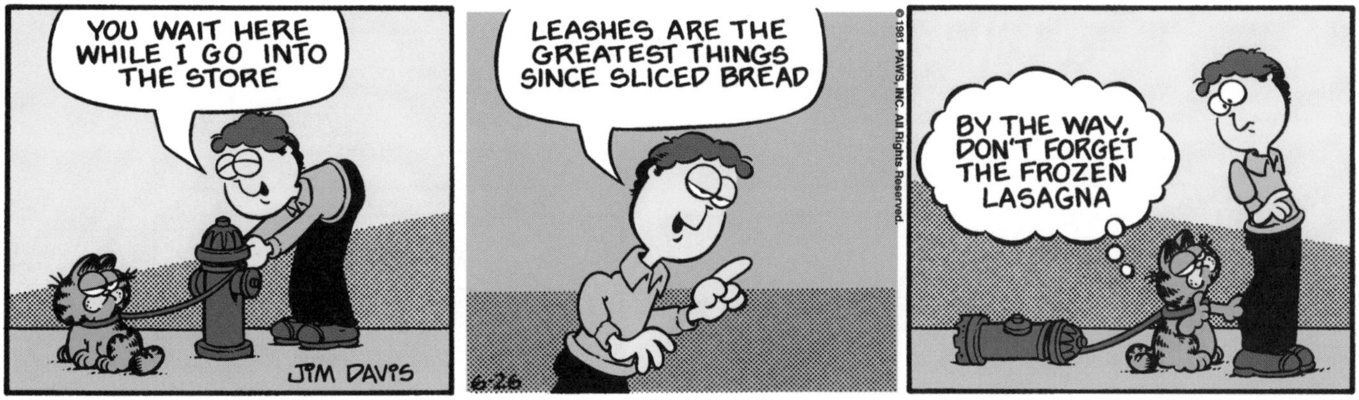
YOU WAIT HERE WHILE I GO INTO THE STORE
JIM DAVIS
LEASHES ARE THE GREATEST THINGS SINCE SLICED BREAD
6-26
© 1981 PAWS, INC. All Rights Reserved.
BY THE WAY, DON'T FORGET THE FROZEN LASAGNA

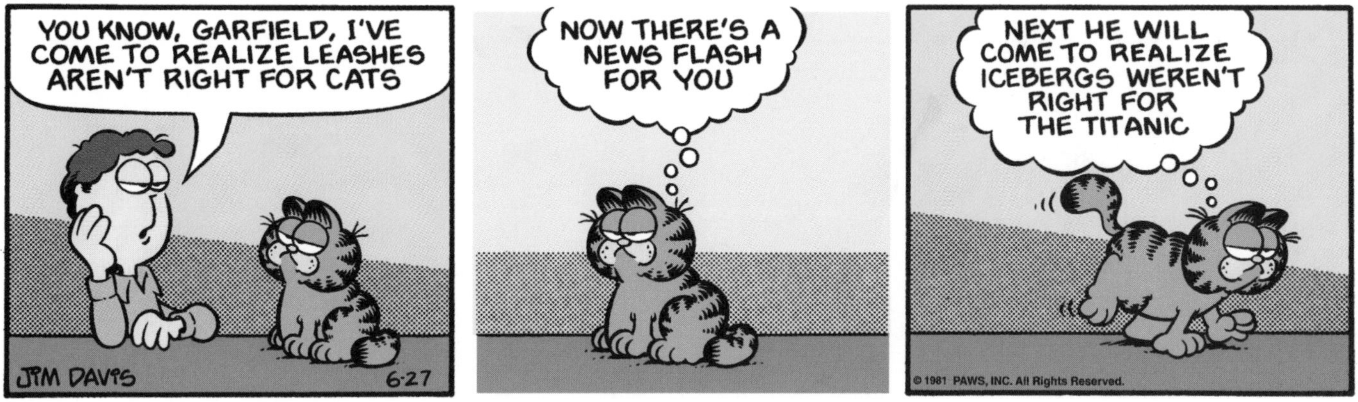
YOU KNOW, GARFIELD, I'VE COME TO REALIZE LEASHES AREN'T RIGHT FOR CATS
JIM DAVIS
6-27
NOW THERE'S A NEWS FLASH FOR YOU
NEXT HE WILL COME TO REALIZE ICEBERGS WEREN'T RIGHT FOR THE TITANIC
© 1981 PAWS, INC. All Rights Reserved.

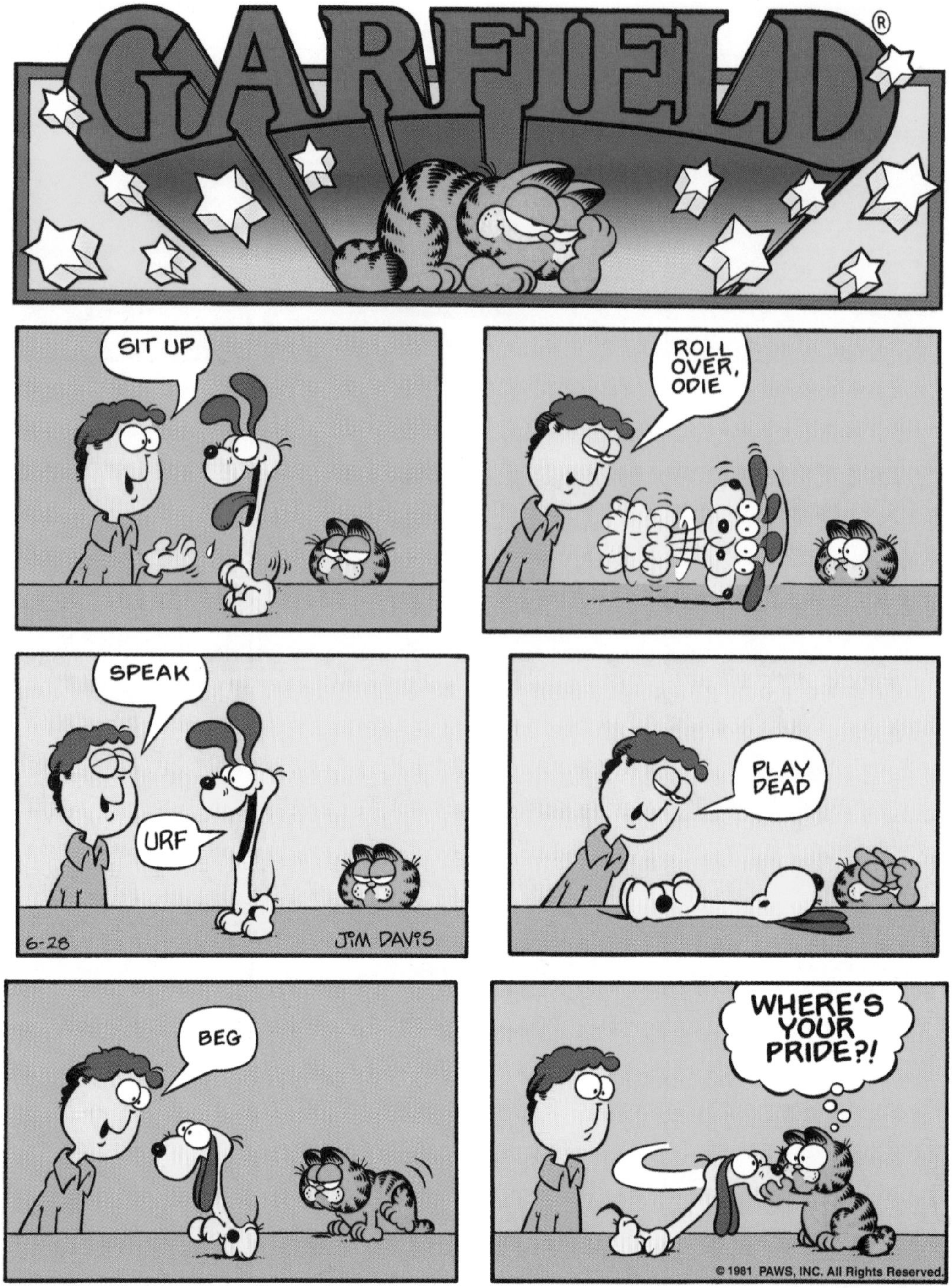
GARFIELD®
SIT UP
ROLL OVER, ODIE
SPEAK
URF
6-28
JIM DAVIS
PLAY DEAD
BEG
WHERE'S YOUR PRIDE?!
© 1981 PAWS, INC. All Rights Reserved.

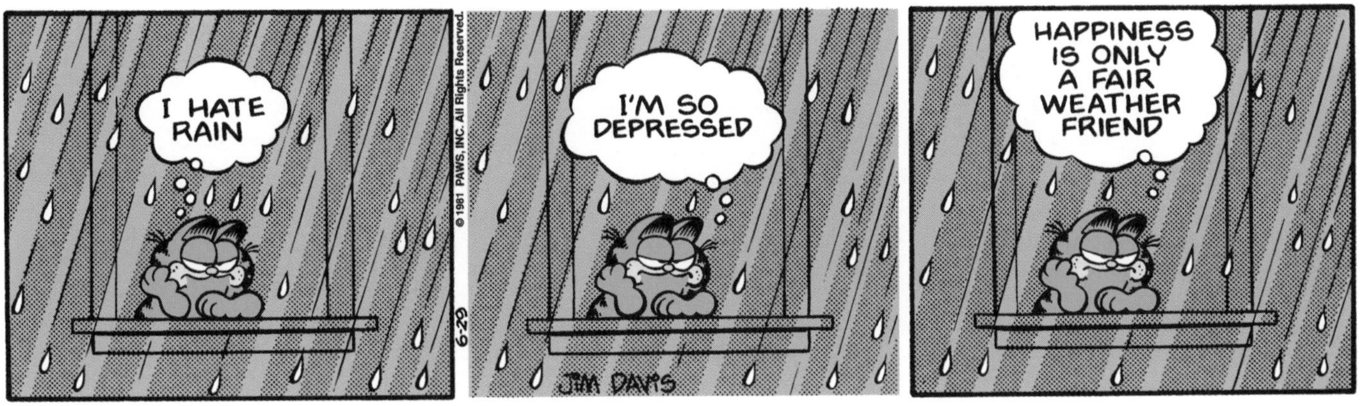
I HATE RAIN
© 1981 PAWS, INC. All Rights Reserved.
6-29
I'M SO DEPRESSED
JIM DAVIS
HAPPINESS IS ONLY A FAIR WEATHER FRIEND

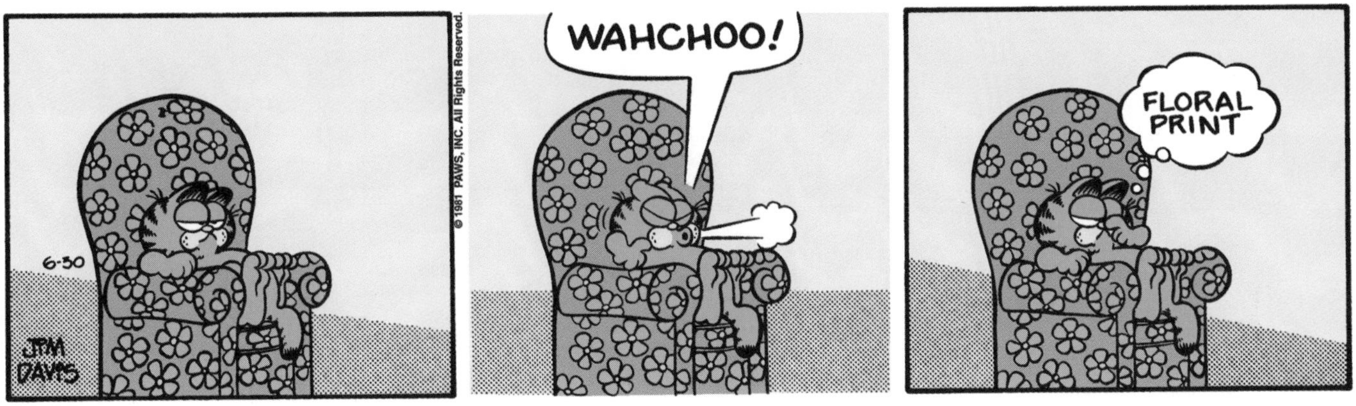
6-30
JIM DAVIS
© 1981 PAWS, INC. All Rights Reserved.
WAHCHOO!
FLORAL PRINT

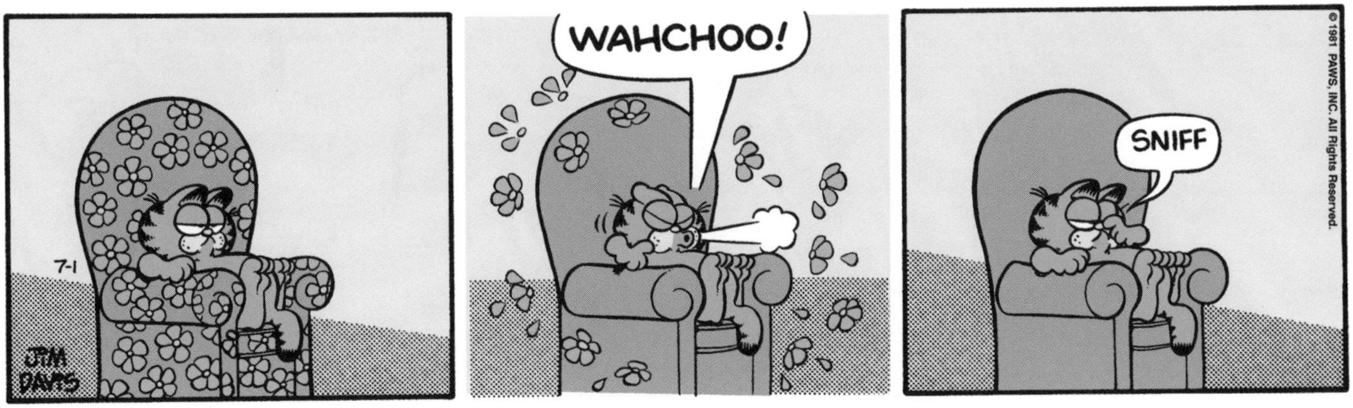
7-1
JIM DAVIS
WAHCHOO!
SNIFF
© 1981 PAWS, INC. All Rights Reserved.

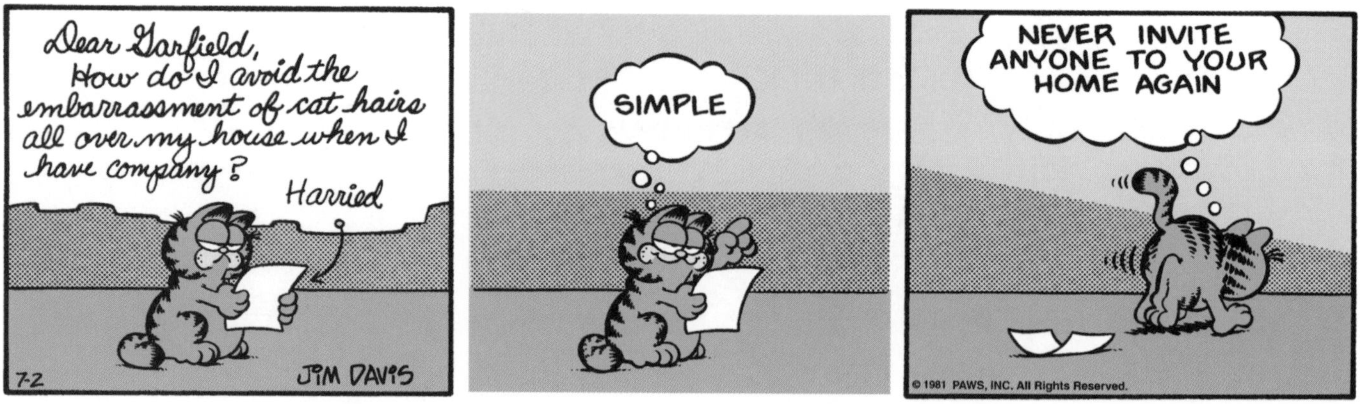
Dear Garfield,
How do I avoid the embarrassment of cat hairs all over my house when I have company?
Harried
7-2
JIM DAVIS
SIMPLE
NEVER INVITE ANYONE TO YOUR HOME AGAIN
© 1981 PAWS, INC. All Rights Reserved.

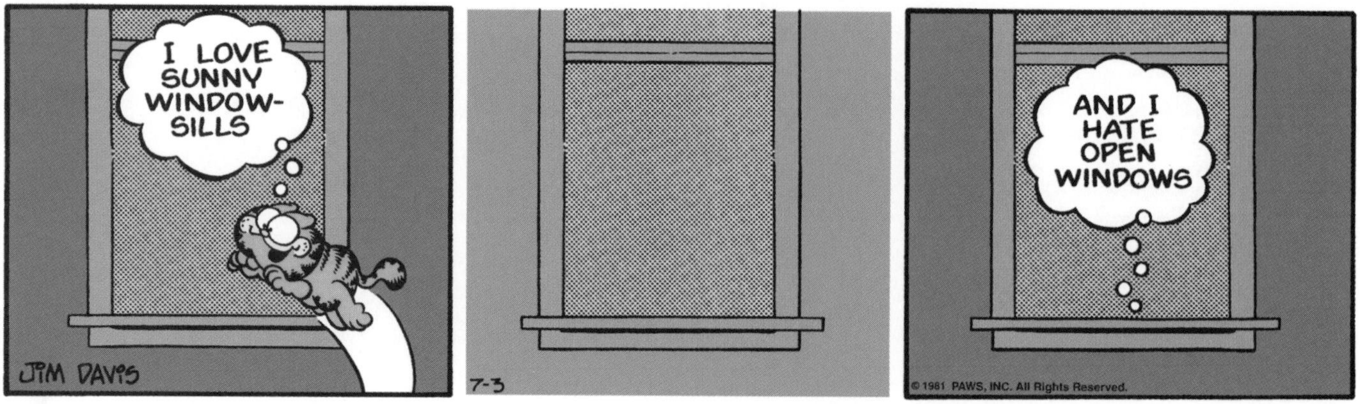
I LOVE SUNNY WINDOW-SILLS
JIM DAVIS
7-3
AND I HATE OPEN WINDOWS
© 1981 PAWS, INC. All Rights Reserved.

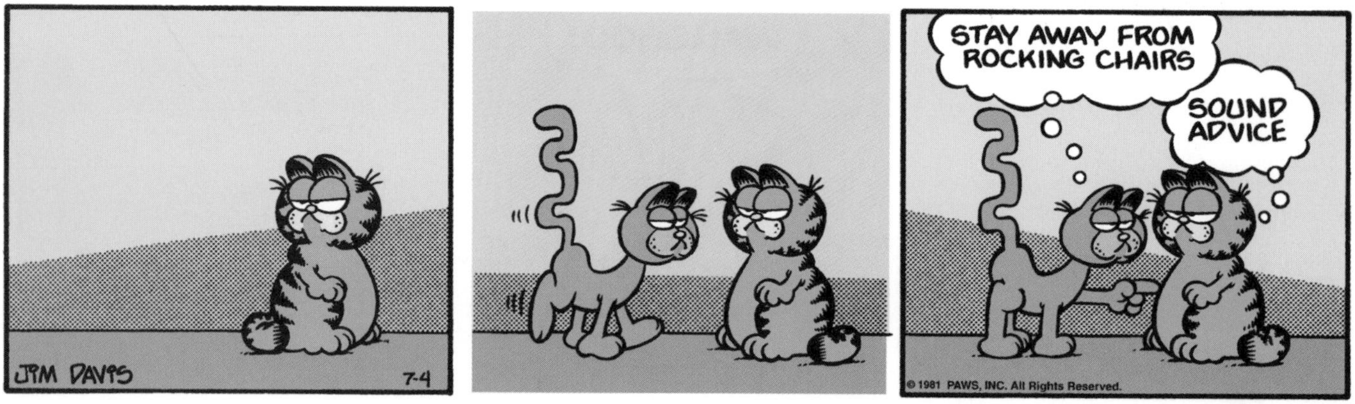
JIM DAVIS
7-4
STAY AWAY FROM ROCKING CHAIRS
SOUND ADVICE
© 1981 PAWS, INC. All Rights Reserved.

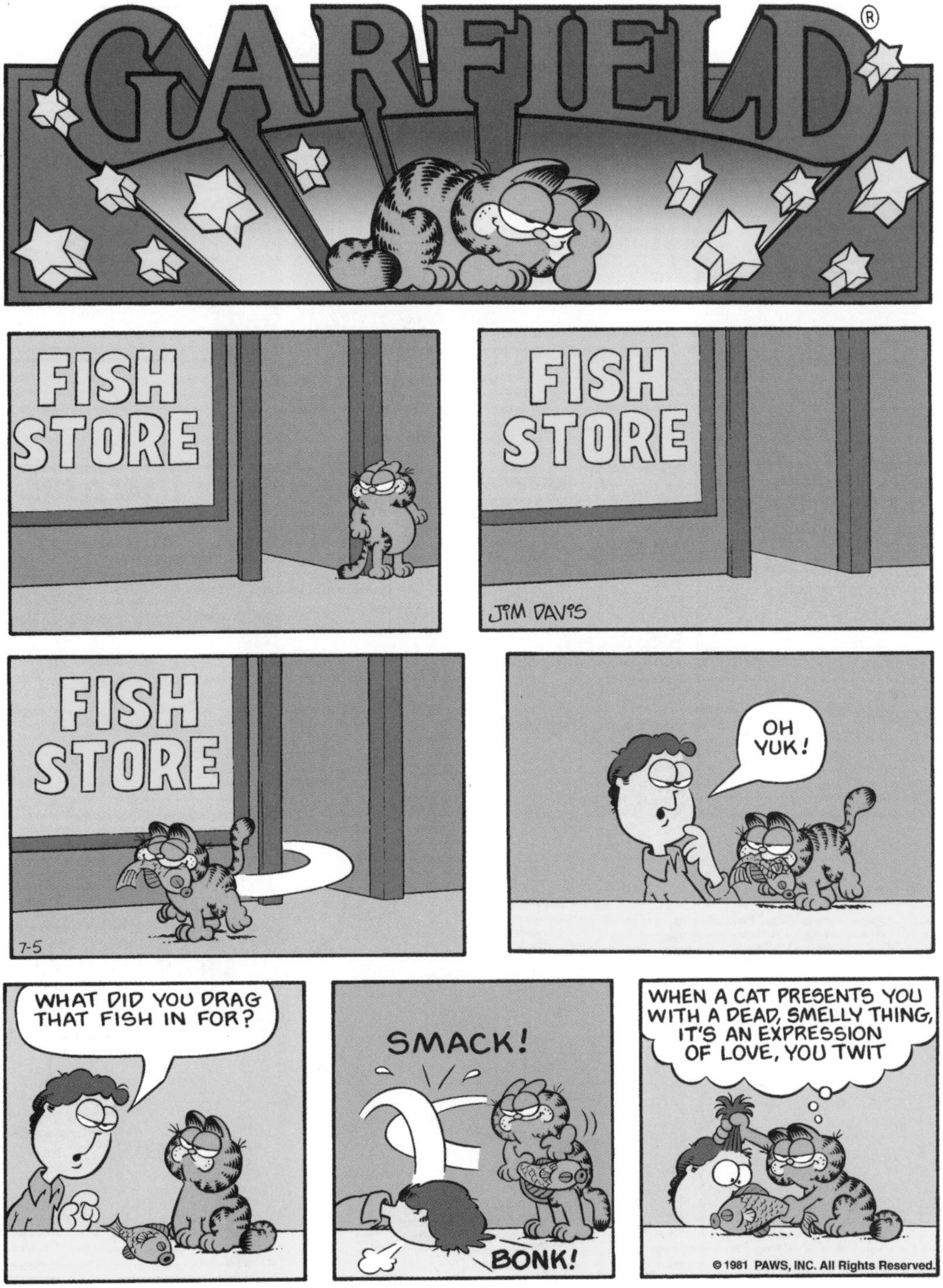
GARFIELD®
FISH STORE
FISH STORE
JIM DAVIS
FISH STORE
7-5
OH YUK!
WHAT DID YOU DRAG THAT FISH IN FOR?
SMACK!
BONK!
WHEN A CAT PRESENTS YOU WITH A DEAD, SMELLY THING, IT'S AN EXPRESSION OF LOVE, YOU TWIT
© 1981 PAWS, INC. All Rights Reserved.

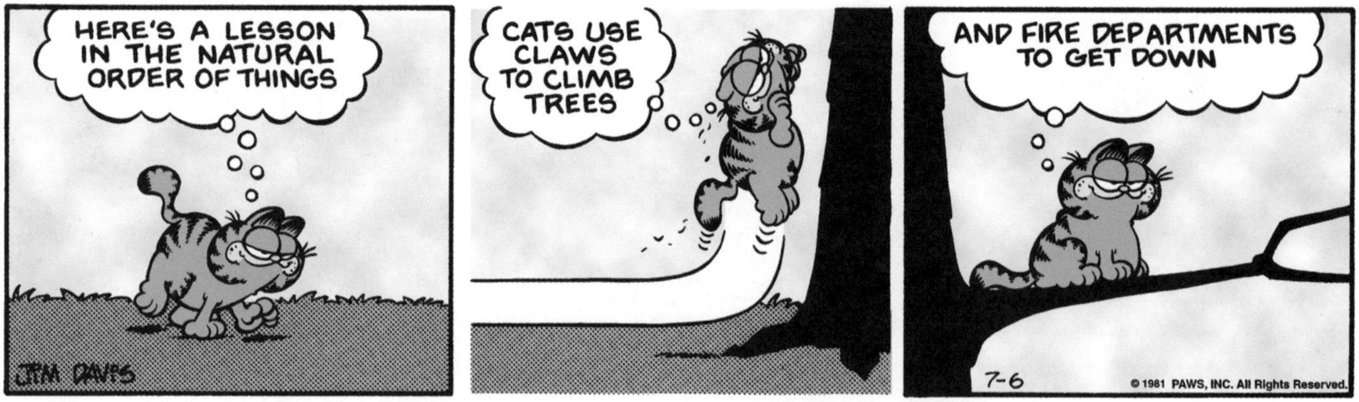
HERE'S A LESSON IN THE NATURAL ORDER OF THINGS
JIM DAVIS
CATS USE CLAWS TO CLIMB TREES
AND FIRE DEPARTMENTS TO GET DOWN
7-6
© 1981 PAWS, INC. All Rights Reserved.

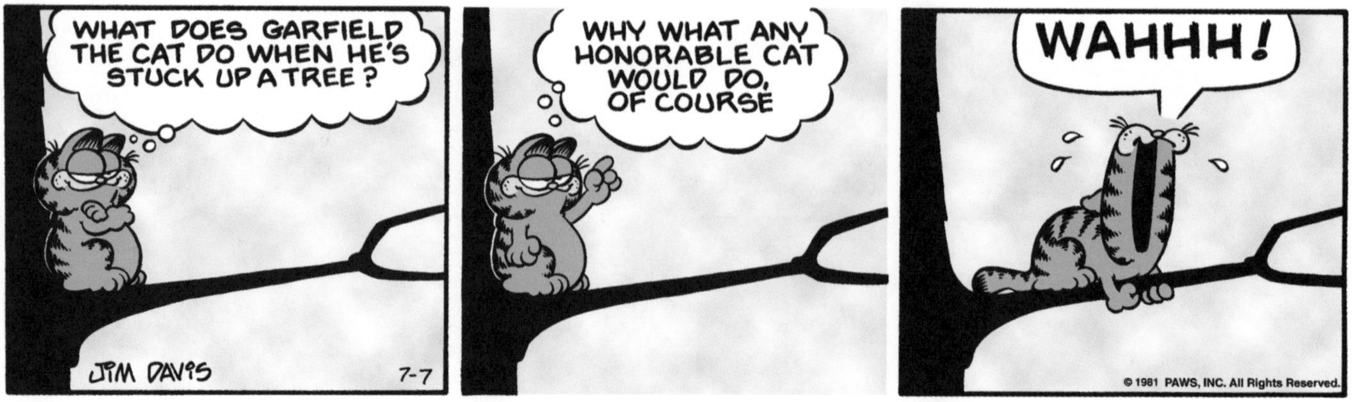
WHAT DOES GARFIELD THE CAT DO WHEN HE'S STUCK UP A TREE?
JIM DAVIS
7-7
WHY WHAT ANY HONORABLE CAT WOULD DO, OF COURSE
WAHHH!
© 1981 PAWS, INC. All Rights Reserved.

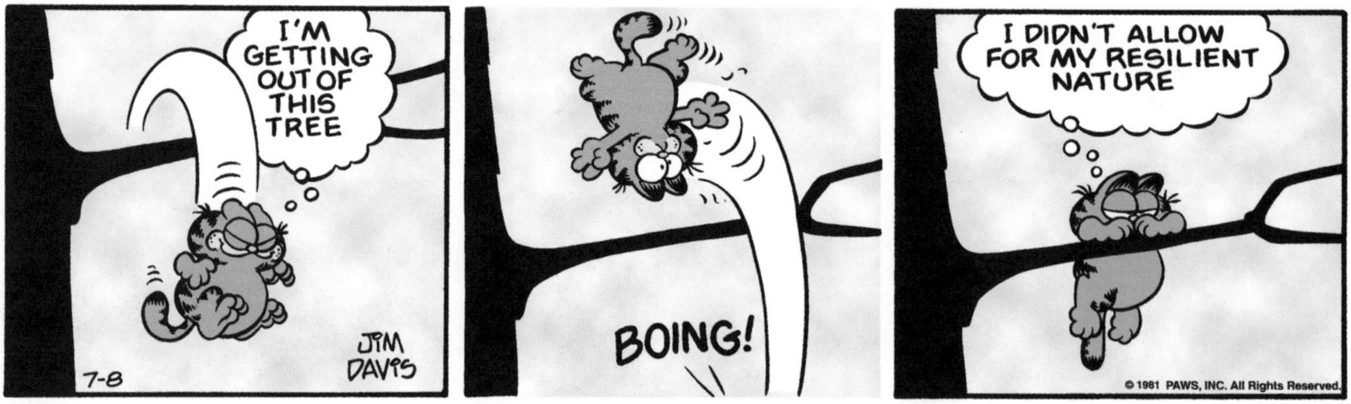
I'M GETTING OUT OF THIS TREE
7-8
JIM DAVIS
BOING!
I DIDN'T ALLOW FOR MY RESILIENT NATURE
© 1981 PAWS, INC. All Rights Reserved.

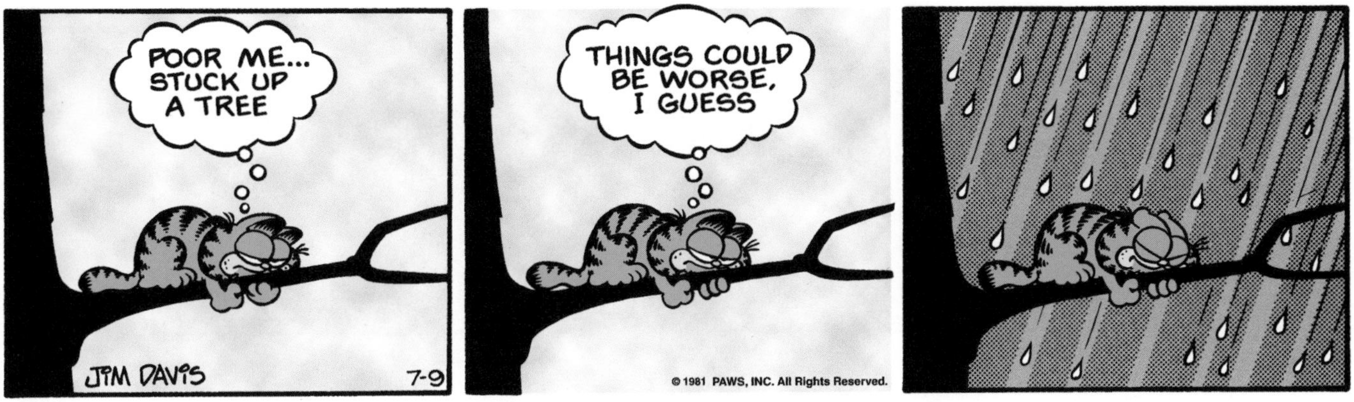
POOR ME... STUCK UP A TREE
JIM DAVIS
7-9
THINGS COULD BE WORSE, I GUESS
© 1981 PAWS, INC. All Rights Reserved.

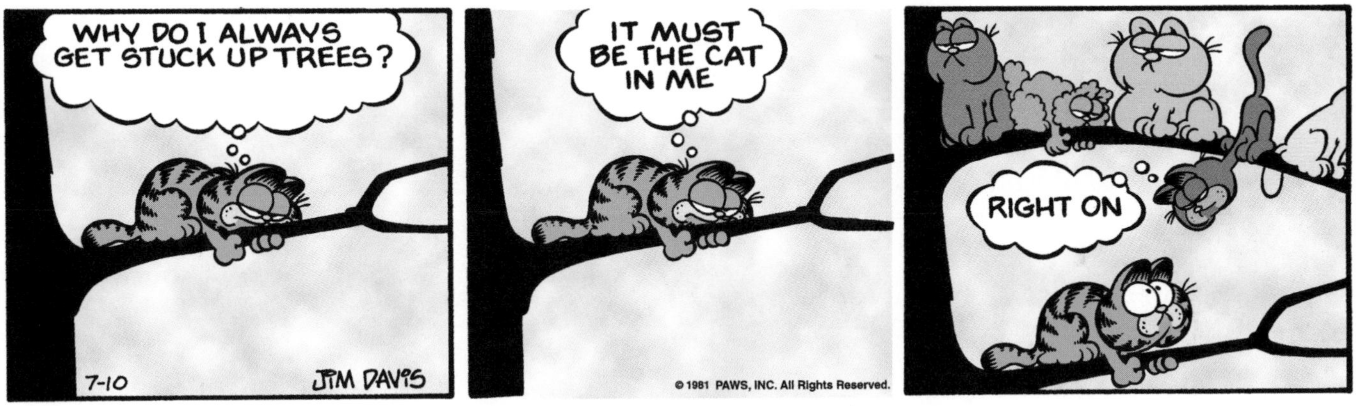
WHY DO I ALWAYS GET STUCK UP TREES?
7-10
JIM DAVIS
IT MUST BE THE CAT IN ME
© 1981 PAWS, INC. All Rights Reserved.
RIGHT ON

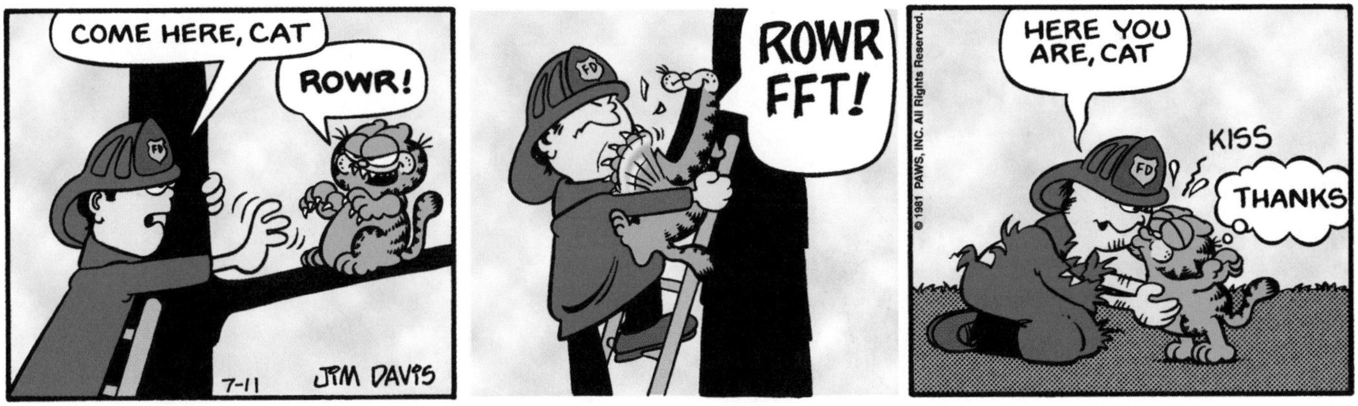
COME HERE, CAT
ROWR!
7-11
JIM DAVIS
ROWR FFT!
© 1981 PAWS, INC. All Rights Reserved.
HERE YOU ARE, CAT
KISS
THANKS

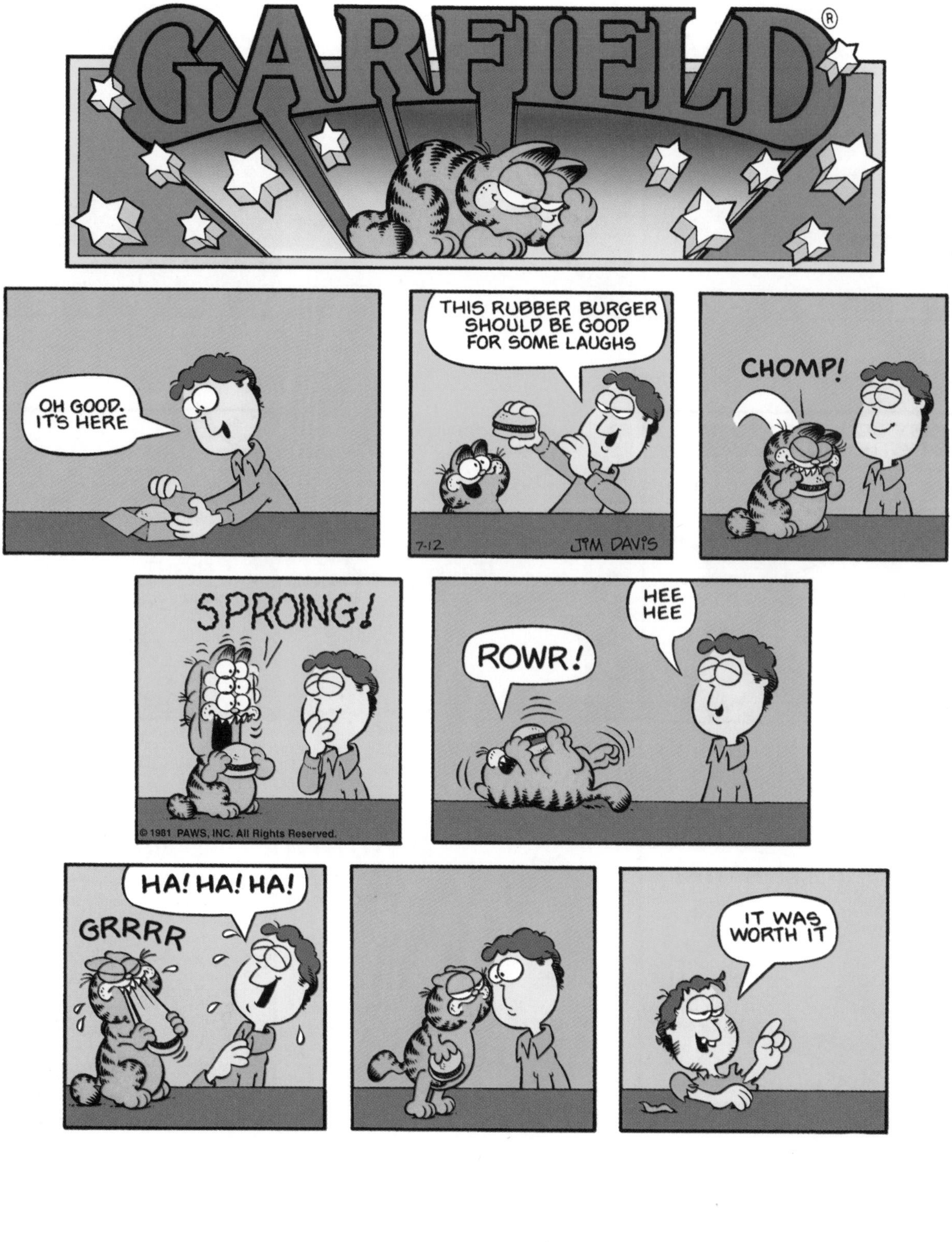
GARFIELD
OH GOOD. IT'S HERE
THIS RUBBER BURGER SHOULD BE GOOD FOR SOME LAUGHS
7-12
JIM DAVIS
CHOMP!
SPROING!
© 1981 PAWS, INC. All Rights Reserved.
ROWR!
HEE HEE
HA! HA! HA!
GRRRR
IT WAS WORTH IT

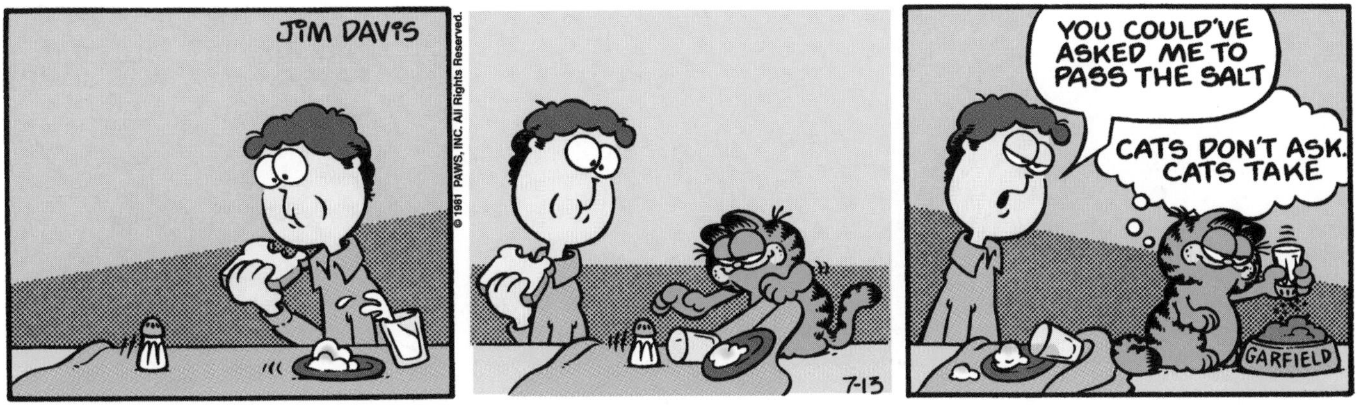
JIM DAVIS
© 1981 PAWS, INC. All Rights Reserved.
7-13
YOU COULD'VE ASKED ME TO PASS THE SALT
CATS DON'T ASK. CATS TAKE
GARFIELD

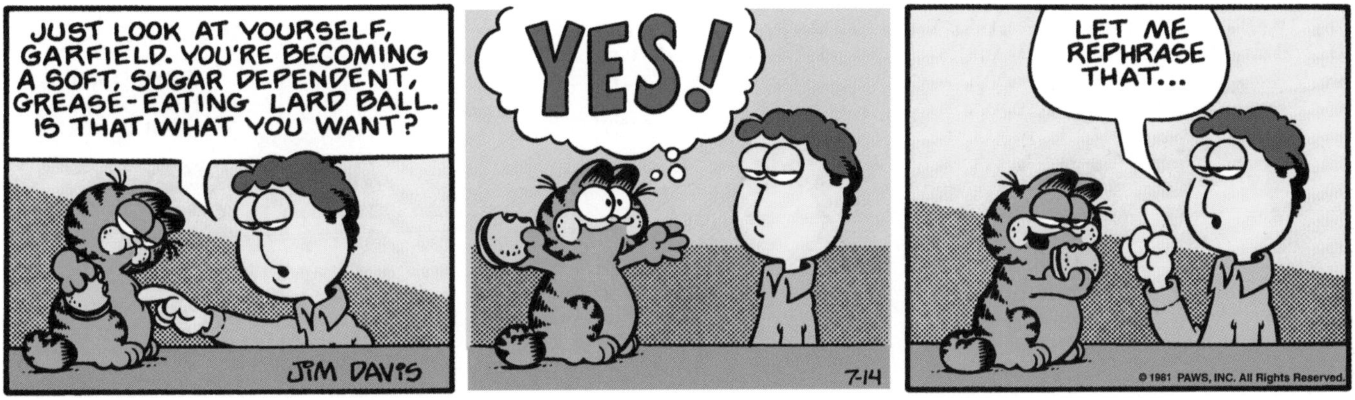
JUST LOOK AT YOURSELF, GARFIELD. YOU'RE BECOMING A SOFT, SUGAR DEPENDENT, GREASE-EATING LARD BALL. IS THAT WHAT YOU WANT?
JIM DAVIS
YES!
7-14
LET ME REPHRASE THAT...
© 1981 PAWS, INC. All Rights Reserved.

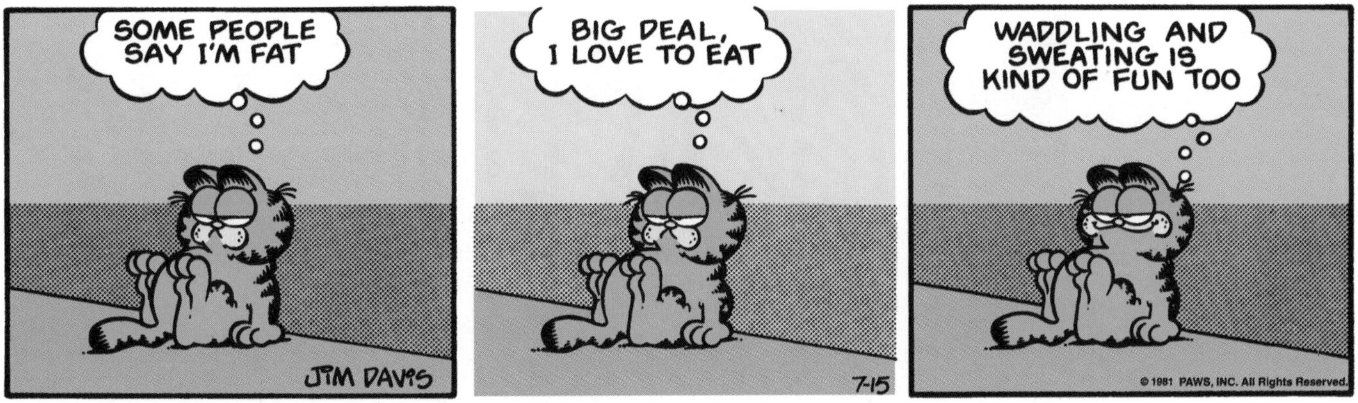
SOME PEOPLE SAY I'M FAT
JIM DAVIS
BIG DEAL, I LOVE TO EAT
7-15
WADDLING AND SWEATING IS KIND OF FUN TOO
© 1981 PAWS, INC. All Rights Reserved.

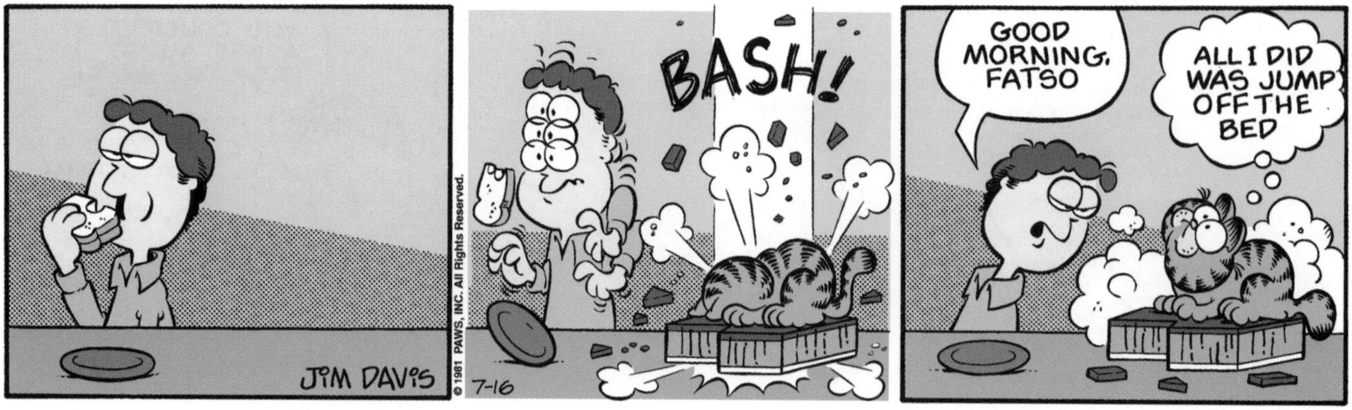
JIM DAVIS
© 1981 PAWS, INC. All Rights Reserved.
7-16
BASH!
GOOD MORNING, FATSO
ALL I DID WAS JUMP OFF THE BED

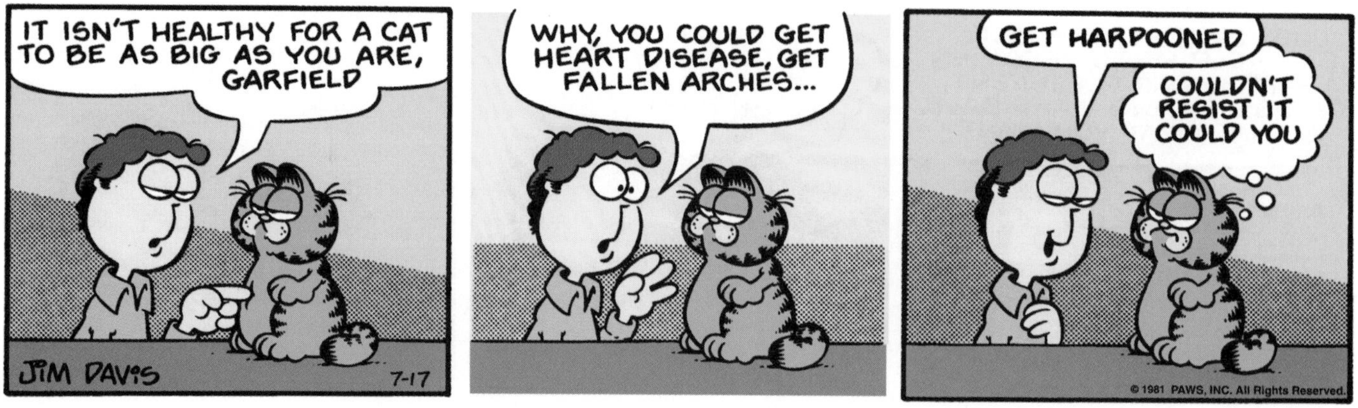
IT ISN'T HEALTHY FOR A CAT TO BE AS BIG AS YOU ARE, GARFIELD
JIM DAVIS
7-17
WHY, YOU COULD GET HEART DISEASE, GET FALLEN ARCHES...
GET HARPOONED
COULDN'T RESIST IT COULD YOU
© 1981 PAWS, INC. All Rights Reserved.

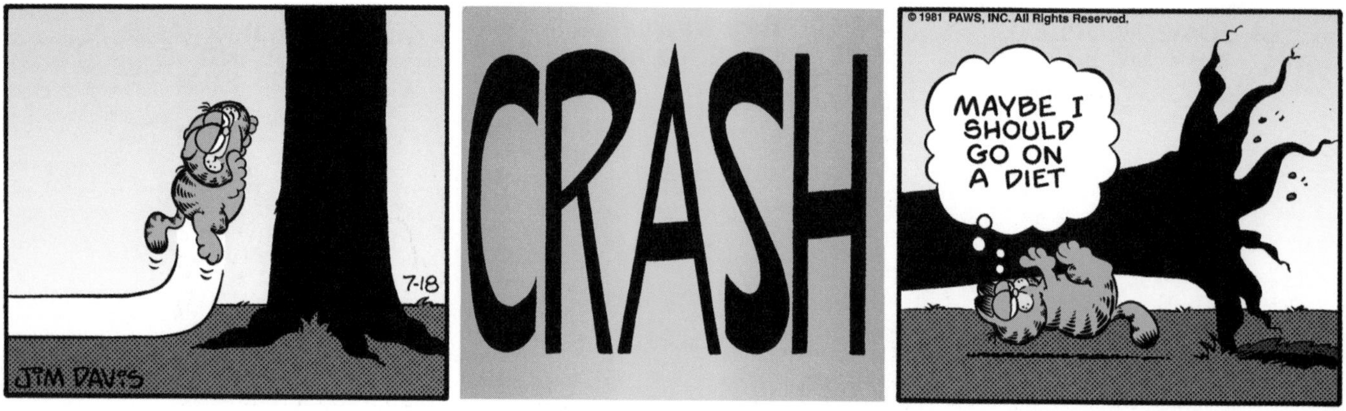
7-18
JIM DAVIS
CRASH
© 1981 PAWS, INC. All Rights Reserved.
MAYBE I SHOULD GO ON A DIET

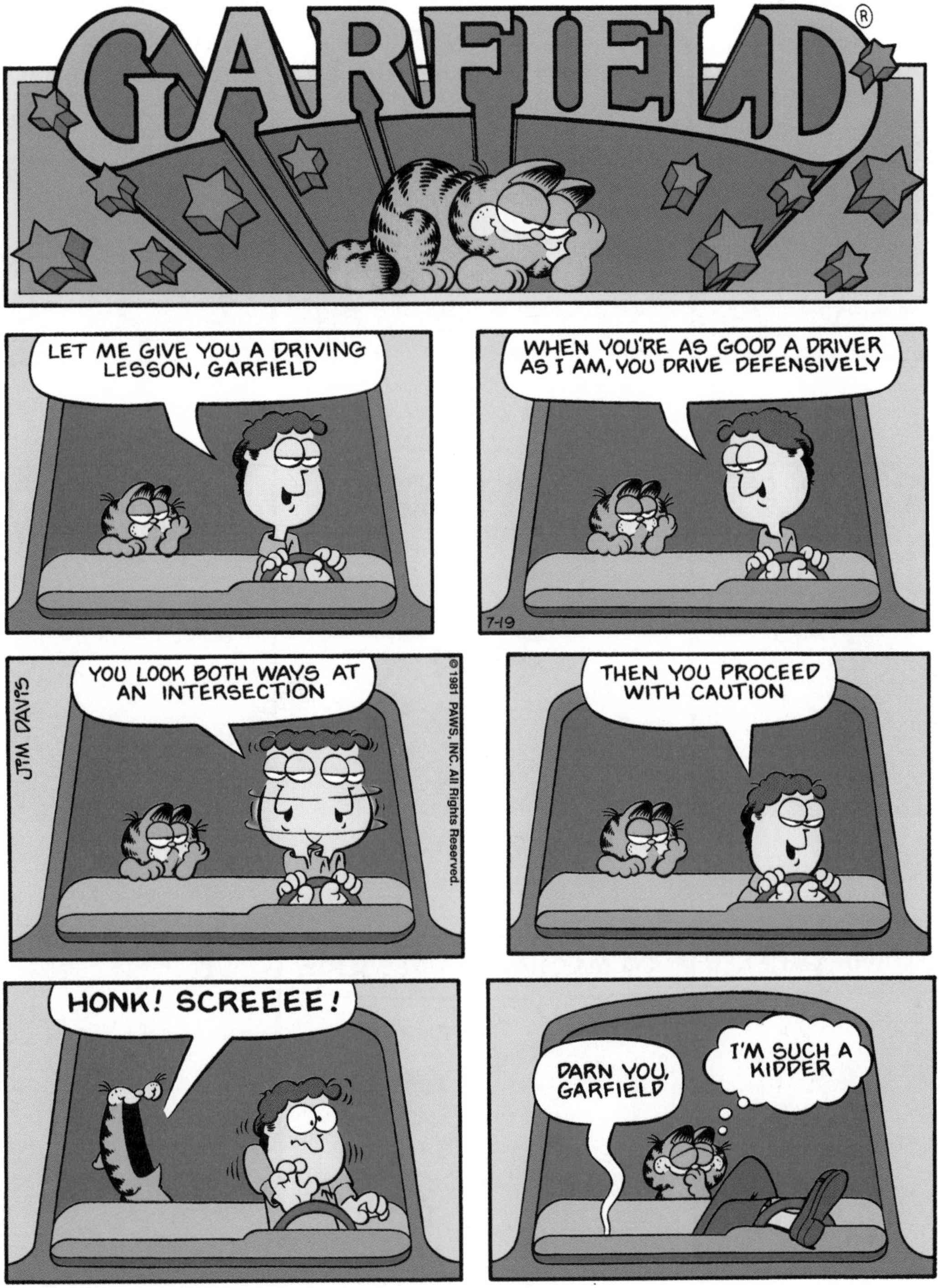
GARFIELD
LET ME GIVE YOU A DRIVING LESSON, GARFIELD
WHEN YOU'RE AS GOOD A DRIVER AS I AM, YOU DRIVE DEFENSIVELY
7-19
JIM DAVIS
© 1981 PAWS, INC. All Rights Reserved.
YOU LOOK BOTH WAYS AT AN INTERSECTION
THEN YOU PROCEED WITH CAUTION
HONK! SCREEEE!
DARN YOU, GARFIELD
I'M SUCH A KIDDER

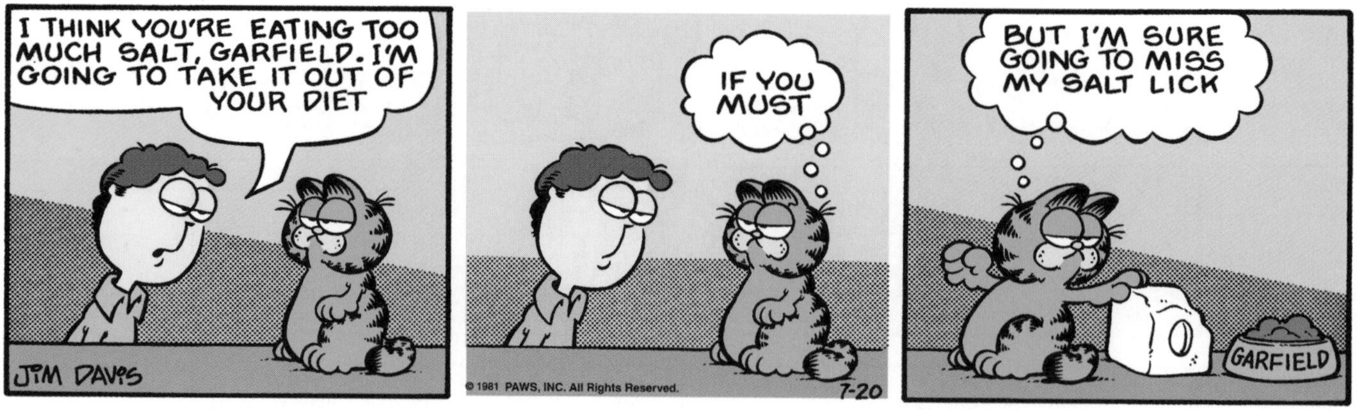
I THINK YOU'RE EATING TOO MUCH SALT, GARFIELD. I'M GOING TO TAKE IT OUT OF YOUR DIET
JIM DAVIS
IF YOU MUST
© 1981 PAWS, INC. All Rights Reserved.
7-20
BUT I'M SURE GOING TO MISS MY SALT LICK
GARFIELD

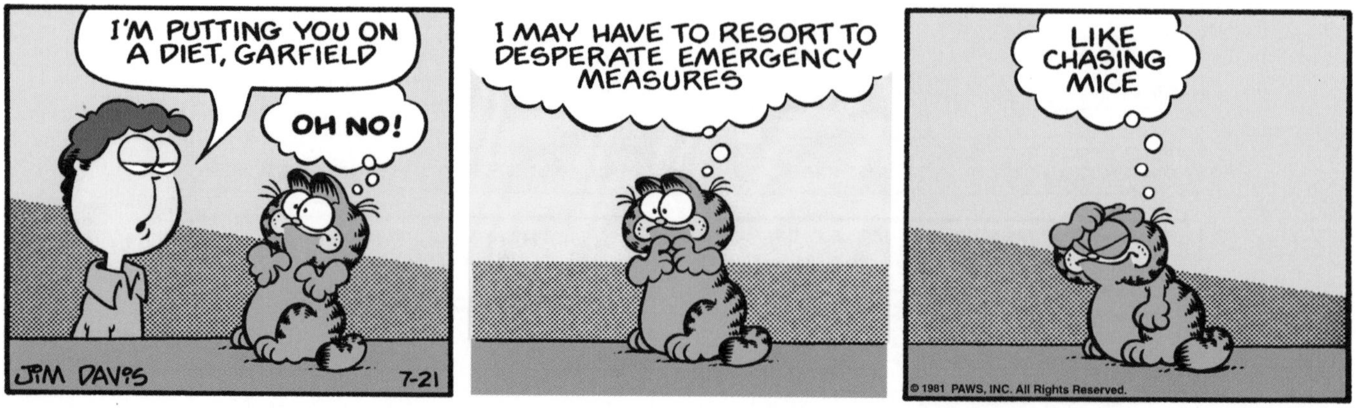
I'M PUTTING YOU ON A DIET, GARFIELD
OH NO!
JIM DAVIS
7-21
I MAY HAVE TO RESORT TO DESPERATE EMERGENCY MEASURES
LIKE CHASING MICE
© 1981 PAWS, INC. All Rights Reserved.

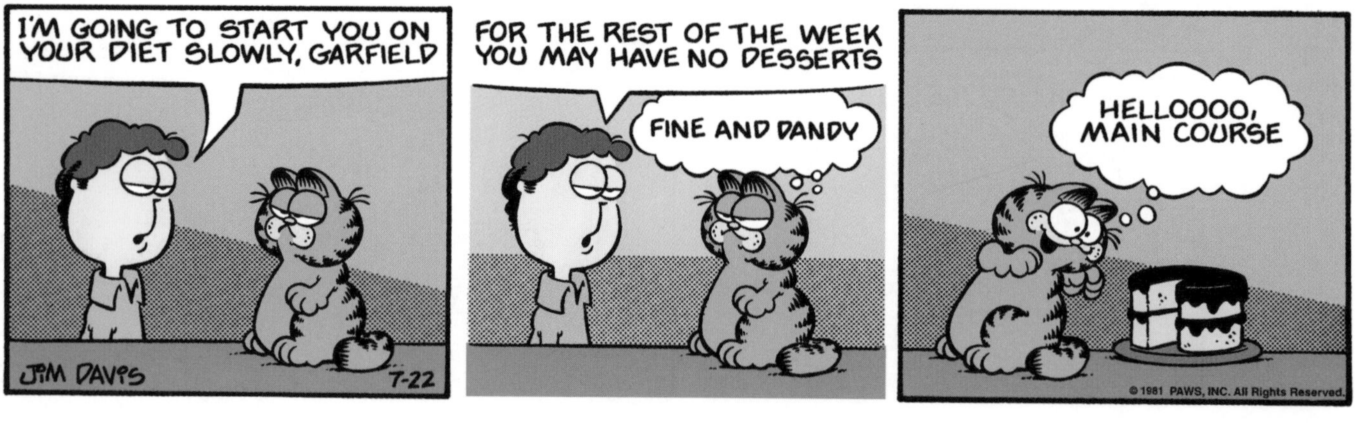
I'M GOING TO START YOU ON YOUR DIET SLOWLY, GARFIELD
JIM DAVIS
7-22
FOR THE REST OF THE WEEK YOU MAY HAVE NO DESSERTS
FINE AND DANDY
HELLOOOO, MAIN COURSE
© 1981 PAWS, INC. All Rights Reserved.

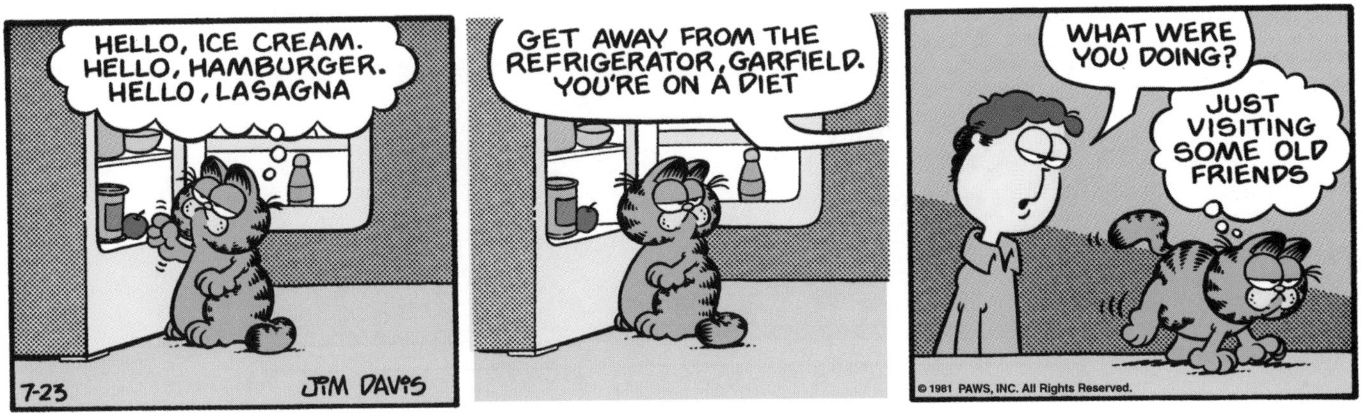
HELLO, ICE CREAM. HELLO, HAMBURGER. HELLO, LASAGNA
7-23
JIM DAVIS
GET AWAY FROM THE REFRIGERATOR, GARFIELD. YOU'RE ON A DIET
WHAT WERE YOU DOING?
JUST VISITING SOME OLD FRIENDS
© 1981 PAWS, INC. All Rights Reserved.

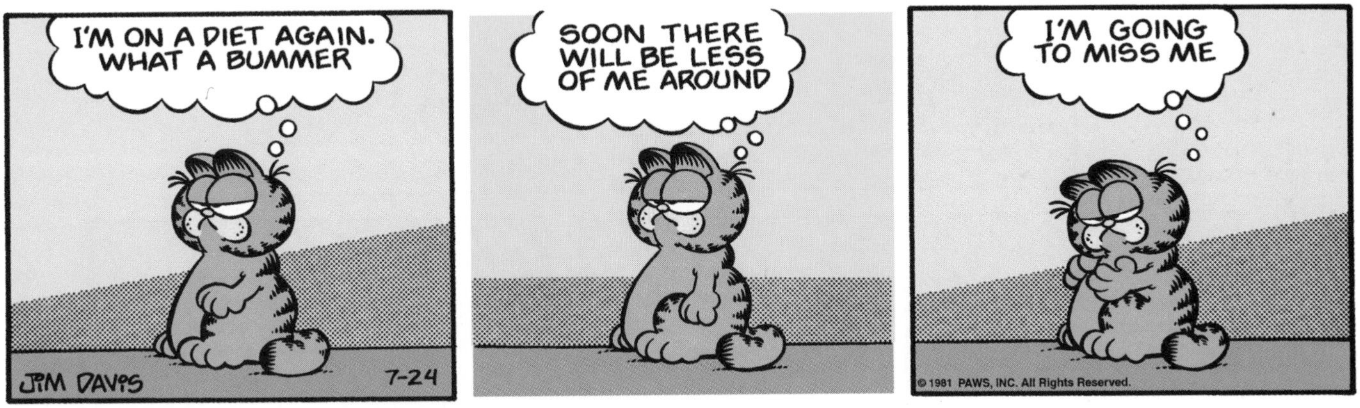
I'M ON A DIET AGAIN. WHAT A BUMMER
JIM DAVIS
7-24
SOON THERE WILL BE LESS OF ME AROUND
I'M GOING TO MISS ME
© 1981 PAWS, INC. All Rights Reserved.

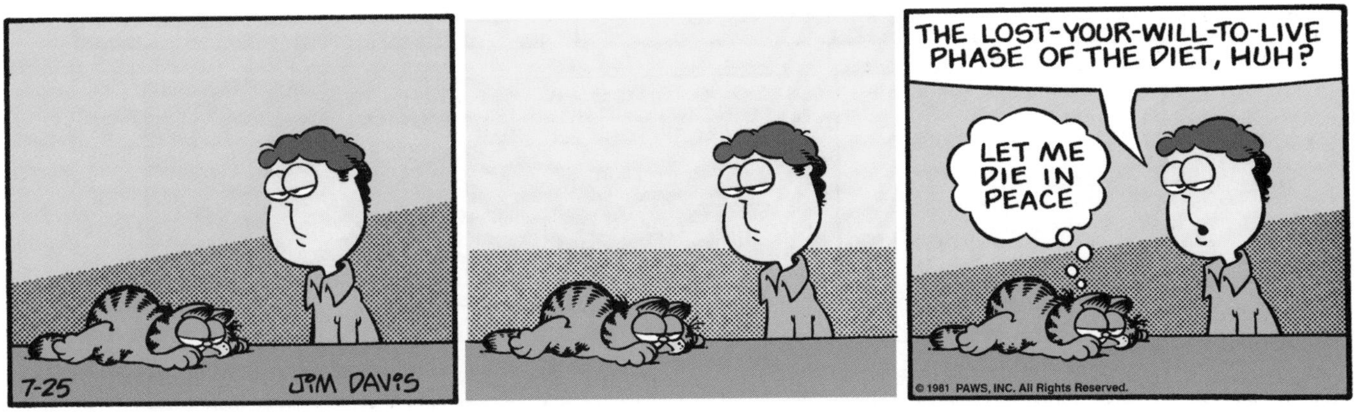
7-25
JIM DAVIS
THE LOST-YOUR-WILL-TO-LIVE PHASE OF THE DIET, HUH?
LET ME DIE IN PEACE
© 1981 PAWS, INC. All Rights Reserved.

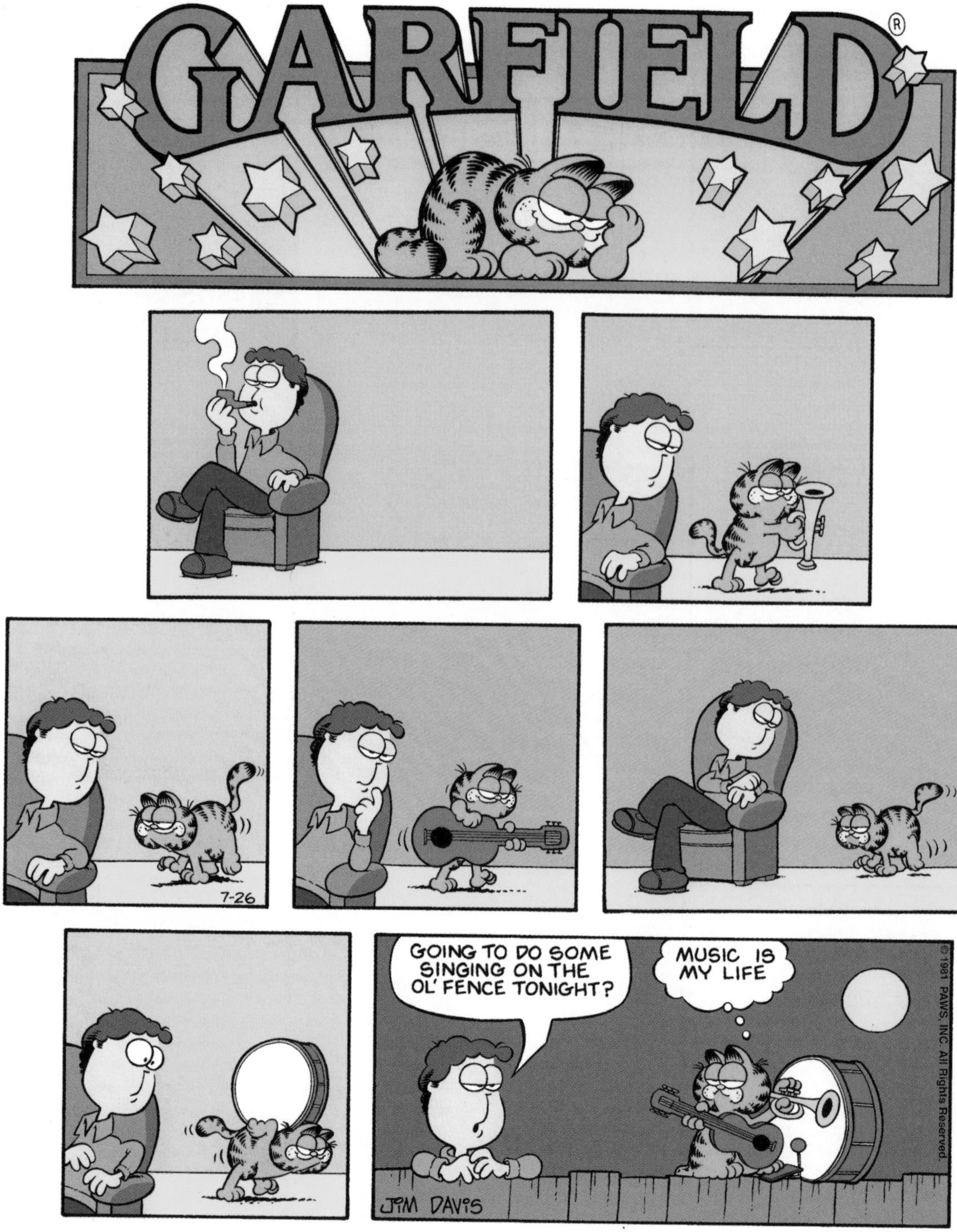
GARFIELD
7-26
GOING TO DO SOME SINGING ON THE OL' FENCE TONIGHT?
MUSIC IS MY LIFE
© 1981 PAWS, INC. All Rights Reserved.
JIM DAVIS

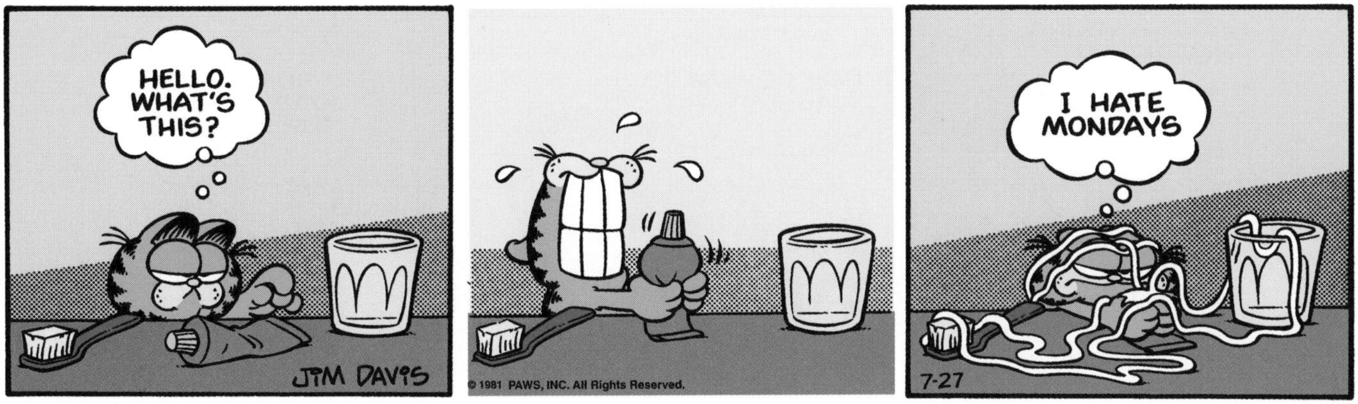
HELLO. WHAT'S THIS?
JIM DAVIS
© 1981 PAWS, INC. All Rights Reserved.
I HATE MONDAYS
7-27

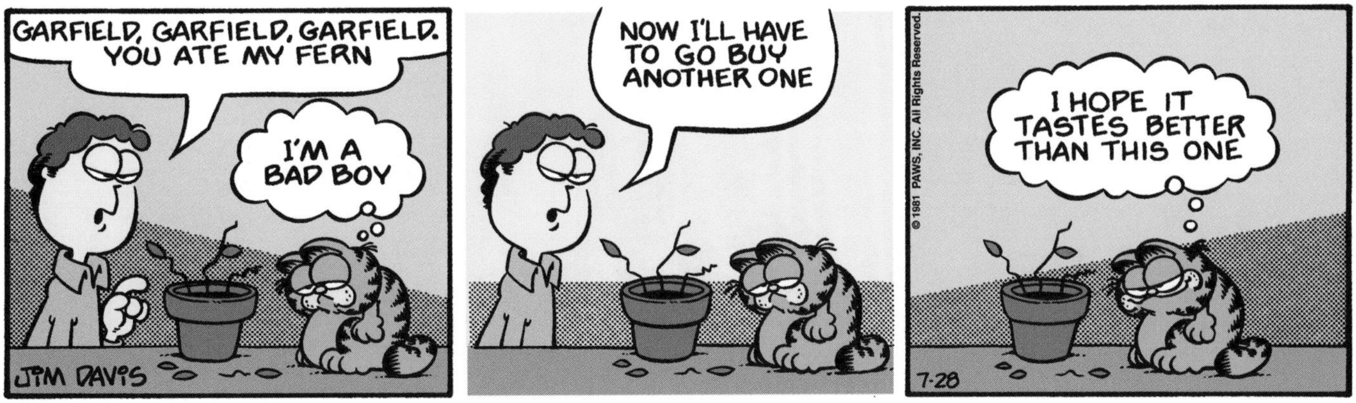
GARFIELD, GARFIELD, GARFIELD. YOU ATE MY FERN
I'M A BAD BOY
JIM DAVIS
NOW I'LL HAVE TO GO BUY ANOTHER ONE
© 1981 PAWS, INC. All Rights Reserved.
I HOPE IT TASTES BETTER THAN THIS ONE
7-28

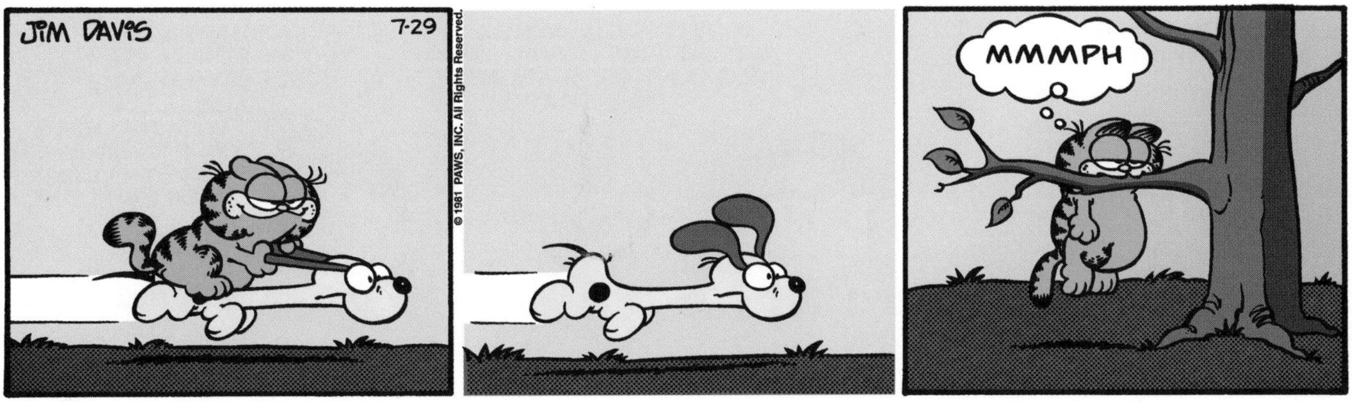
JIM DAVIS
7-29
© 1981 PAWS, INC. All Rights Reserved.
MMMPH

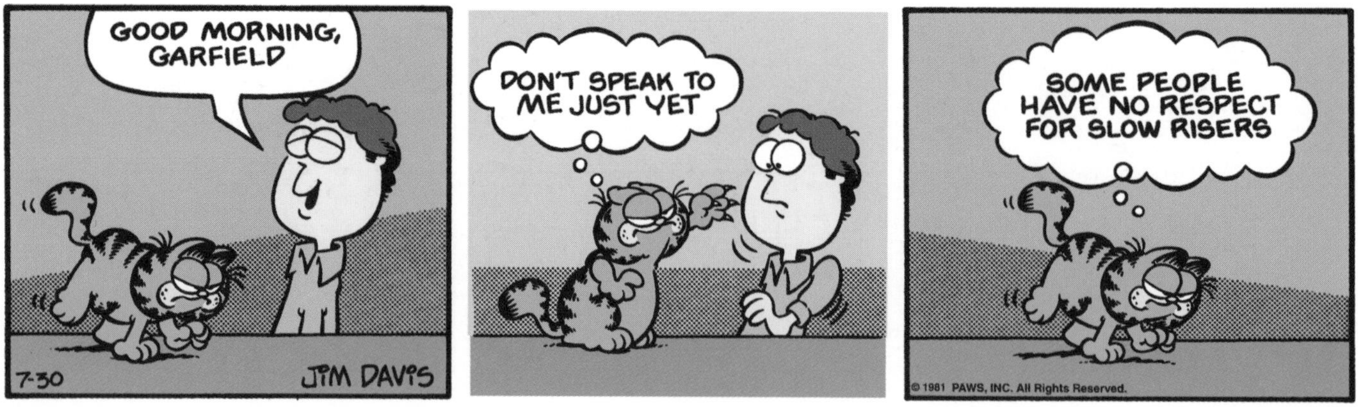
GOOD MORNING, GARFIELD
7-30
JIM DAVIS
DON'T SPEAK TO ME JUST YET
SOME PEOPLE HAVE NO RESPECT FOR SLOW RISERS
© 1981 PAWS, INC. All Rights Reserved.

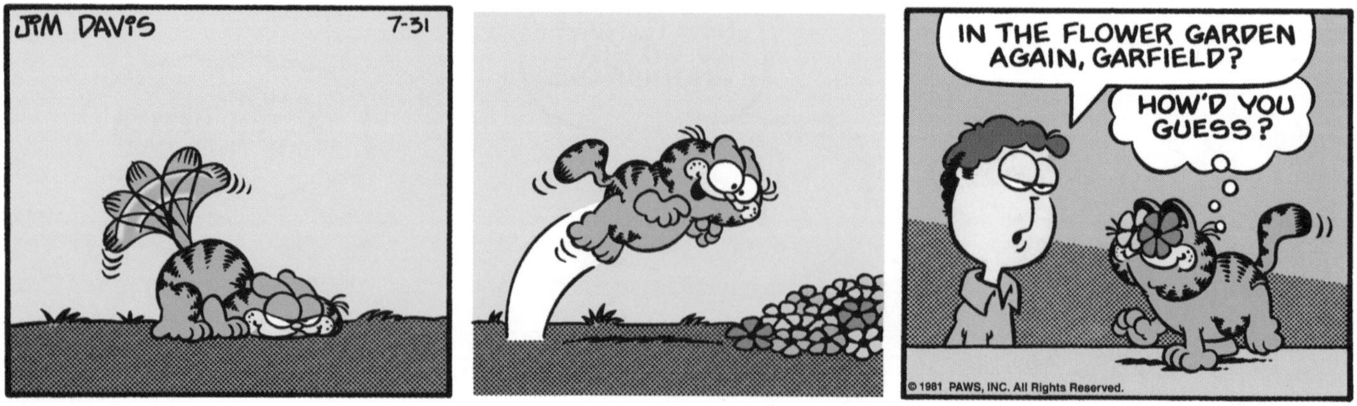
JIM DAVIS
7-31
IN THE FLOWER GARDEN AGAIN, GARFIELD?
HOW'D YOU GUESS?
© 1981 PAWS, INC. All Rights Reserved.

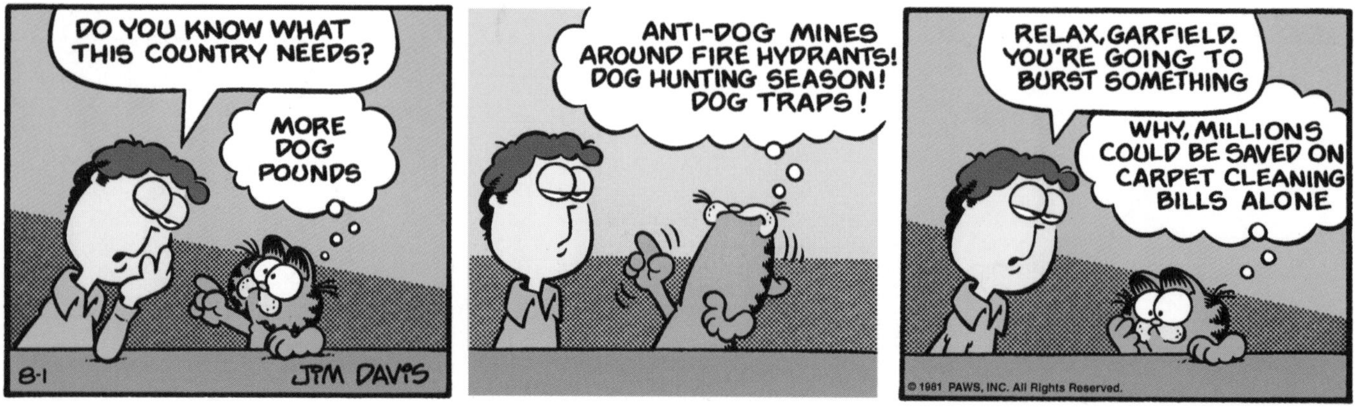
DO YOU KNOW WHAT THIS COUNTRY NEEDS?
MORE DOG POUNDS
8-1
JIM DAVIS
ANTI-DOG MINES AROUND FIRE HYDRANTS! DOG HUNTING SEASON! DOG TRAPS!
RELAX, GARFIELD. YOU'RE GOING TO BURST SOMETHING
WHY, MILLIONS COULD BE SAVED ON CARPET CLEANING BILLS ALONE
© 1981 PAWS, INC. All Rights Reserved.

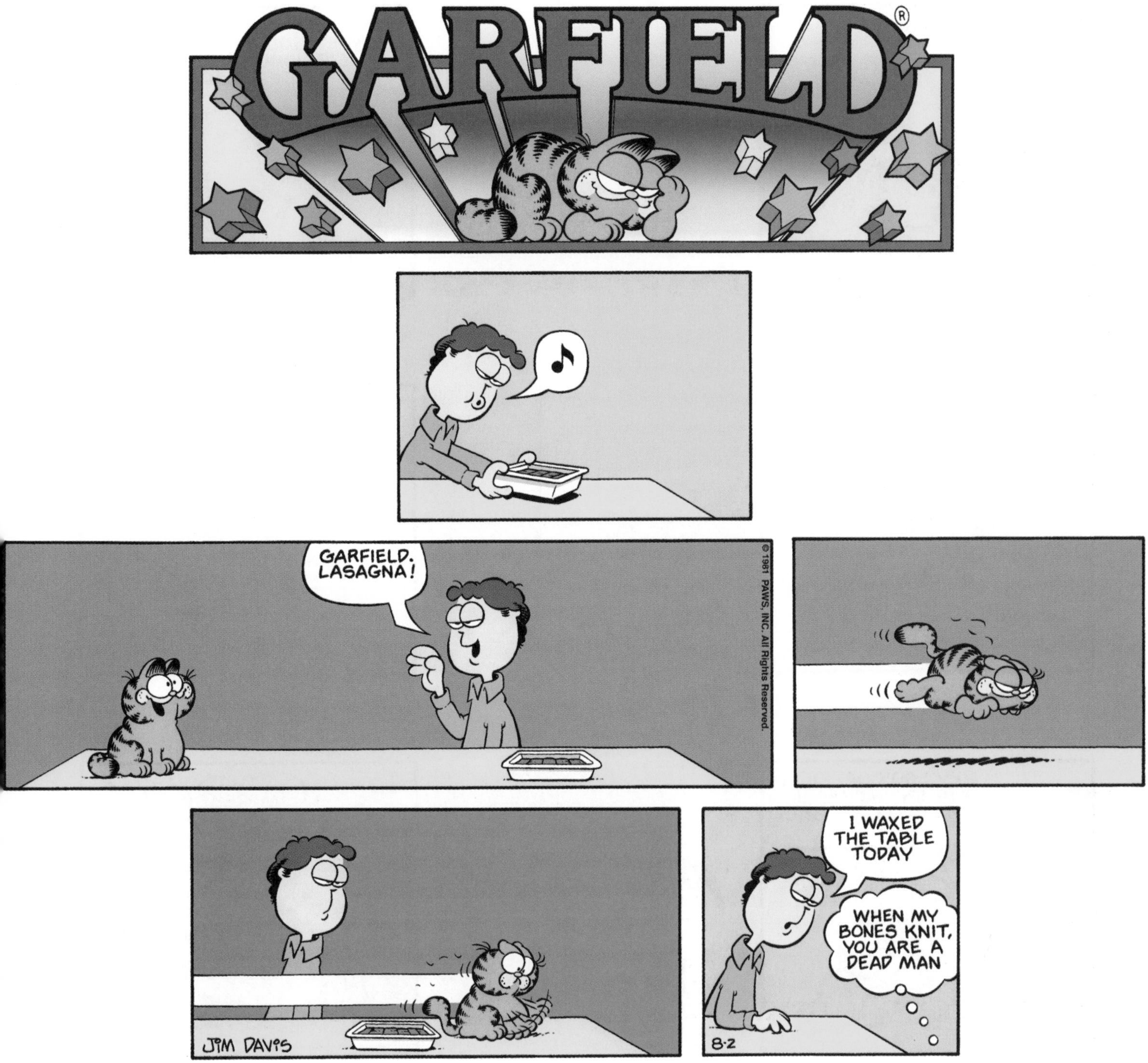
GARFIELD®
GARFIELD. LASAGNA!
© 1981 PAWS, INC. All Rights Reserved.
JIM DAVIS
I WAXED THE TABLE TODAY
WHEN MY BONES KNIT, YOU ARE A DEAD MAN
8-2

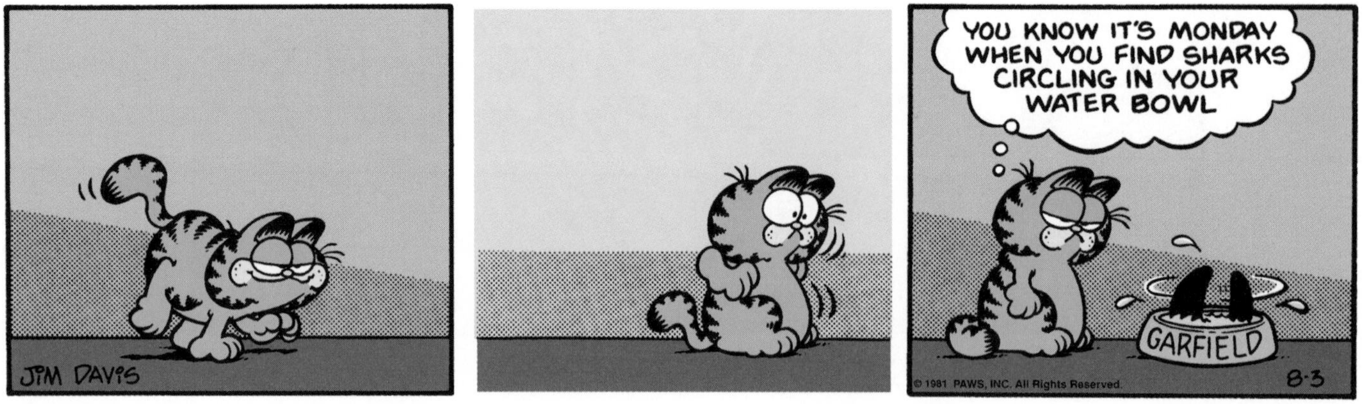
JIM DAVIS
YOU KNOW IT'S MONDAY WHEN YOU FIND SHARKS CIRCLING IN YOUR WATER BOWL
GARFIELD
© 1981 PAWS, INC. All Rights Reserved.
8-3

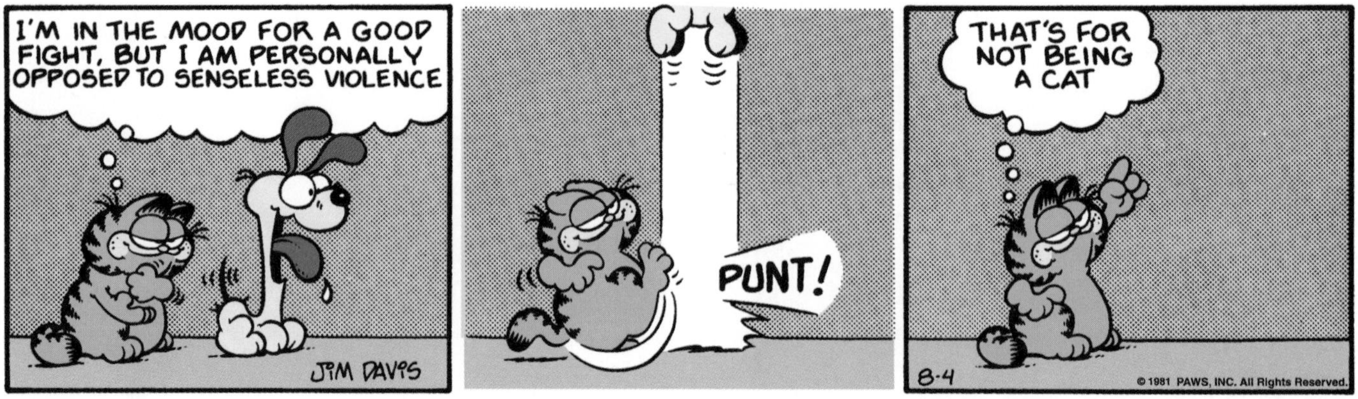
I'M IN THE MOOD FOR A GOOD FIGHT, BUT I AM PERSONALLY OPPOSED TO SENSELESS VIOLENCE
JIM DAVIS
PUNT!
THAT'S FOR NOT BEING A CAT
8-4
© 1981 PAWS, INC. All Rights Reserved.

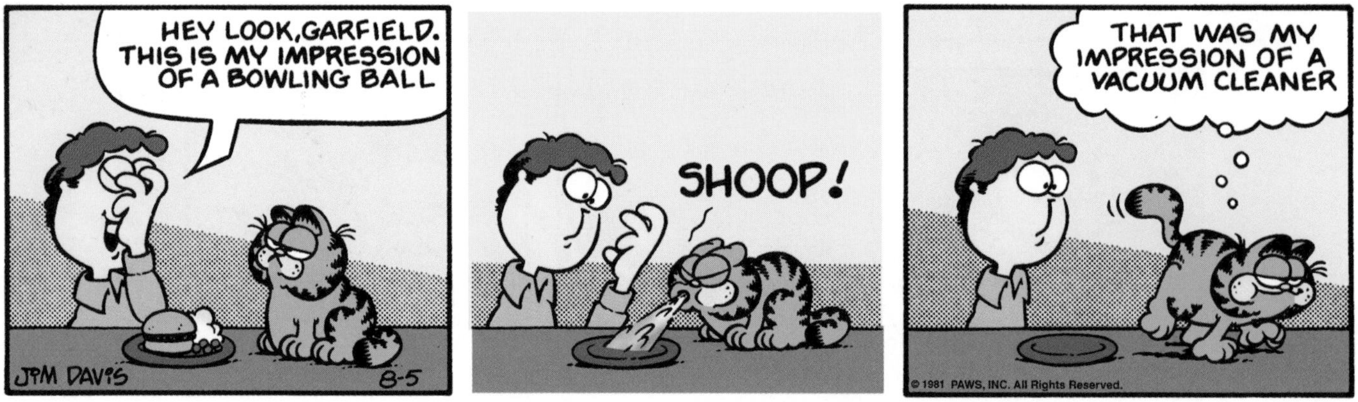
HEY LOOK,GARFIELD. THIS IS MY IMPRESSION OF A BOWLING BALL
JIM DAVIS
8-5
SHOOP!
THAT WAS MY IMPRESSION OF A VACUUM CLEANER
© 1981 PAWS, INC. All Rights Reserved.

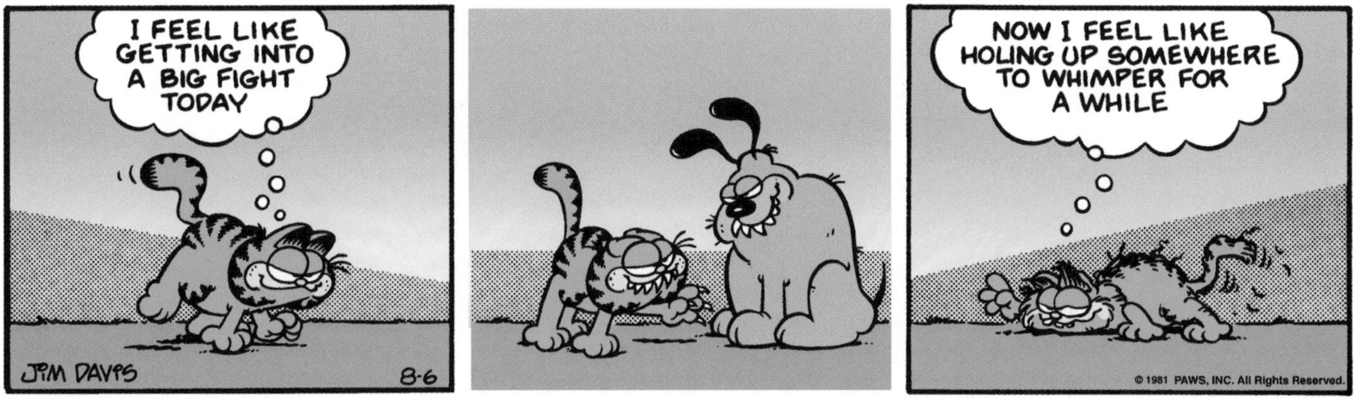
I FEEL LIKE GETTING INTO A BIG FIGHT TODAY
JIM DAVIS
8-6
NOW I FEEL LIKE HOLING UP SOMEWHERE TO WHIMPER FOR A WHILE
© 1981 PAWS, INC. All Rights Reserved.

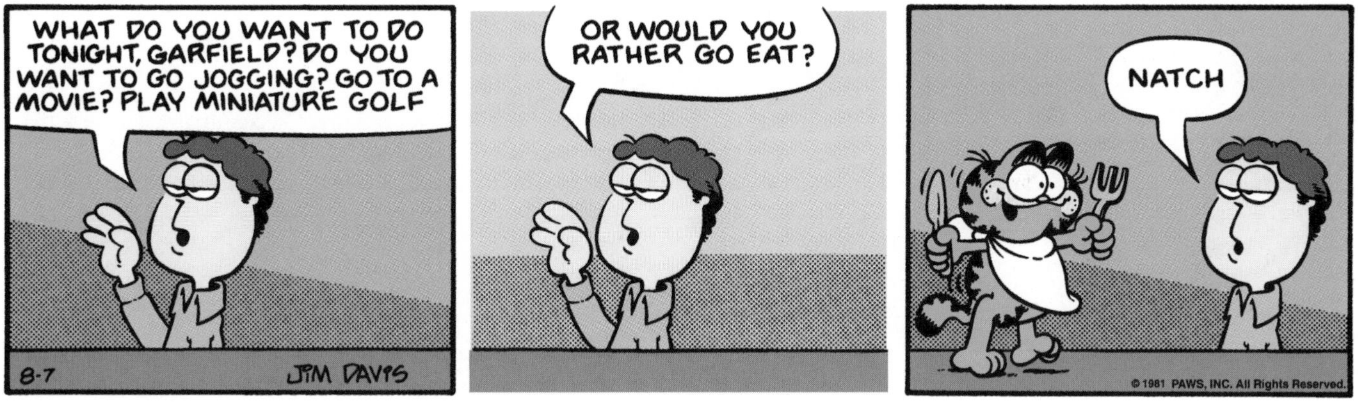
WHAT DO YOU WANT TO DO TONIGHT, GARFIELD? DO YOU WANT TO GO JOGGING? GO TO A MOVIE? PLAY MINIATURE GOLF
8-7
JIM DAVIS
OR WOULD YOU RATHER GO EAT?
NATCH
© 1981 PAWS, INC. All Rights Reserved.

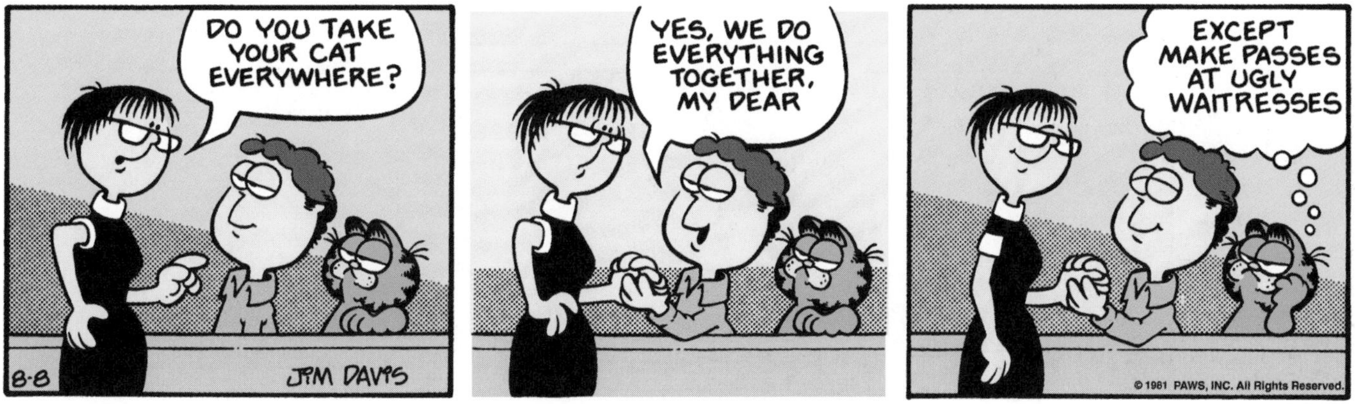
DO YOU TAKE YOUR CAT EVERYWHERE?
8-8
JIM DAVIS
YES, WE DO EVERYTHING TOGETHER, MY DEAR
EXCEPT MAKE PASSES AT UGLY WAITRESSES
© 1981 PAWS, INC. All Rights Reserved.

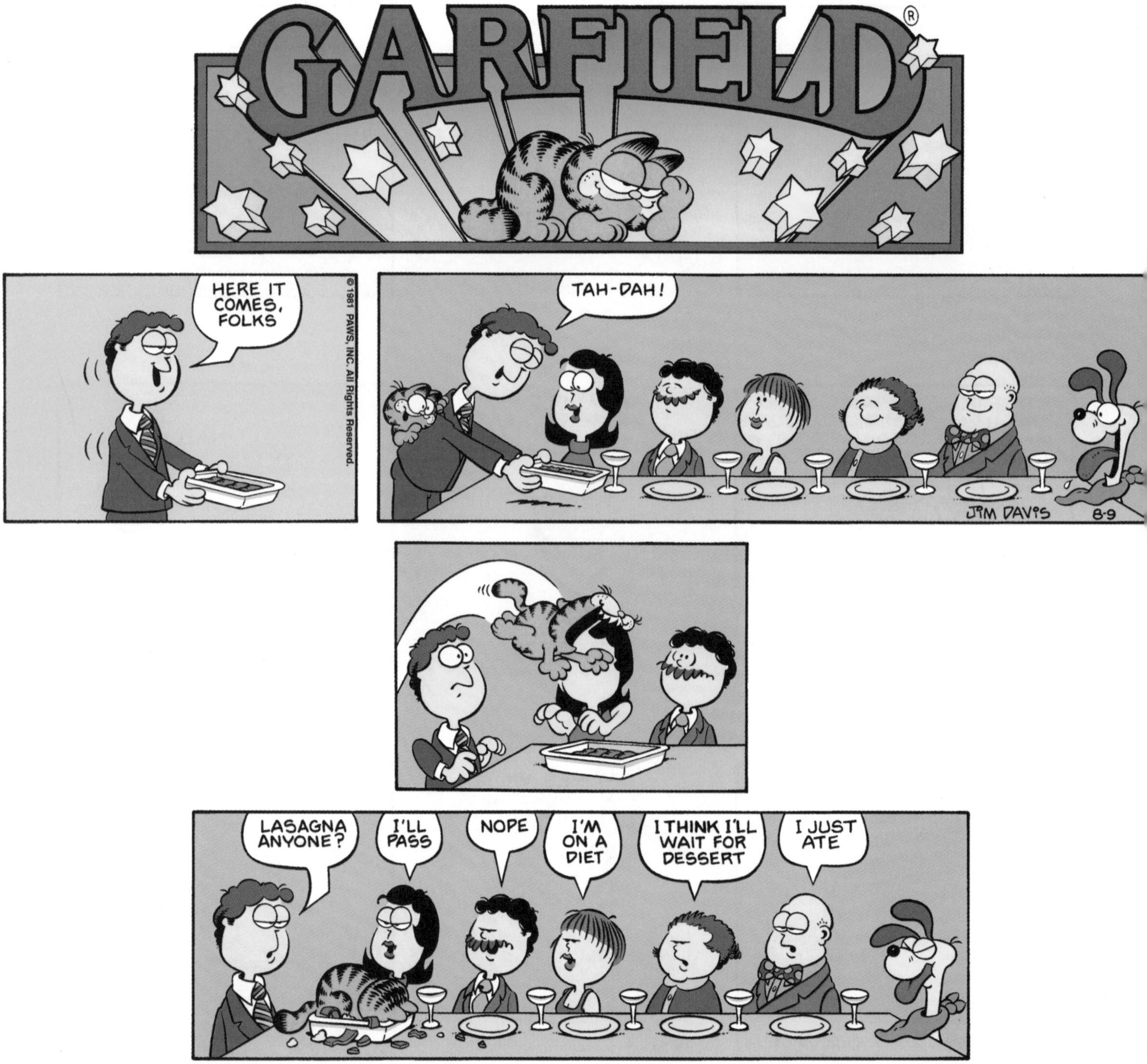
GARFIELD®
HERE IT COMES, FOLKS
© 1981 PAWS, INC. All Rights Reserved.
TAH-DAH!
JIM DAVIS 8-9
LASAGNA ANYONE?
I'LL PASS
NOPE
I'M ON A DIET
I THINK I'LL WAIT FOR DESSERT
I JUST ATE

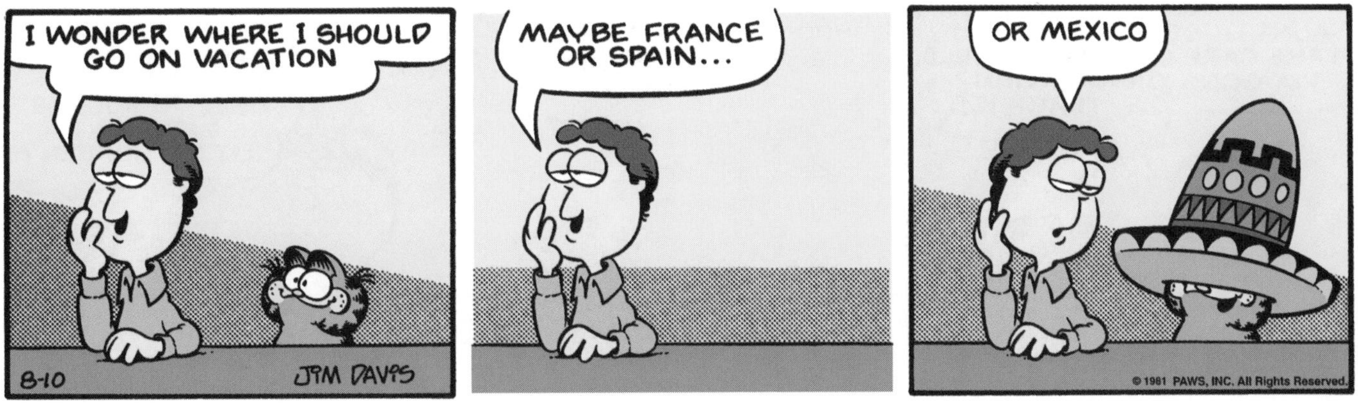
I WONDER WHERE I SHOULD GO ON VACATION
8-10
JIM DAVIS
MAYBE FRANCE OR SPAIN...
OR MEXICO
© 1981 PAWS, INC. All Rights Reserved.

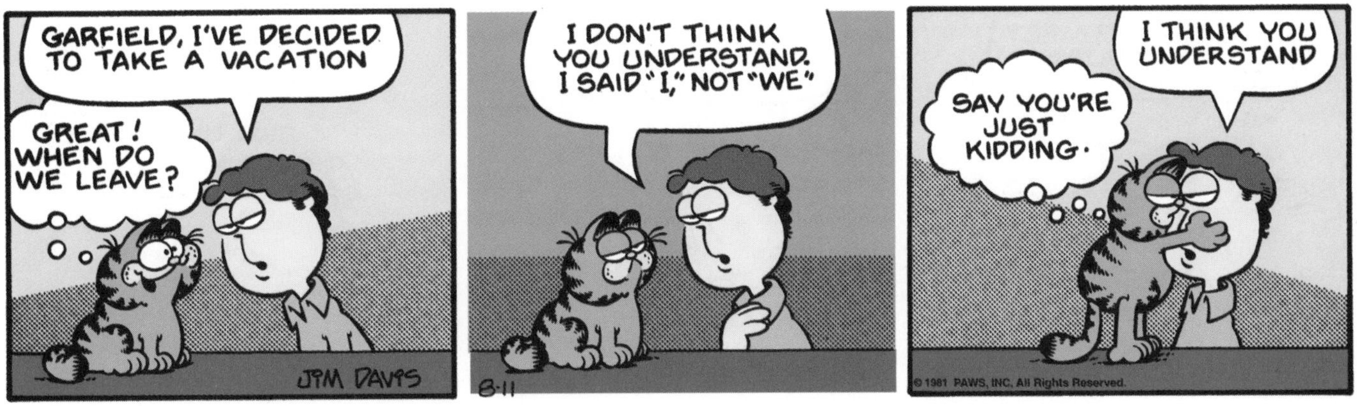
GARFIELD, I'VE DECIDED TO TAKE A VACATION
GREAT! WHEN DO WE LEAVE?
JIM DAVIS
I DON'T THINK YOU UNDERSTAND. I SAID "I," NOT "WE"
8-11
I THINK YOU UNDERSTAND
SAY YOU'RE JUST KIDDING.
© 1981 PAWS, INC. All Rights Reserved.

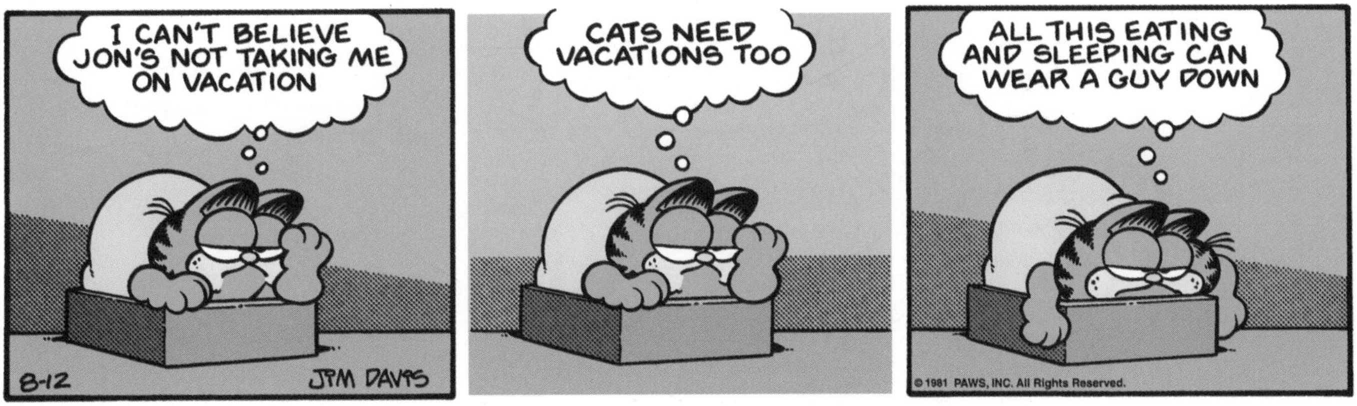
I CAN'T BELIEVE JON'S NOT TAKING ME ON VACATION
8-12
JIM DAVIS
CATS NEED VACATIONS TOO
ALL THIS EATING AND SLEEPING CAN WEAR A GUY DOWN
© 1981 PAWS, INC. All Rights Reserved.

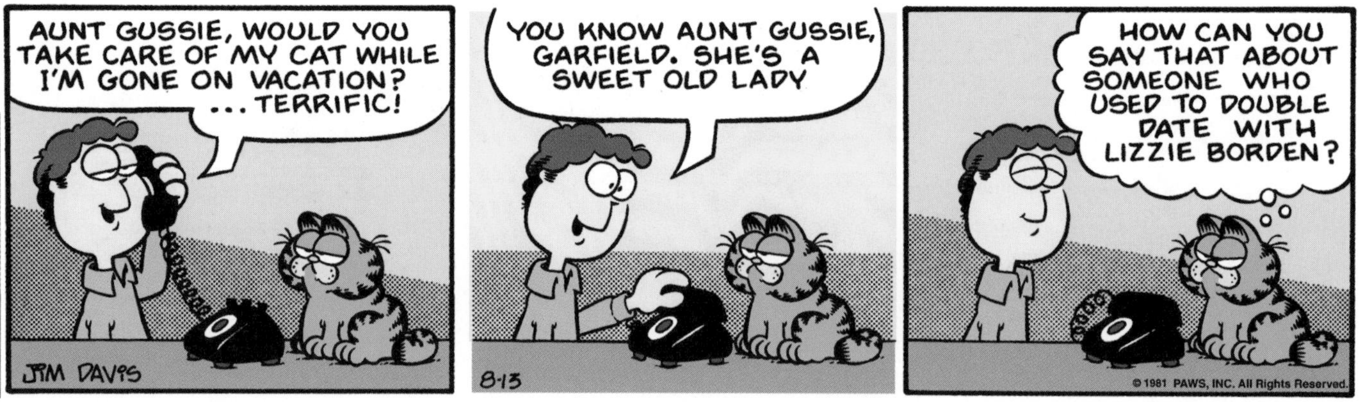
AUNT GUSSIE, WOULD YOU TAKE CARE OF MY CAT WHILE I'M GONE ON VACATION? ... TERRIFIC!
JIM DAVIS
YOU KNOW AUNT GUSSIE, GARFIELD. SHE'S A SWEET OLD LADY
8-13
HOW CAN YOU SAY THAT ABOUT SOMEONE WHO USED TO DOUBLE DATE WITH LIZZIE BORDEN?
© 1981 PAWS, INC. All Rights Reserved.

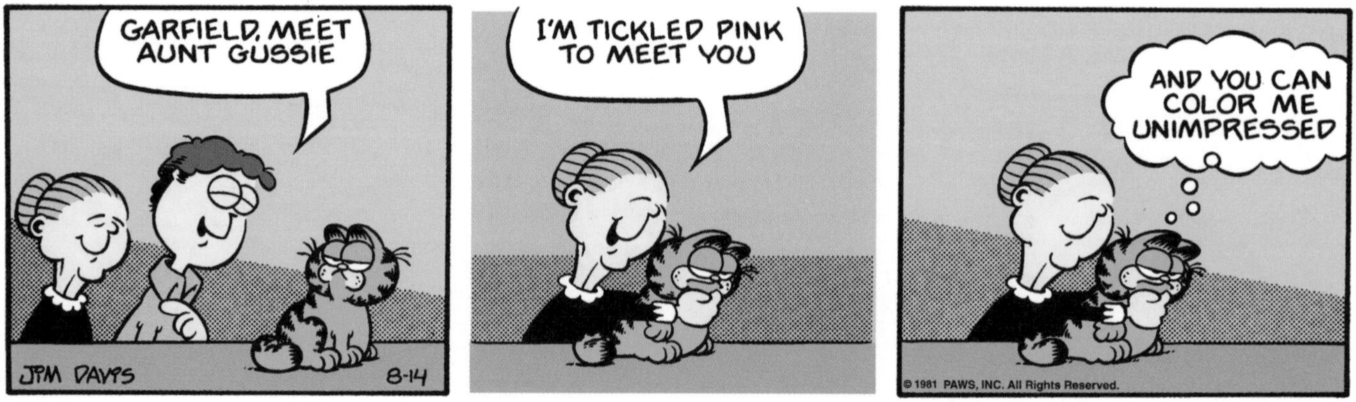
GARFIELD, MEET AUNT GUSSIE
JIM DAVIS
8-14
I'M TICKLED PINK TO MEET YOU
AND YOU CAN COLOR ME UNIMPRESSED
© 1981 PAWS, INC. All Rights Reserved.

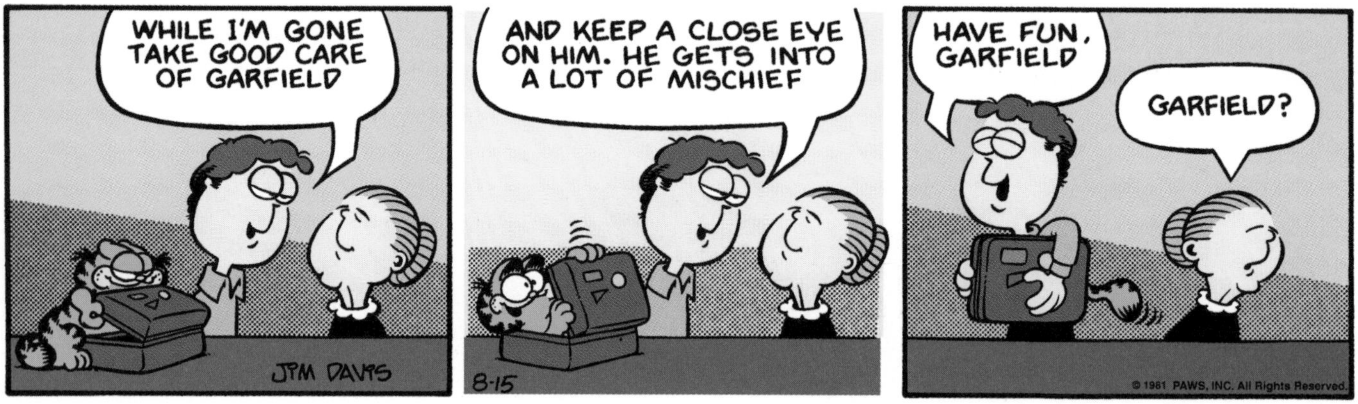
WHILE I'M GONE TAKE GOOD CARE OF GARFIELD
JIM DAVIS
AND KEEP A CLOSE EYE ON HIM. HE GETS INTO A LOT OF MISCHIEF
8-15
HAVE FUN, GARFIELD
GARFIELD?
© 1981 PAWS, INC. All Rights Reserved.

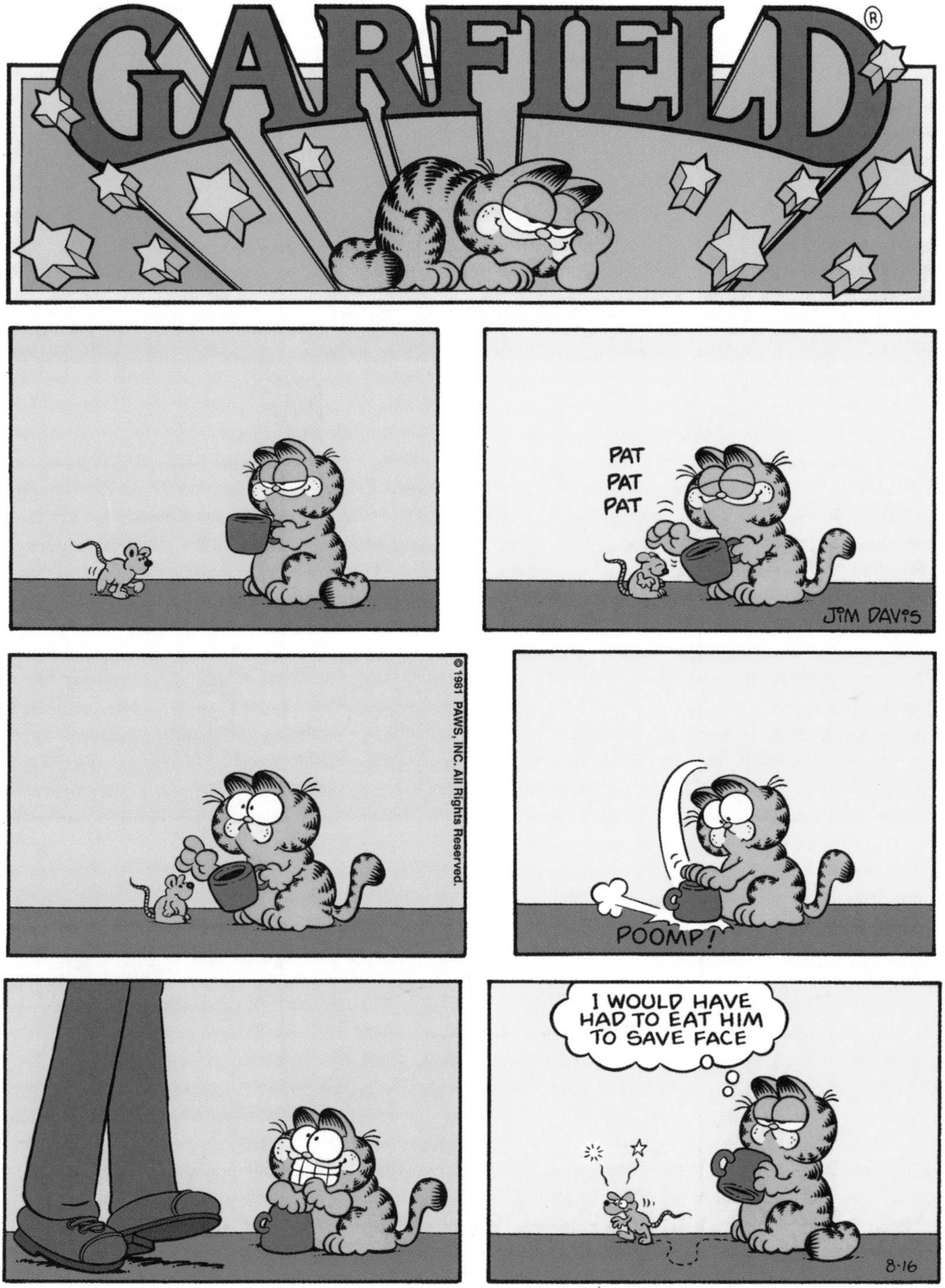
GARFIELD®
PAT
PAT
PAT
JIM DAVIS
© 1981 PAWS, INC. All Rights Reserved.
POOMP!
I WOULD HAVE HAD TO EAT HIM TO SAVE FACE
8-16

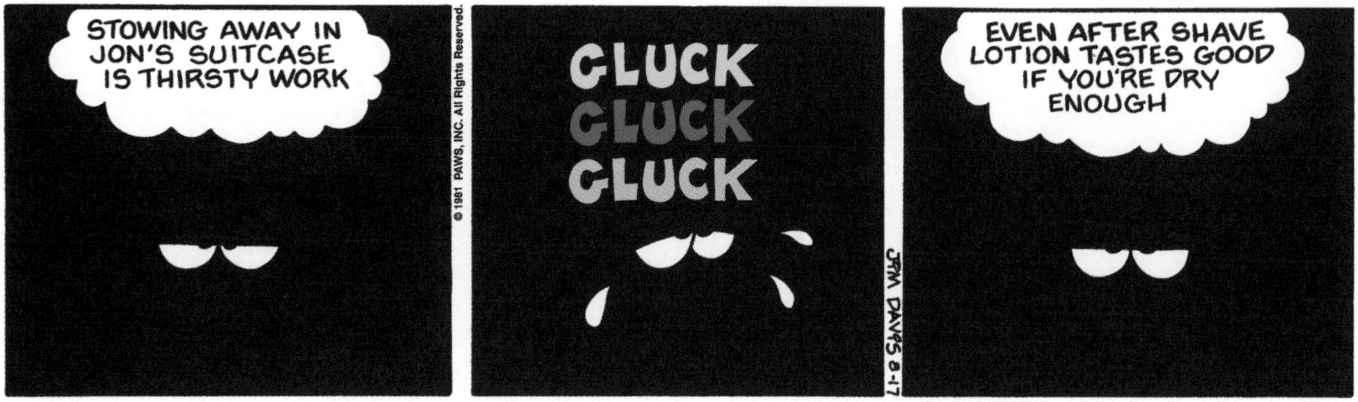
STOWING AWAY IN JON'S SUITCASE IS THIRSTY WORK
GLUCK
GLUCK
GLUCK
EVEN AFTER SHAVE LOTION TASTES GOOD IF YOU'RE DRY ENOUGH
JIM DAVIS 8-17
© 1981 PAWS, INC. All Rights Reserved.

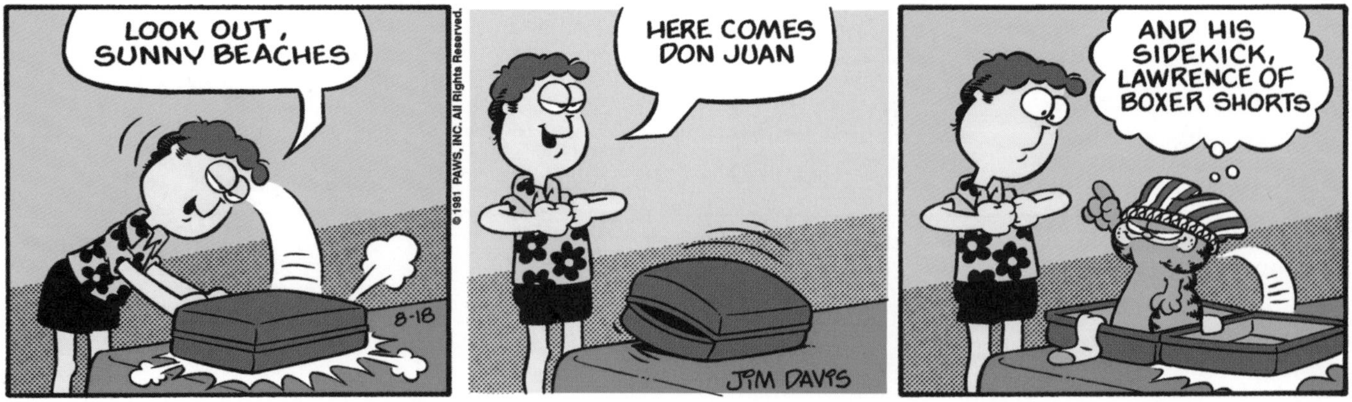
LOOK OUT, SUNNY BEACHES
8-18
HERE COMES DON JUAN
JIM DAVIS
AND HIS SIDEKICK, LAWRENCE OF BOXER SHORTS
© 1981 PAWS, INC. All Rights Reserved.

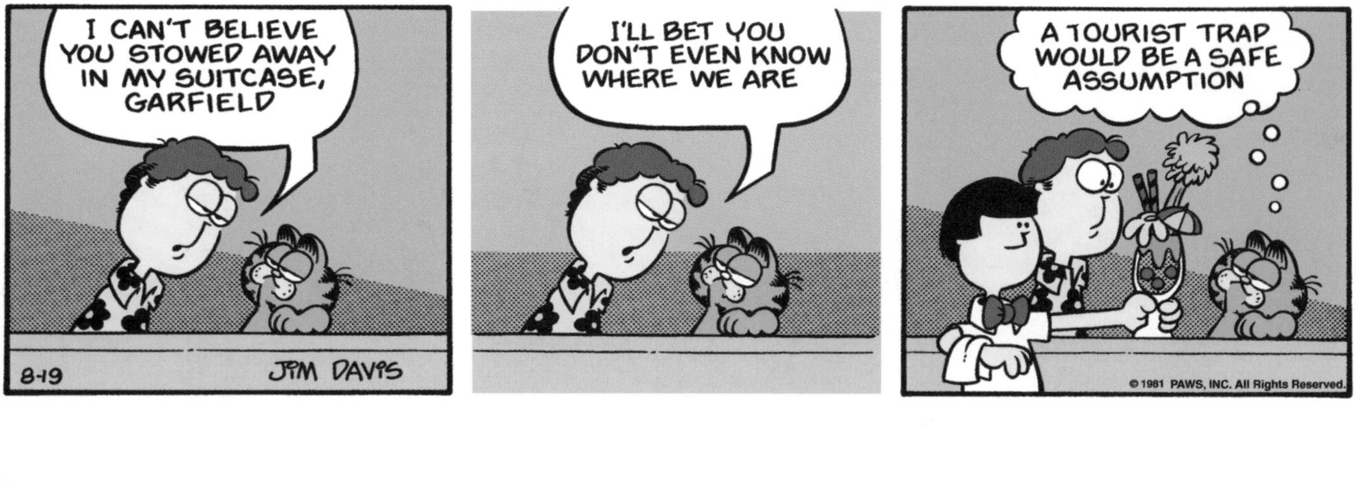
I CAN'T BELIEVE YOU STOWED AWAY IN MY SUITCASE, GARFIELD
8-19
JIM DAVIS
I'LL BET YOU DON'T EVEN KNOW WHERE WE ARE
A TOURIST TRAP WOULD BE A SAFE ASSUMPTION
© 1981 PAWS, INC. All Rights Reserved.

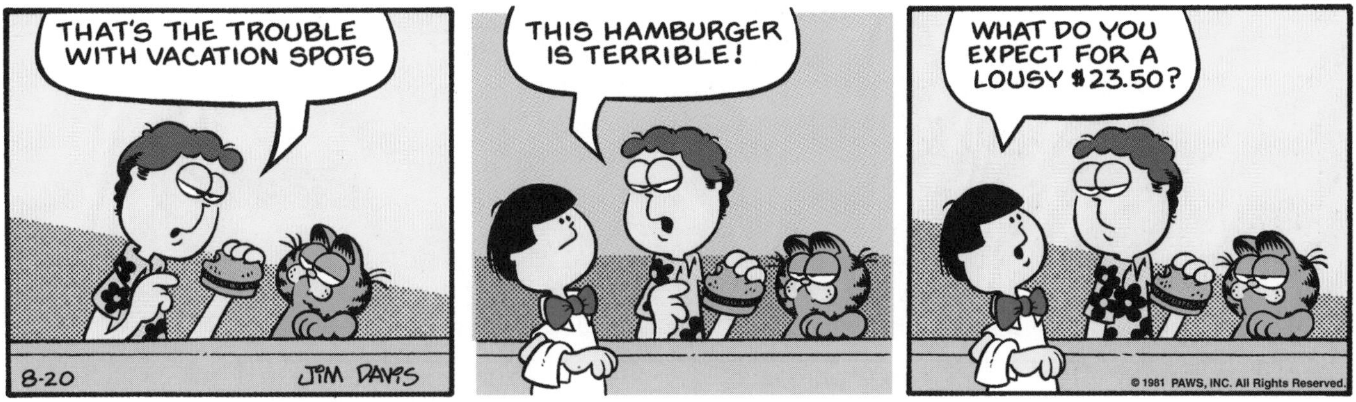
THAT'S THE TROUBLE WITH VACATION SPOTS
8-20
JIM DAVIS
THIS HAMBURGER IS TERRIBLE!
WHAT DO YOU EXPECT FOR A LOUSY $23.50?
© 1981 PAWS, INC. All Rights Reserved.

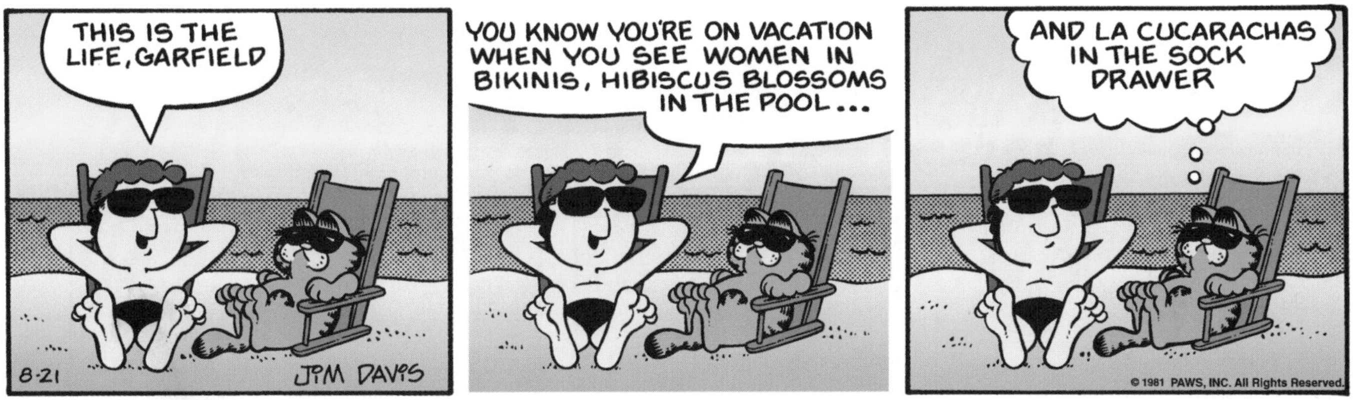
THIS IS THE LIFE, GARFIELD
8-21
JIM DAVIS
YOU KNOW YOU'RE ON VACATION WHEN YOU SEE WOMEN IN BIKINIS, HIBISCUS BLOSSOMS IN THE POOL...
AND LA CUCARACHAS IN THE SOCK DRAWER
© 1981 PAWS, INC. All Rights Reserved.

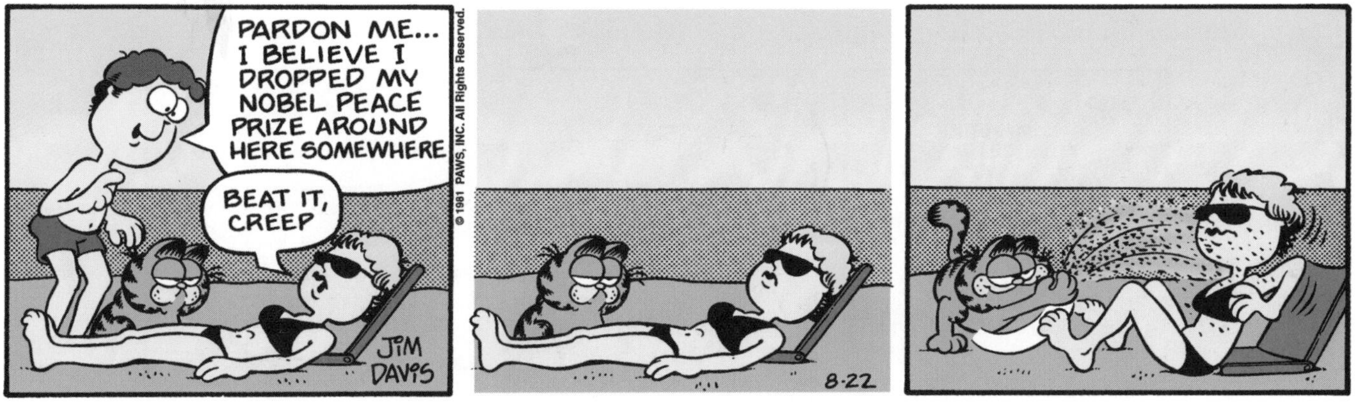
PARDON ME... I BELIEVE I DROPPED MY NOBEL PEACE PRIZE AROUND HERE SOMEWHERE
BEAT IT, CREEP
JIM DAVIS
© 1981 PAWS, INC. All Rights Reserved.
8-22

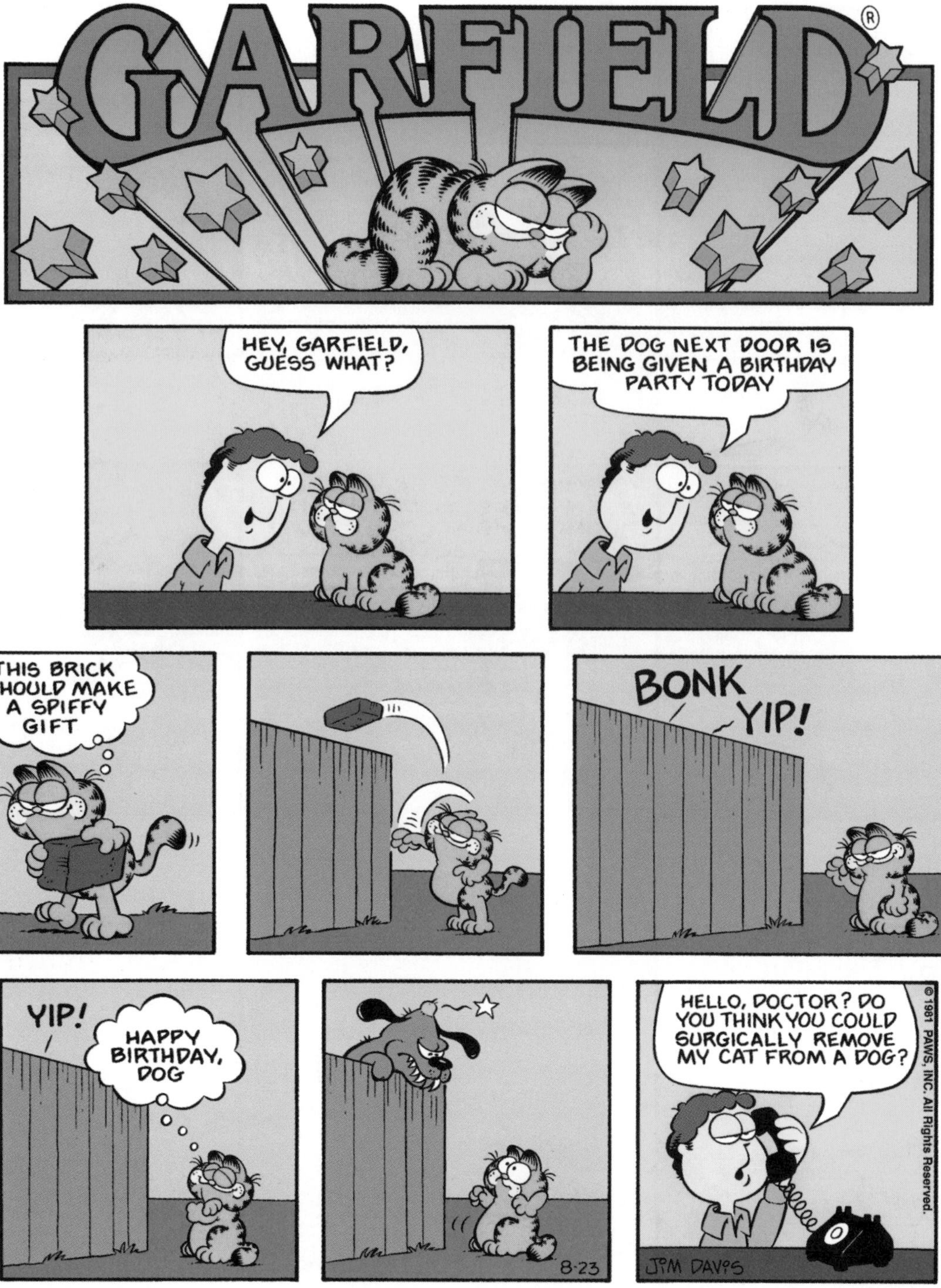
GARFIELD®
HEY, GARFIELD, GUESS WHAT?
THE DOG NEXT DOOR IS BEING GIVEN A BIRTHDAY PARTY TODAY
THIS BRICK SHOULD MAKE A SPIFFY GIFT
BONK
YIP!
YIP!
HAPPY BIRTHDAY, DOG
8-23
HELLO, DOCTOR? DO YOU THINK YOU COULD SURGICALLY REMOVE MY CAT FROM A DOG?
JIM DAVIS
© 1981 PAWS, INC. All Rights Reserved.

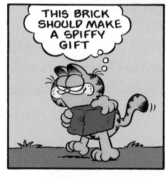

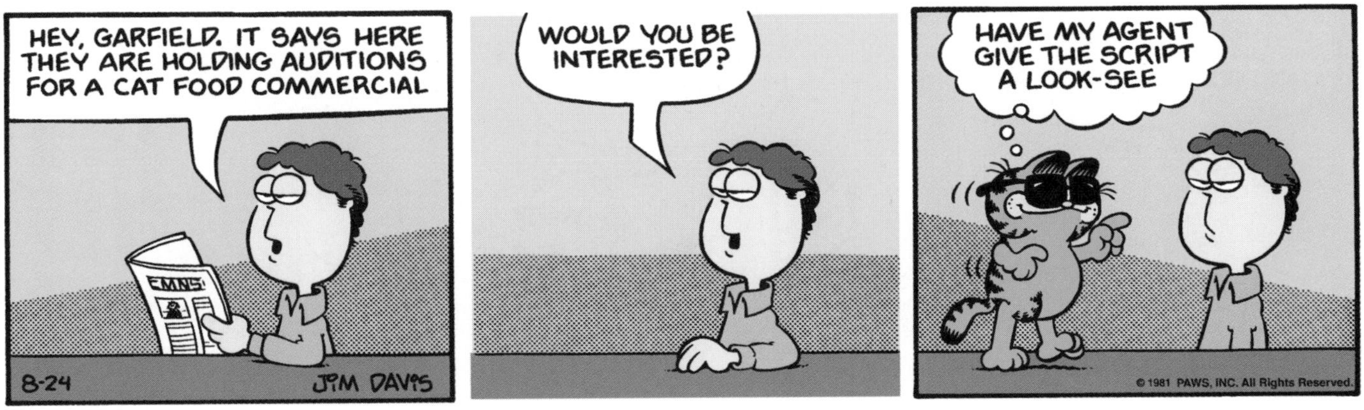
HEY, GARFIELD. IT SAYS HERE THEY ARE HOLDING AUDITIONS FOR A CAT FOOD COMMERCIAL
8-24
JIM DAVIS
WOULD YOU BE INTERESTED?
HAVE MY AGENT GIVE THE SCRIPT A LOOK-SEE
© 1981 PAWS, INC. All Rights Reserved.

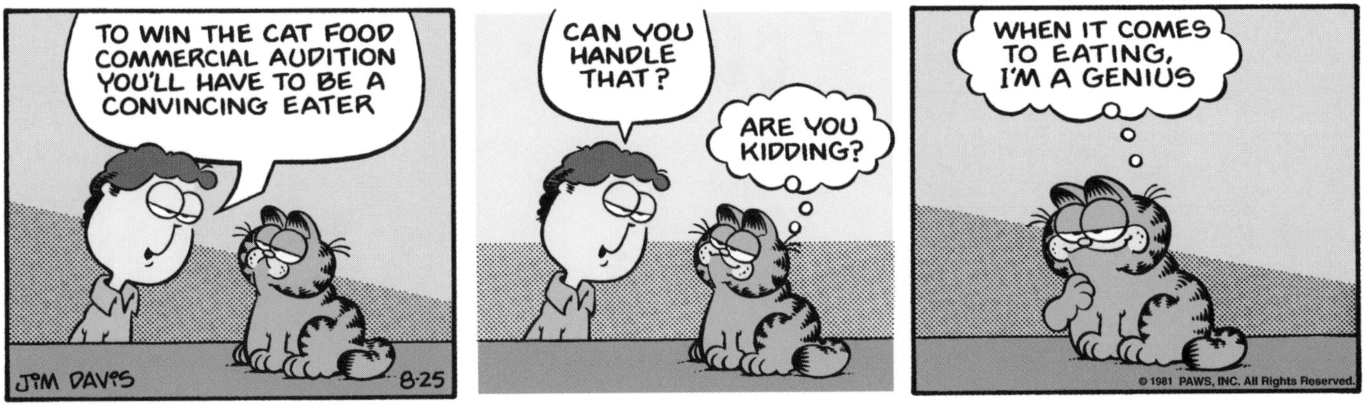
TO WIN THE CAT FOOD COMMERCIAL AUDITION YOU'LL HAVE TO BE A CONVINCING EATER
JIM DAVIS
8-25
CAN YOU HANDLE THAT?
ARE YOU KIDDING?
WHEN IT COMES TO EATING, I'M A GENIUS
© 1981 PAWS, INC. All Rights Reserved.

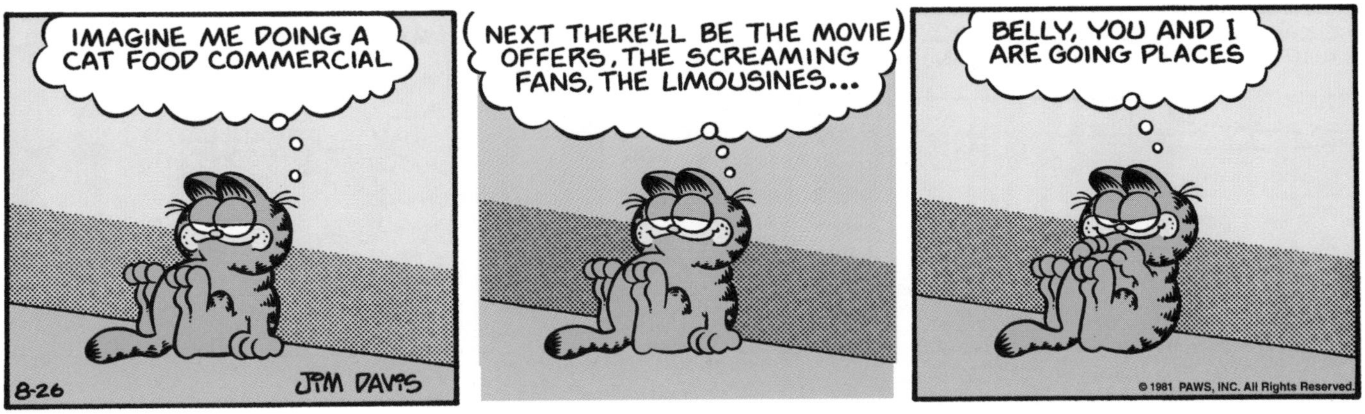
IMAGINE ME DOING A CAT FOOD COMMERCIAL
8-26
JIM DAVIS
NEXT THERE'LL BE THE MOVIE OFFERS, THE SCREAMING FANS, THE LIMOUSINES...
BELLY, YOU AND I ARE GOING PLACES
© 1981 PAWS, INC. All Rights Reserved.

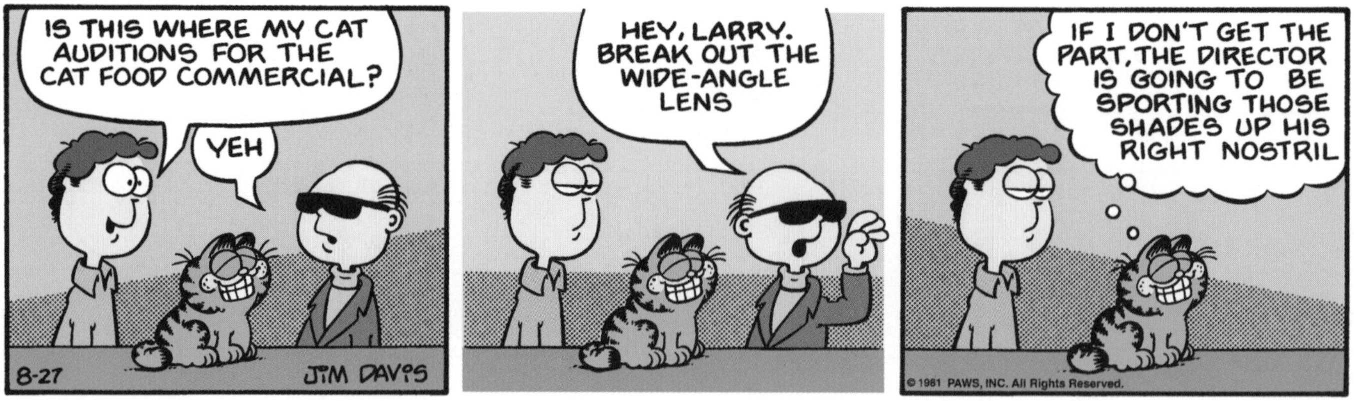
IS THIS WHERE MY CAT AUDITIONS FOR THE CAT FOOD COMMERCIAL?
YEH
8-27
JIM DAVIS
HEY, LARRY. BREAK OUT THE WIDE-ANGLE LENS
IF I DON'T GET THE PART, THE DIRECTOR IS GOING TO BE SPORTING THOSE SHADES UP HIS RIGHT NOSTRIL
© 1981 PAWS, INC. All Rights Reserved.

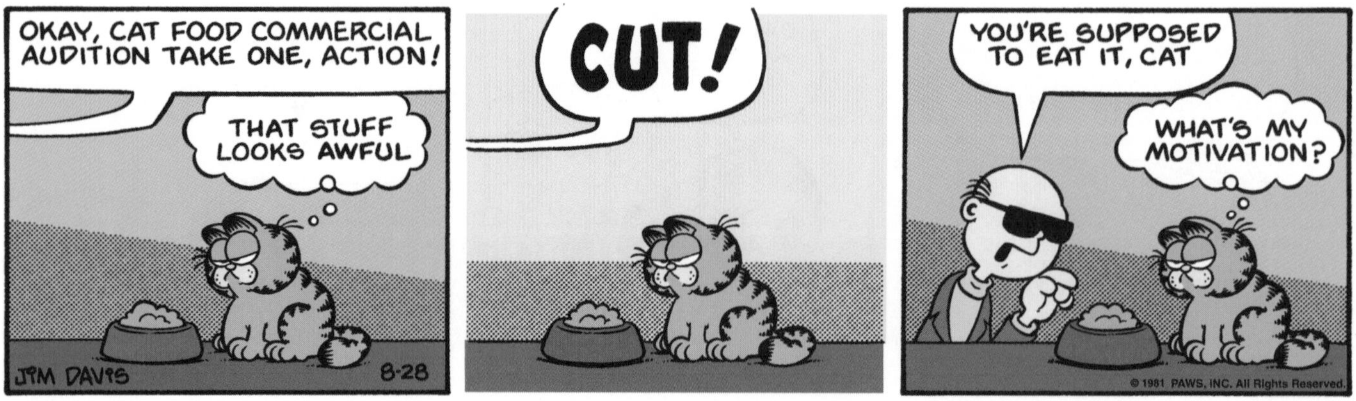
OKAY, CAT FOOD COMMERCIAL AUDITION TAKE ONE, ACTION!
THAT STUFF LOOKS AWFUL
JIM DAVIS
8-28
CUT!
YOU'RE SUPPOSED TO EAT IT, CAT
WHAT'S MY MOTIVATION?
© 1981 PAWS, INC. All Rights Reserved.

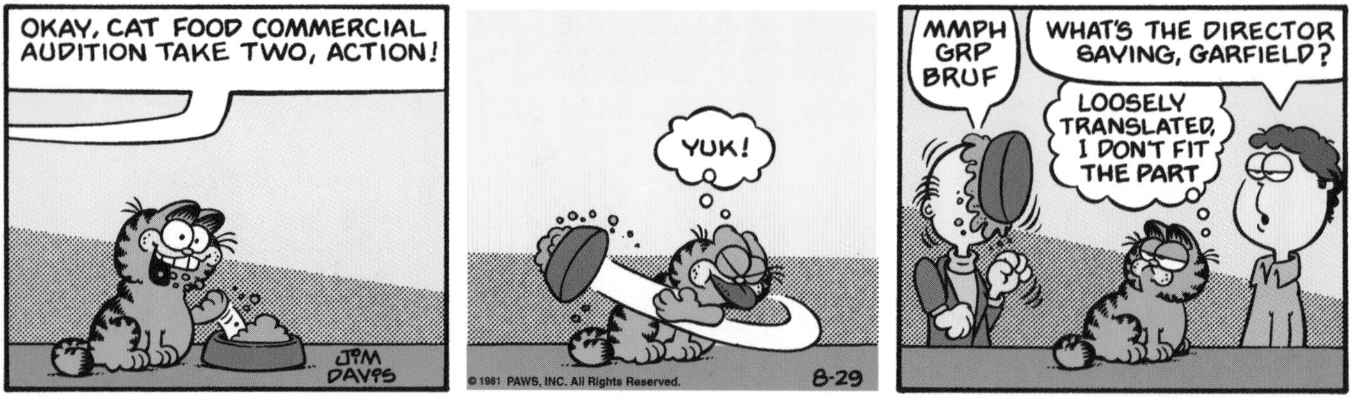
OKAY, CAT FOOD COMMERCIAL AUDITION TAKE TWO, ACTION!
JIM DAVIS
YUK!
© 1981 PAWS, INC. All Rights Reserved.
8-29
MMPH GRP BRUF
WHAT'S THE DIRECTOR SAYING, GARFIELD?
LOOSELY TRANSLATED, I DON'T FIT THE PART

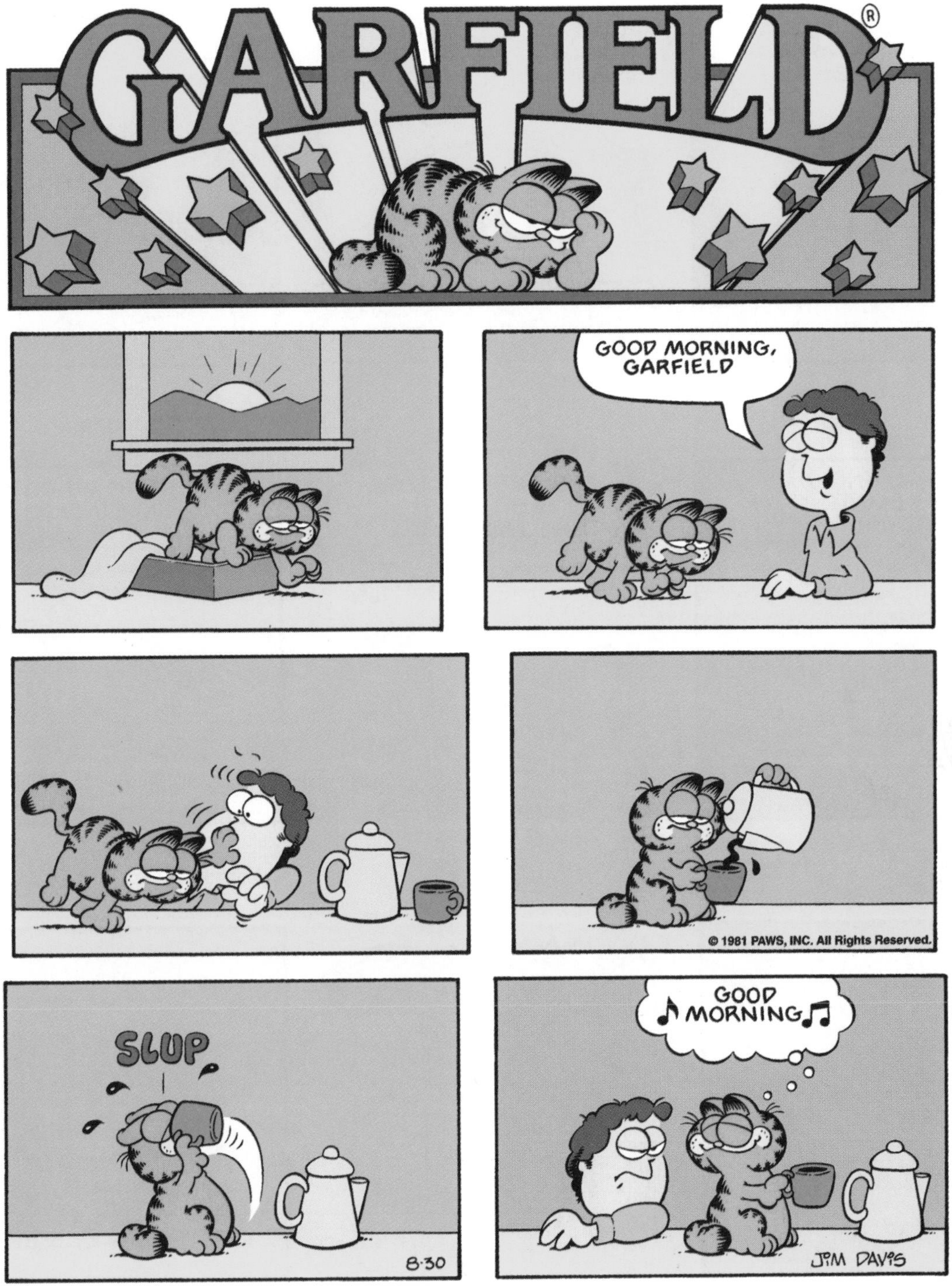
GARFIELD®
GOOD MORNING, GARFIELD
SLUP
8·30
GOOD MORNING
JIM DAVIS

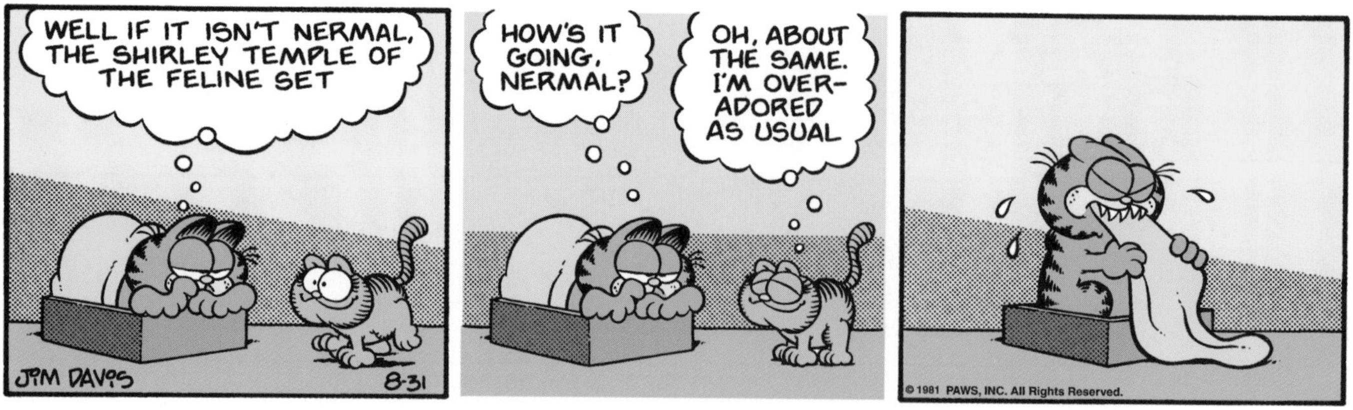
WELL IF IT ISN'T NERMAL, THE SHIRLEY TEMPLE OF THE FELINE SET
JIM DAVIS
8-31
HOW'S IT GOING, NERMAL?
OH, ABOUT THE SAME. I'M OVER-ADORED AS USUAL
© 1981 PAWS, INC. All Rights Reserved.

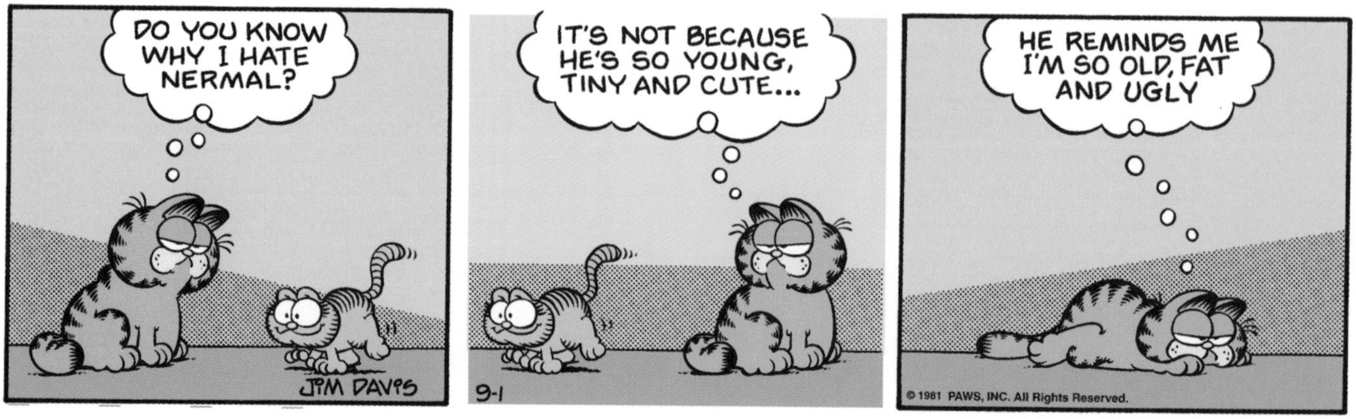
DO YOU KNOW WHY I HATE NERMAL?
JIM DAVIS
9-1
IT'S NOT BECAUSE HE'S SO YOUNG, TINY AND CUTE...
HE REMINDS ME I'M SO OLD, FAT AND UGLY
© 1981 PAWS, INC. All Rights Reserved.

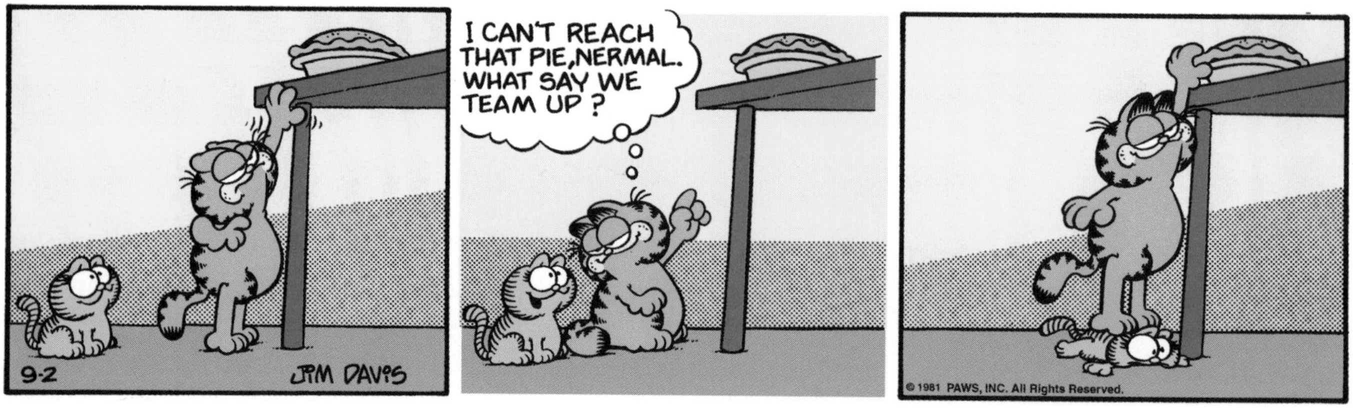
9-2
JIM DAVIS
I CAN'T REACH THAT PIE, NERMAL. WHAT SAY WE TEAM UP ?
© 1981 PAWS, INC. All Rights Reserved.

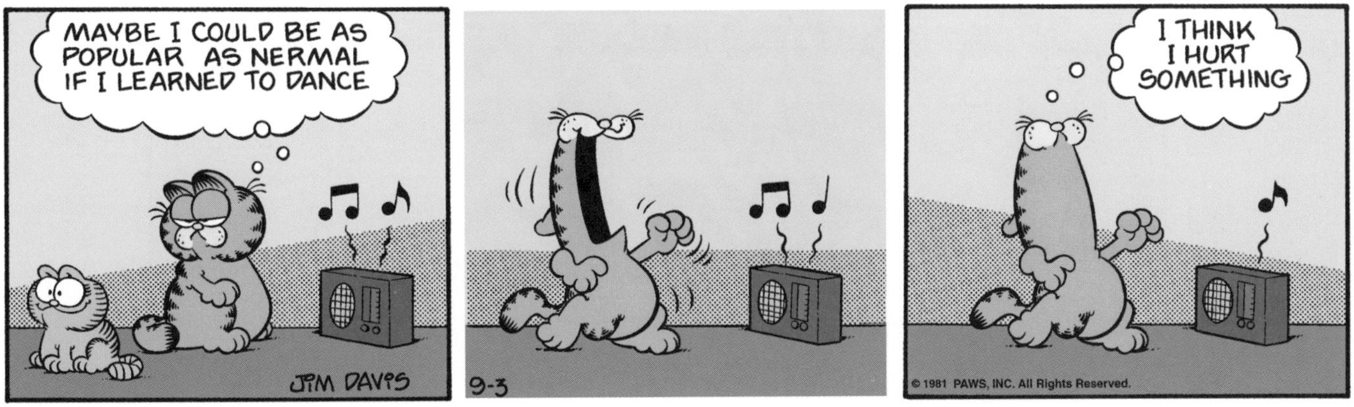
MAYBE I COULD BE AS POPULAR AS NERMAL IF I LEARNED TO DANCE
JIM DAVIS
9-3
I THINK I HURT SOMETHING
© 1981 PAWS, INC. All Rights Reserved.

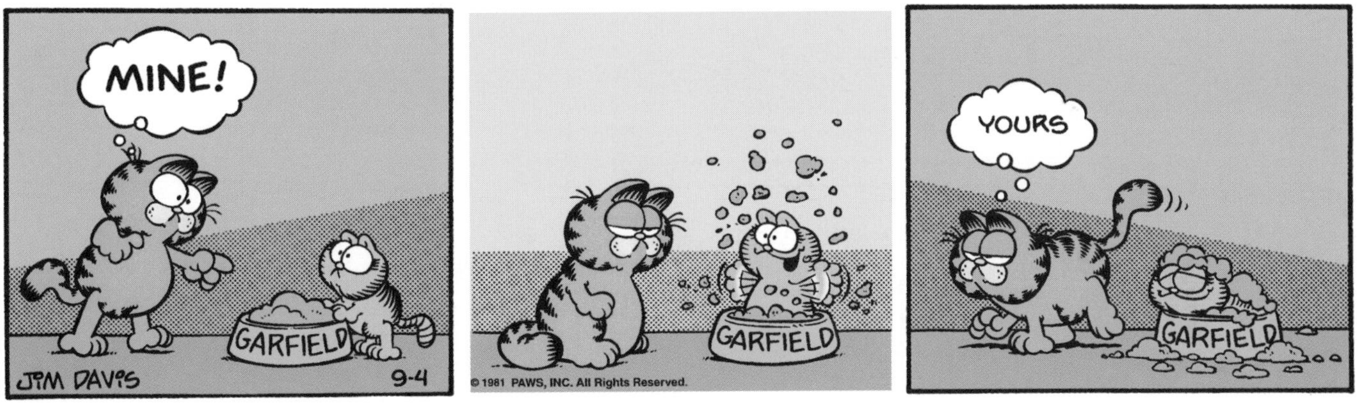
MINE!
GARFIELD
JIM DAVIS
9-4
GARFIELD
© 1981 PAWS, INC. All Rights Reserved.
YOURS
GARFIELD

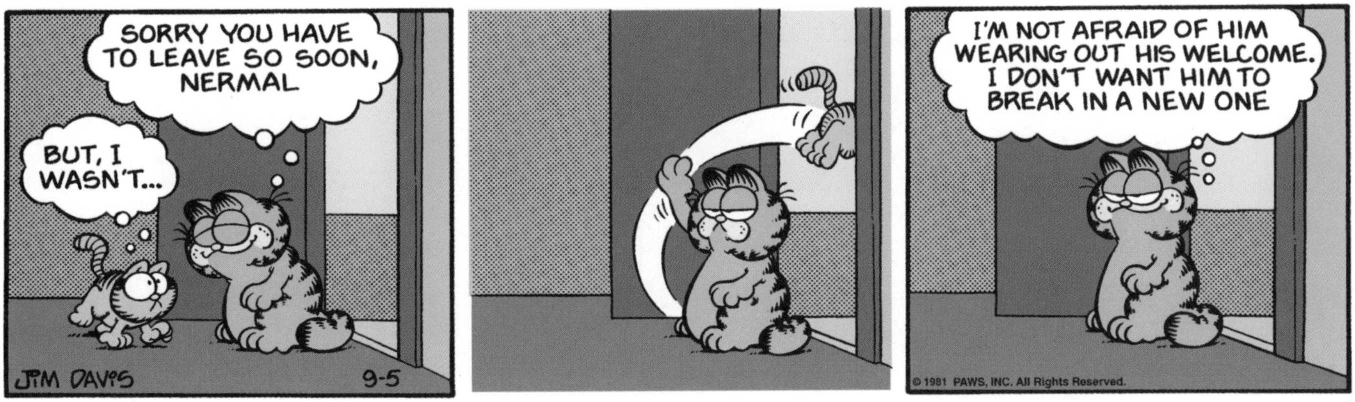
SORRY YOU HAVE TO LEAVE SO SOON, NERMAL
BUT, I WASN'T...
JIM DAVIS
9-5
I'M NOT AFRAID OF HIM WEARING OUT HIS WELCOME. I DON'T WANT HIM TO BREAK IN A NEW ONE
© 1981 PAWS, INC. All Rights Reserved.

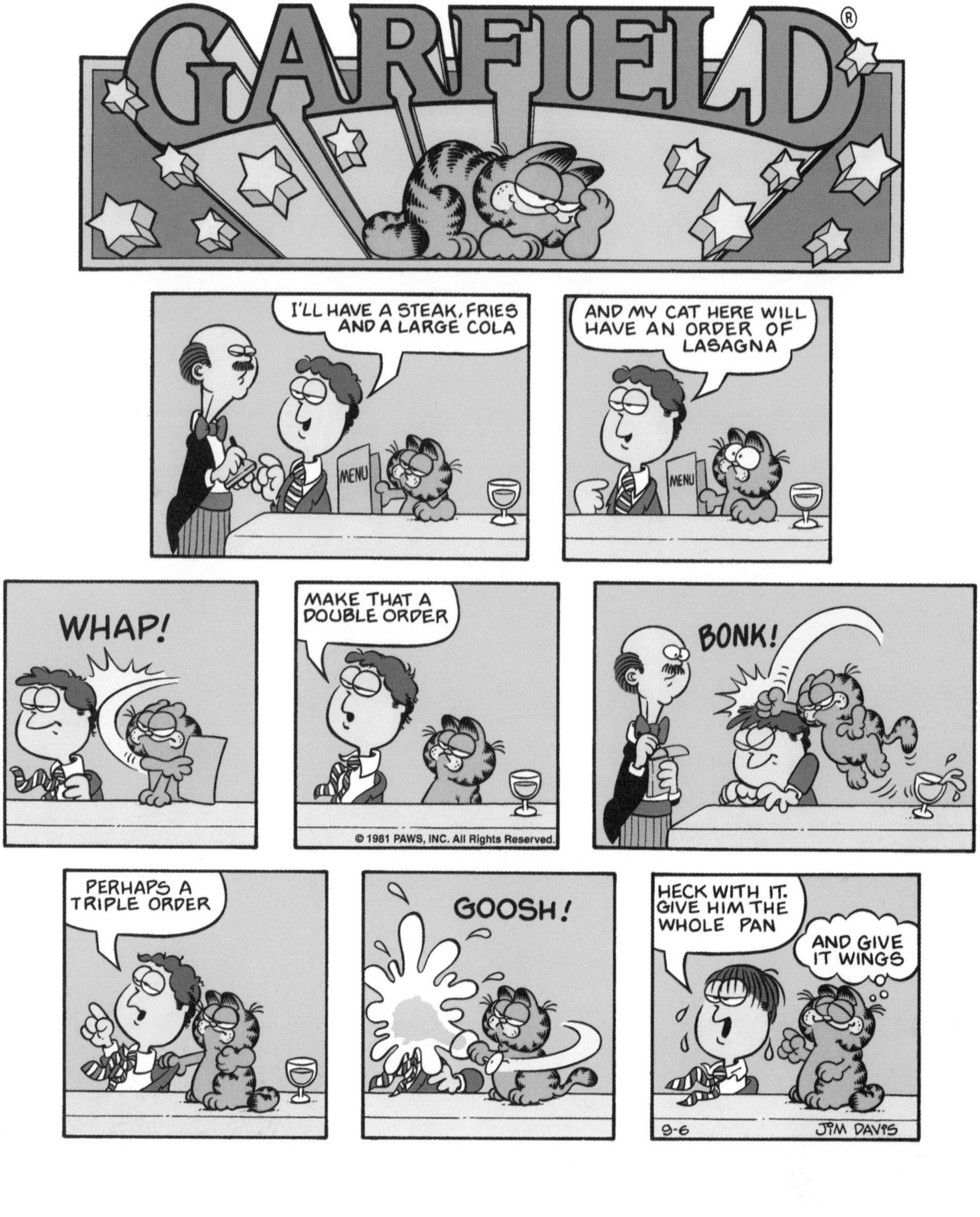
GARFIELD®
I'LL HAVE A STEAK, FRIES AND A LARGE COLA
MENU
AND MY CAT HERE WILL HAVE AN ORDER OF LASAGNA
MENU
WHAP!
MAKE THAT A DOUBLE ORDER
© 1981 PAWS, INC. All Rights Reserved.
BONK!
PERHAPS A TRIPLE ORDER
GOOSH!
HECK WITH IT. GIVE HIM THE WHOLE PAN
AND GIVE IT WINGS
9-6
JIM DAVIS

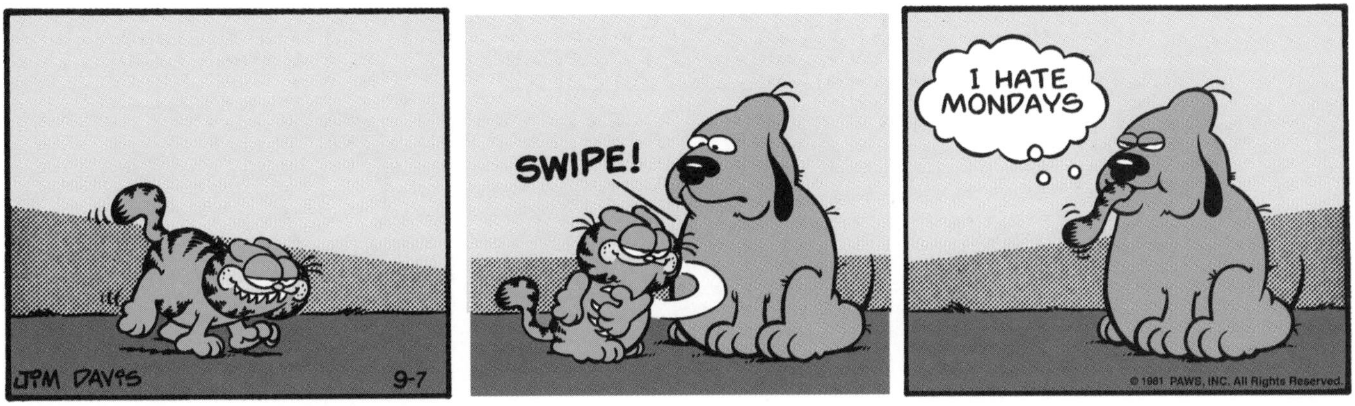
JIM DAVIS
9-7
SWIPE!
I HATE MONDAYS
© 1981 PAWS, INC. All Rights Reserved.

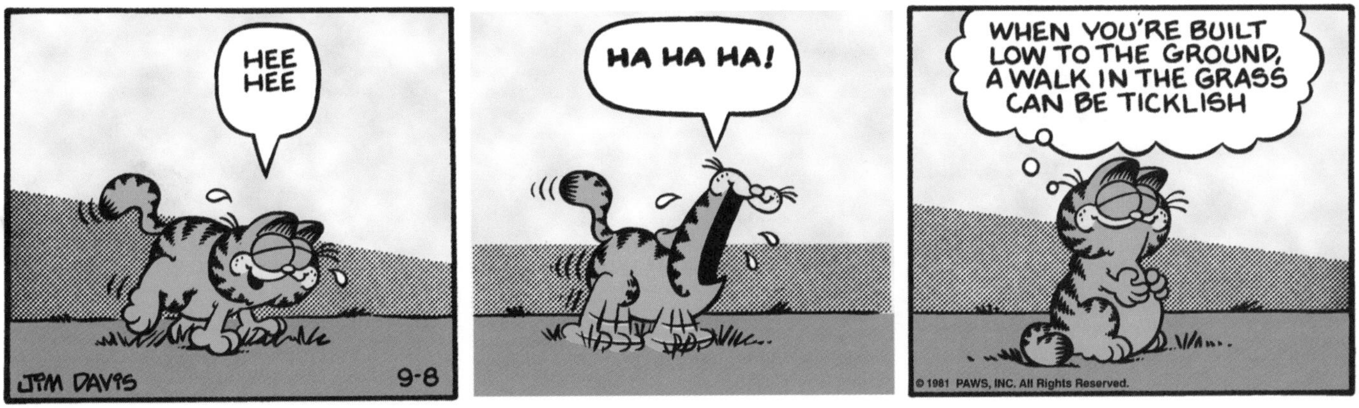
HEE HEE
JIM DAVIS
9-8
HA HA HA!
WHEN YOU'RE BUILT LOW TO THE GROUND, A WALK IN THE GRASS CAN BE TICKLISH
© 1981 PAWS, INC. All Rights Reserved.

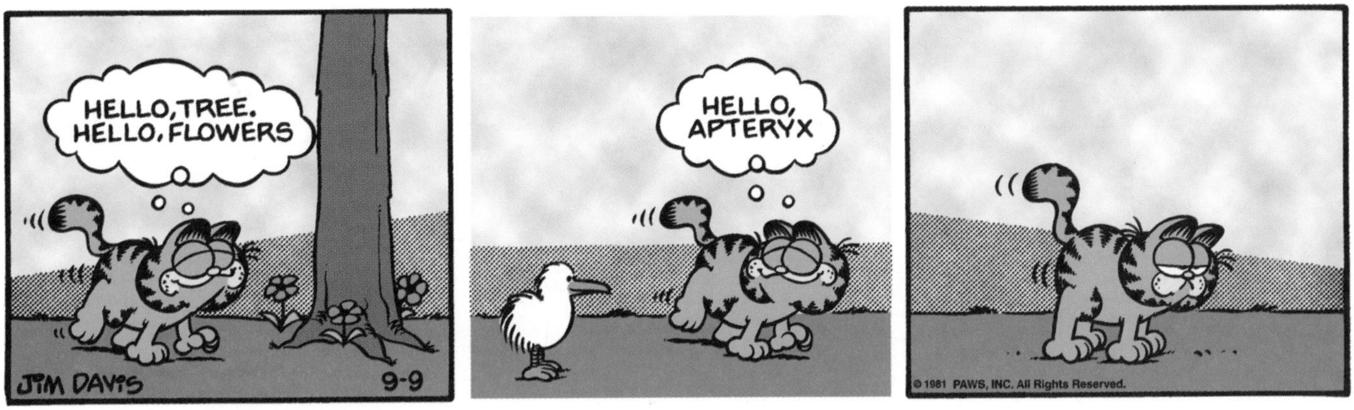
HELLO, TREE. HELLO, FLOWERS
JIM DAVIS
9-9
HELLO, APTERYX
© 1981 PAWS, INC. All Rights Reserved.

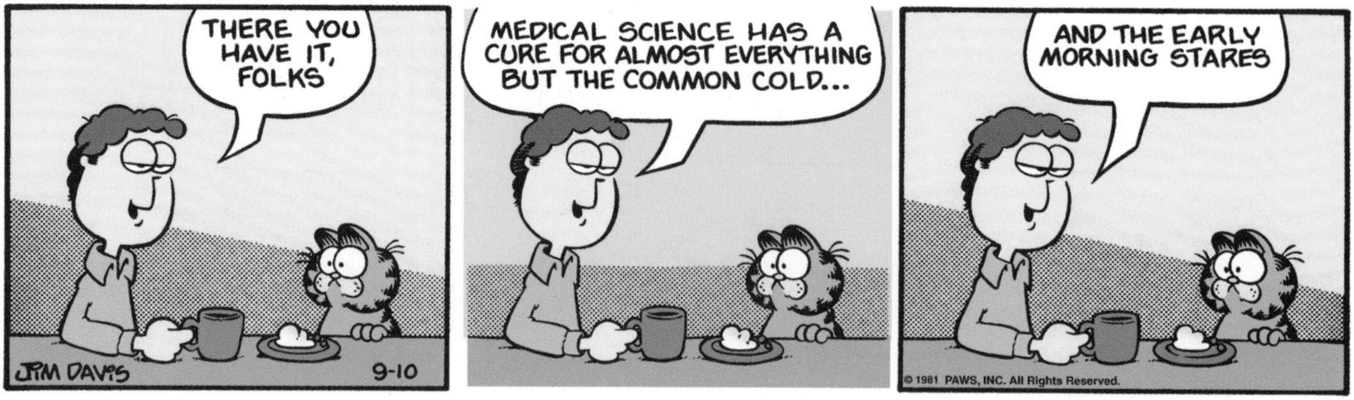
THERE YOU HAVE IT, FOLKS
JIM DAVIS
9-10
MEDICAL SCIENCE HAS A CURE FOR ALMOST EVERYTHING BUT THE COMMON COLD...
AND THE EARLY MORNING STARES
© 1981 PAWS, INC. All Rights Reserved.

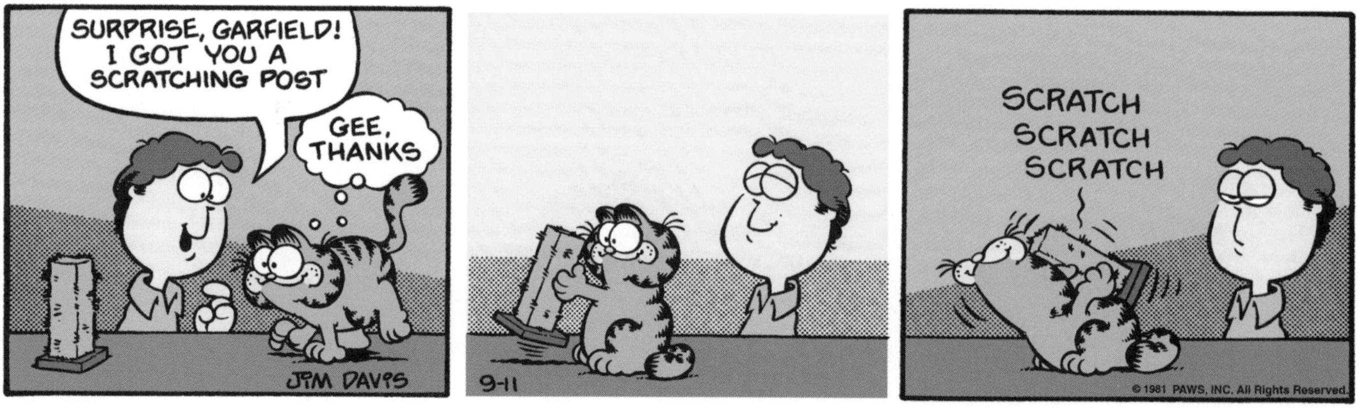
SURPRISE, GARFIELD! I GOT YOU A SCRATCHING POST
GEE, THANKS
JIM DAVIS
9-11
SCRATCH
SCRATCH
SCRATCH
© 1981 PAWS, INC. All Rights Reserved.

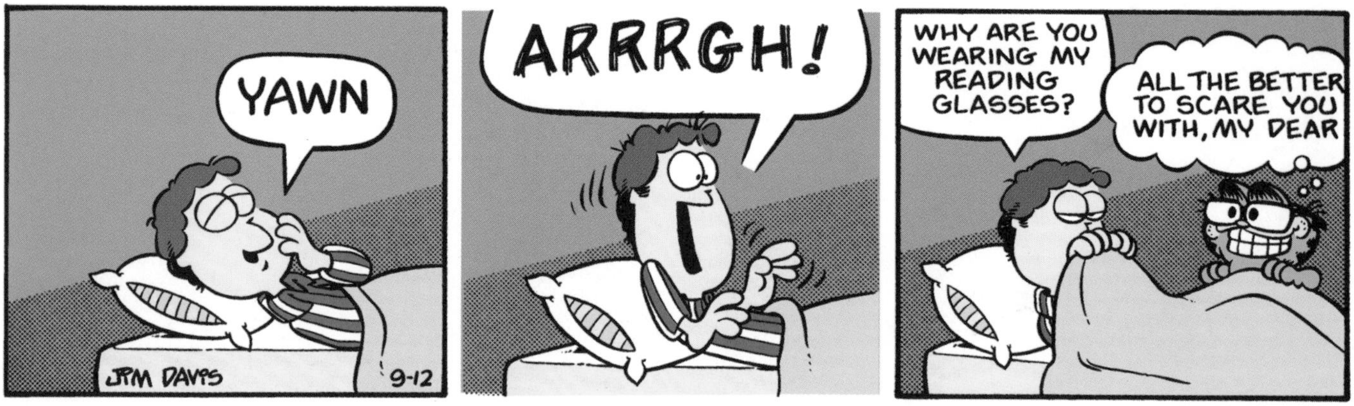
YAWN
JIM DAVIS
9-12
ARRRGH!
WHY ARE YOU WEARING MY READING GLASSES?
ALL THE BETTER TO SCARE YOU WITH, MY DEAR

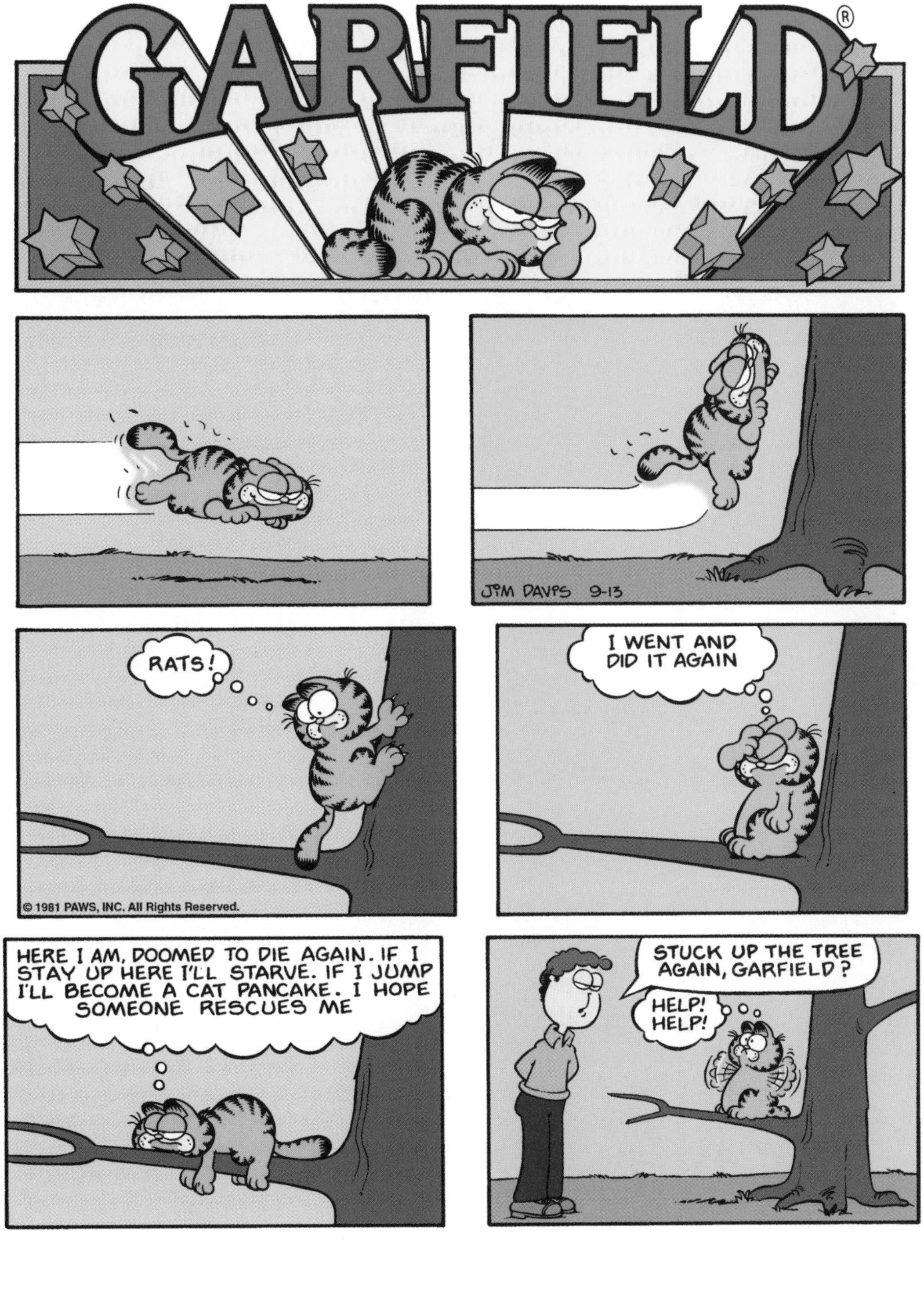
GARFIELD®
JIM DAVIS 9-13
RATS!
I WENT AND DID IT AGAIN
© 1981 PAWS, INC. All Rights Reserved.
HERE I AM, DOOMED TO DIE AGAIN. IF I STAY UP HERE I'LL STARVE. IF I JUMP I'LL BECOME A CAT PANCAKE. I HOPE SOMEONE RESCUES ME
STUCK UP THE TREE AGAIN, GARFIELD?
HELP! HELP!

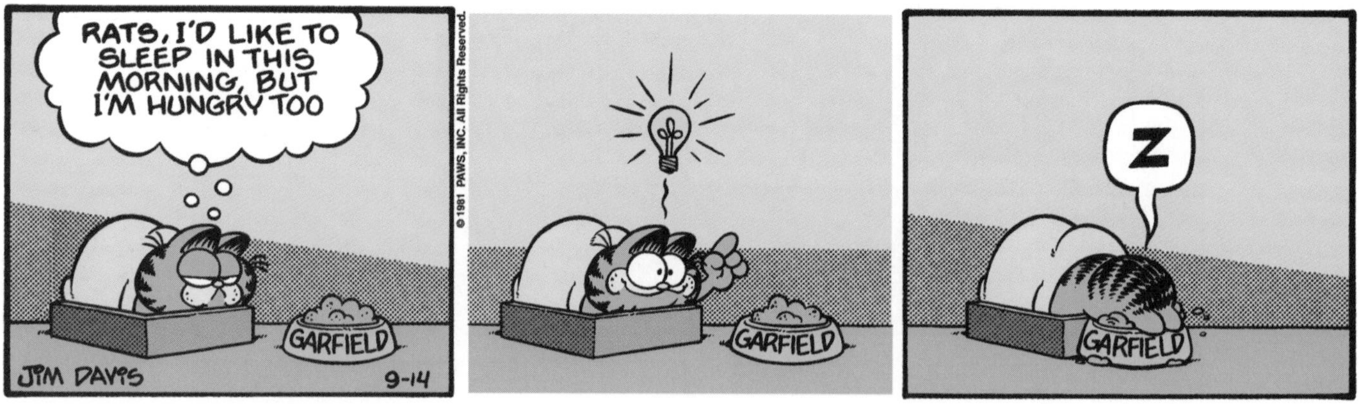
RATS, I'D LIKE TO SLEEP IN THIS MORNING, BUT I'M HUNGRY TOO
JIM DAVIS
9-14
GARFIELD
© 1981 PAWS, INC. All Rights Reserved.
GARFIELD
Z
GARFIELD

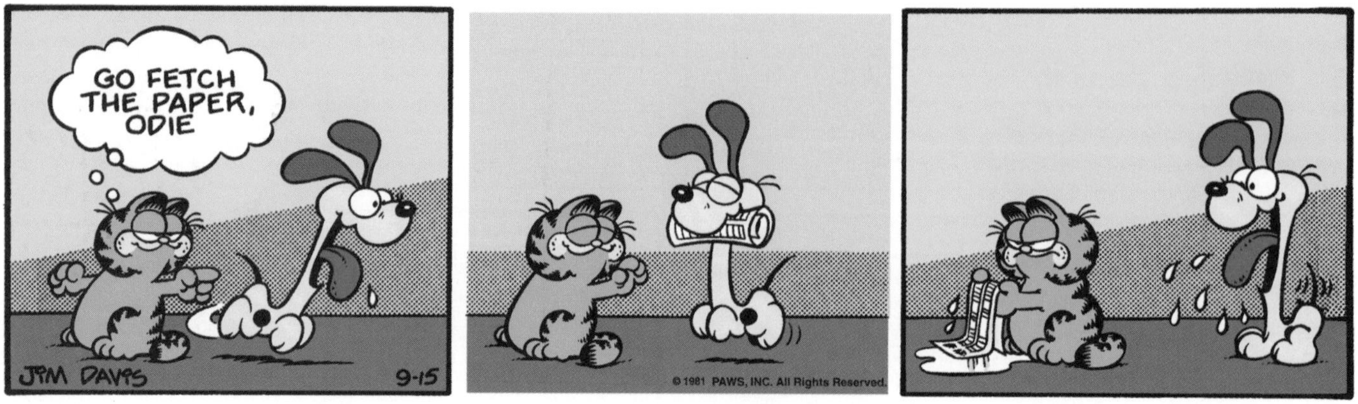
GO FETCH THE PAPER, ODIE
JIM DAVIS
9-15
© 1981 PAWS, INC. All Rights Reserved.

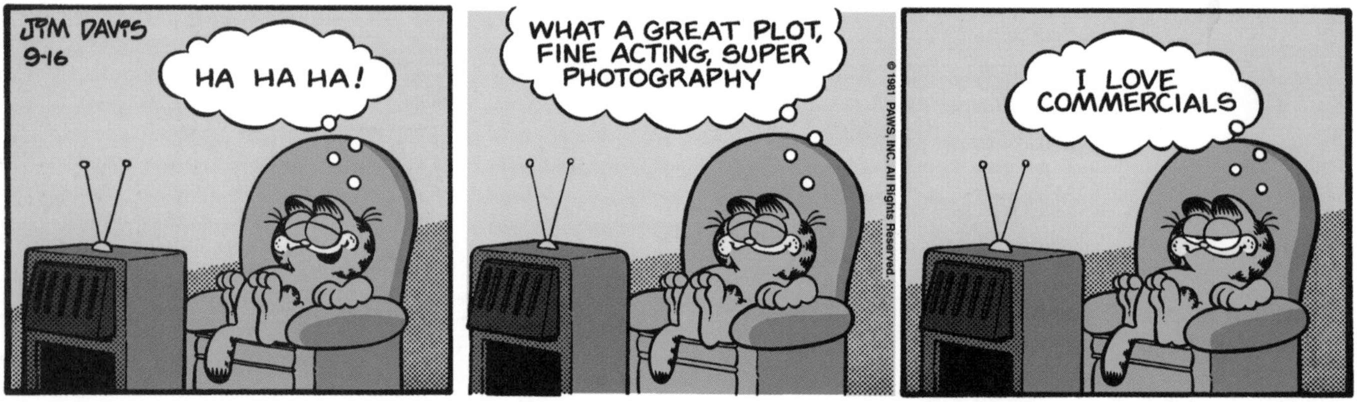
JIM DAVIS
9-16
HA HA HA!
WHAT A GREAT PLOT, FINE ACTING, SUPER PHOTOGRAPHY
© 1981 PAWS, INC. All Rights Reserved.
I LOVE COMMERCIALS

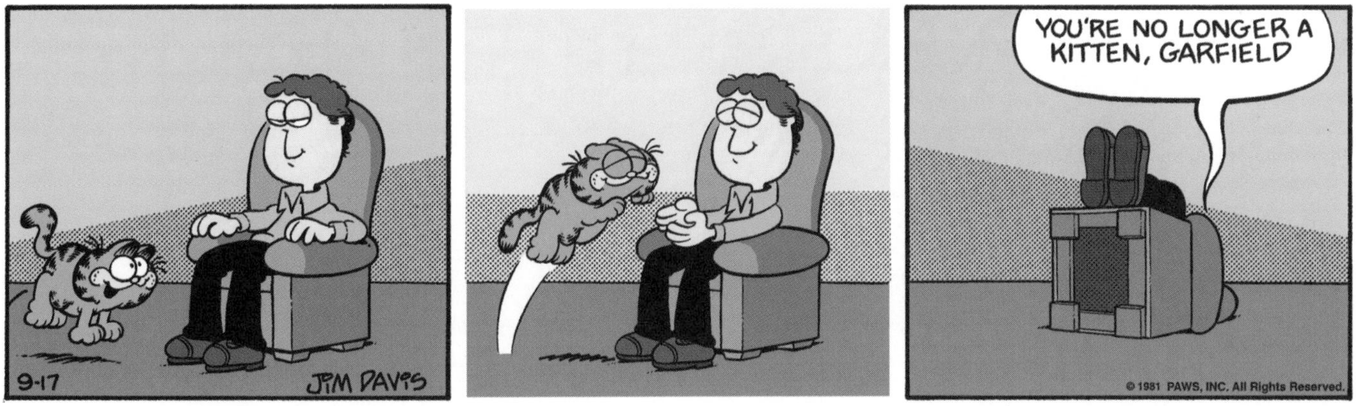
9-17
JIM DAVIS
YOU'RE NO LONGER A KITTEN, GARFIELD
© 1981 PAWS, INC. All Rights Reserved.

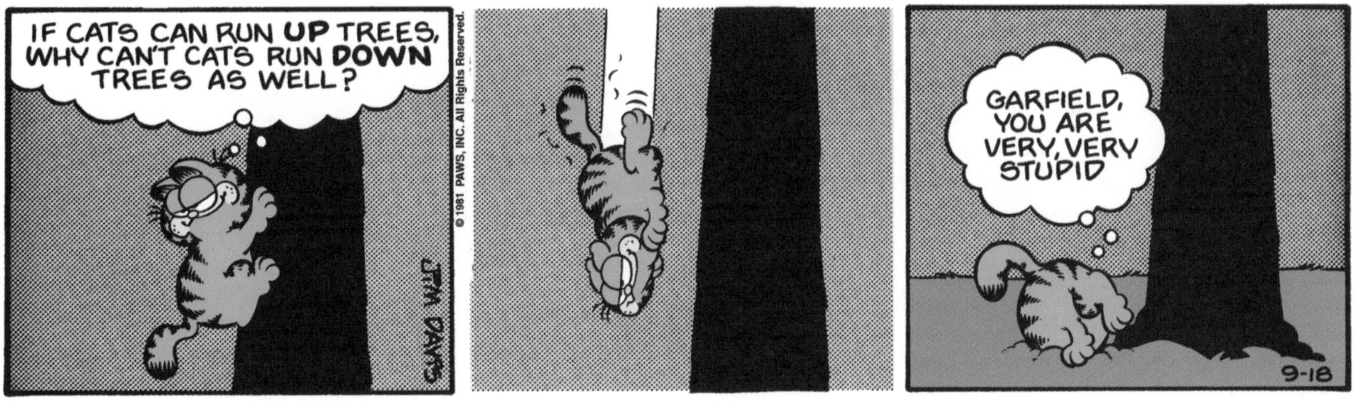
IF CATS CAN RUN UP TREES, WHY CAN'T CATS RUN DOWN TREES AS WELL?
JIM DAVIS
© 1981 PAWS, INC. All Rights Reserved.
GARFIELD, YOU ARE VERY, VERY STUPID
9-18

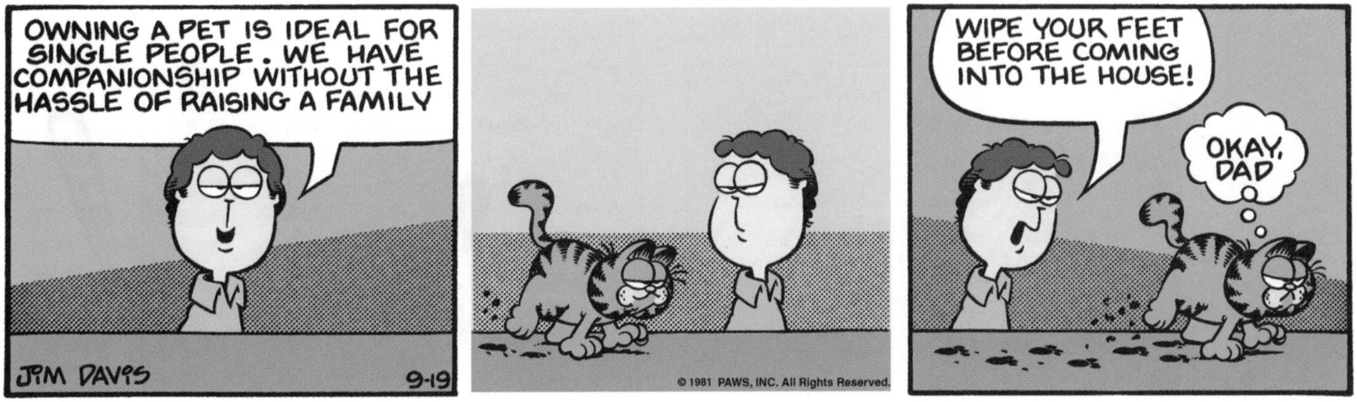
OWNING A PET IS IDEAL FOR SINGLE PEOPLE. WE HAVE COMPANIONSHIP WITHOUT THE HASSLE OF RAISING A FAMILY
JIM DAVIS
9-19
© 1981 PAWS, INC. All Rights Reserved.
WIPE YOUR FEET BEFORE COMING INTO THE HOUSE!
OKAY, DAD

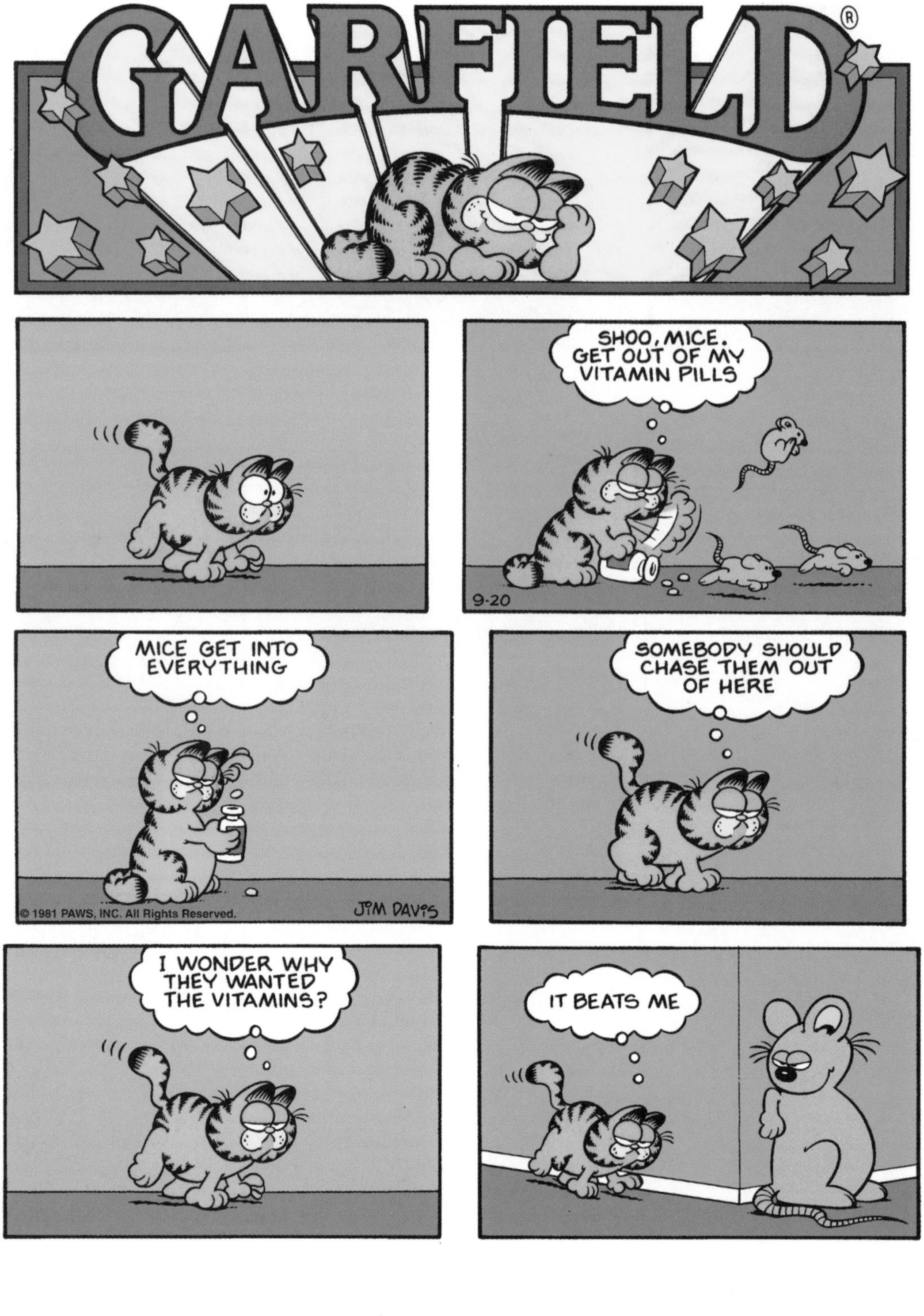
GARFIELD®
SHOO, MICE. GET OUT OF MY VITAMIN PILLS
9-20
MICE GET INTO EVERYTHING
© 1981 PAWS, INC. All Rights Reserved.
JIM DAVIS
SOMEBODY SHOULD CHASE THEM OUT OF HERE
I WONDER WHY THEY WANTED THE VITAMINS?
IT BEATS ME

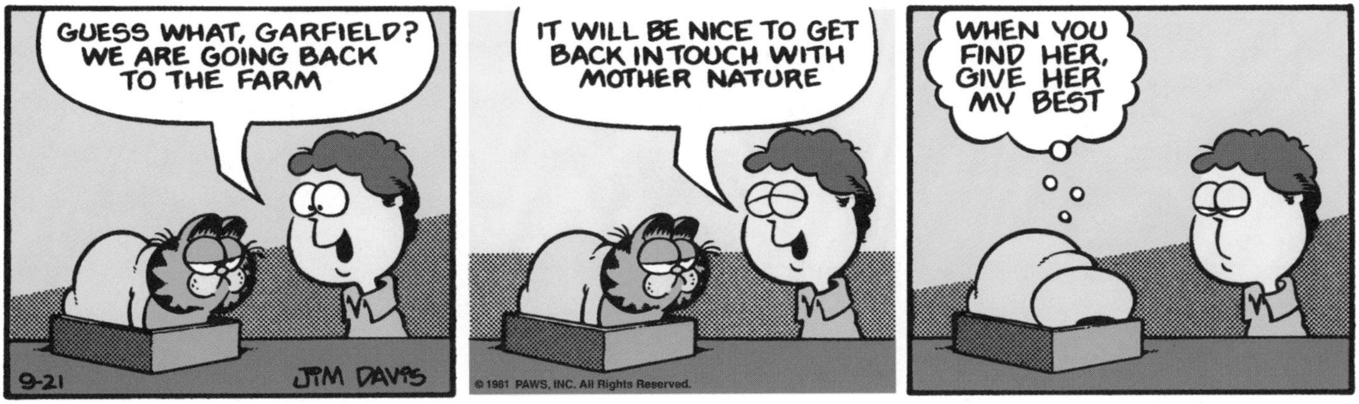
GUESS WHAT, GARFIELD? WE ARE GOING BACK TO THE FARM
9-21
JIM DAVIS
IT WILL BE NICE TO GET BACK IN TOUCH WITH MOTHER NATURE
© 1981 PAWS, INC. All Rights Reserved.
WHEN YOU FIND HER, GIVE HER MY BEST

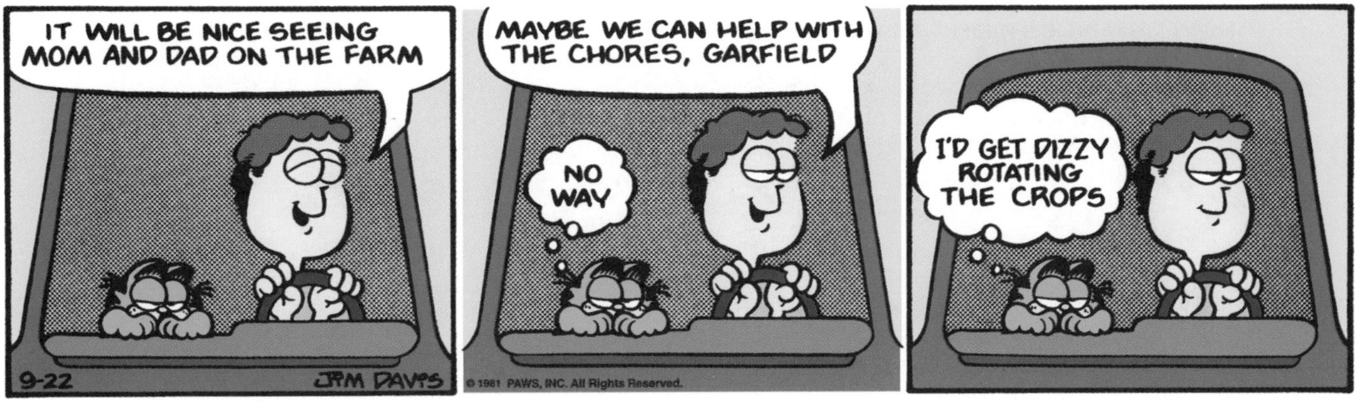
IT WILL BE NICE SEEING MOM AND DAD ON THE FARM
9-22
JIM DAVIS
MAYBE WE CAN HELP WITH THE CHORES, GARFIELD
NO WAY
© 1981 PAWS, INC. All Rights Reserved.
I'D GET DIZZY ROTATING THE CROPS

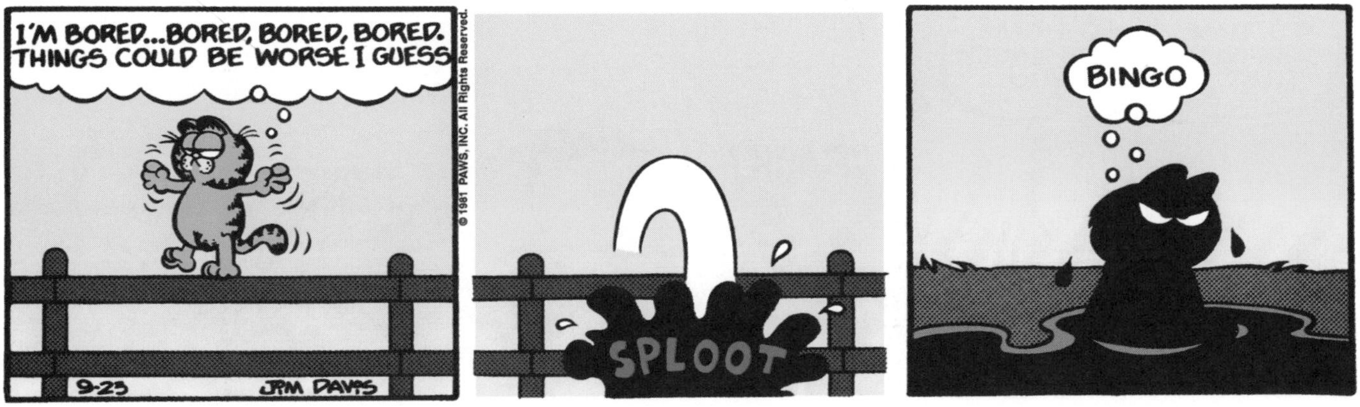
I'M BORED...BORED, BORED, BORED. THINGS COULD BE WORSE I GUESS
9-23
JIM DAVIS
© 1981 PAWS, INC. All Rights Reserved.
SPLOOT
BINGO

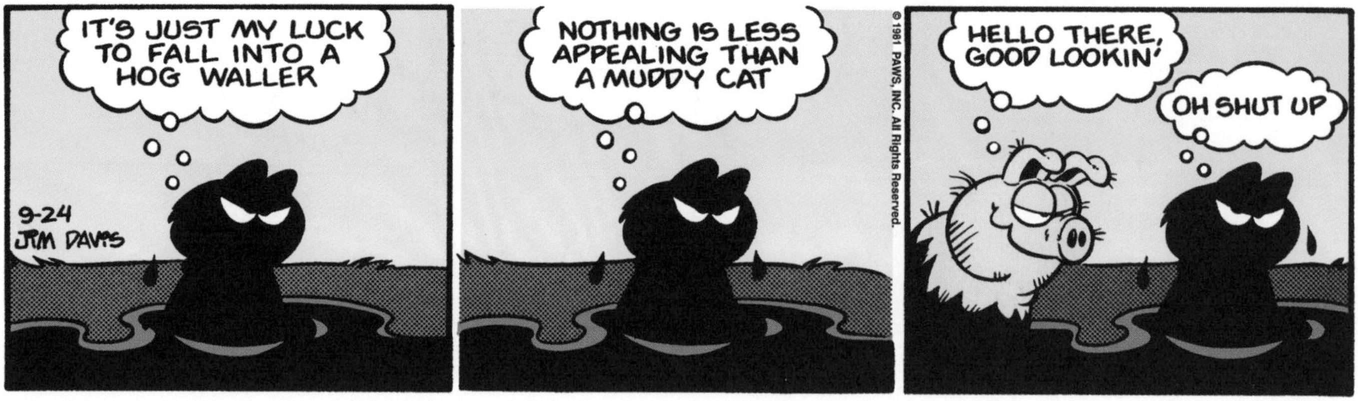
IT'S JUST MY LUCK TO FALL INTO A HOG WALLER
9-24
JIM DAVIS
NOTHING IS LESS APPEALING THAN A MUDDY CAT
© 1981 PAWS, INC. All Rights Reserved.
HELLO THERE, GOOD LOOKIN'
OH SHUT UP

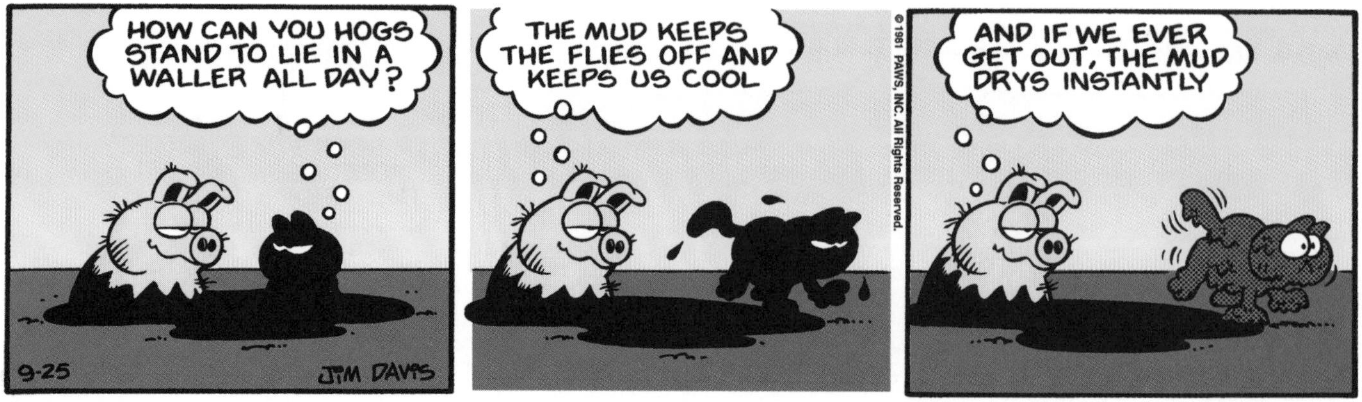
HOW CAN YOU HOGS STAND TO LIE IN A WALLER ALL DAY?
9-25
JIM DAVIS
THE MUD KEEPS THE FLIES OFF AND KEEPS US COOL
© 1981 PAWS, INC. All Rights Reserved.
AND IF WE EVER GET OUT, THE MUD DRYS INSTANTLY

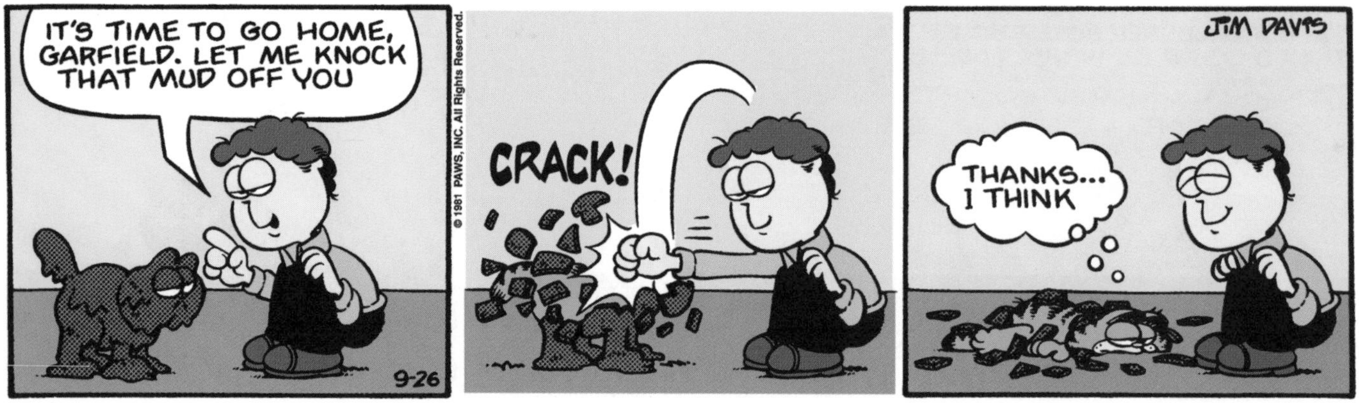
IT'S TIME TO GO HOME, GARFIELD. LET ME KNOCK THAT MUD OFF YOU
9-26
© 1981 PAWS, INC. All Rights Reserved.
CRACK!
JIM DAVIS
THANKS... I THINK

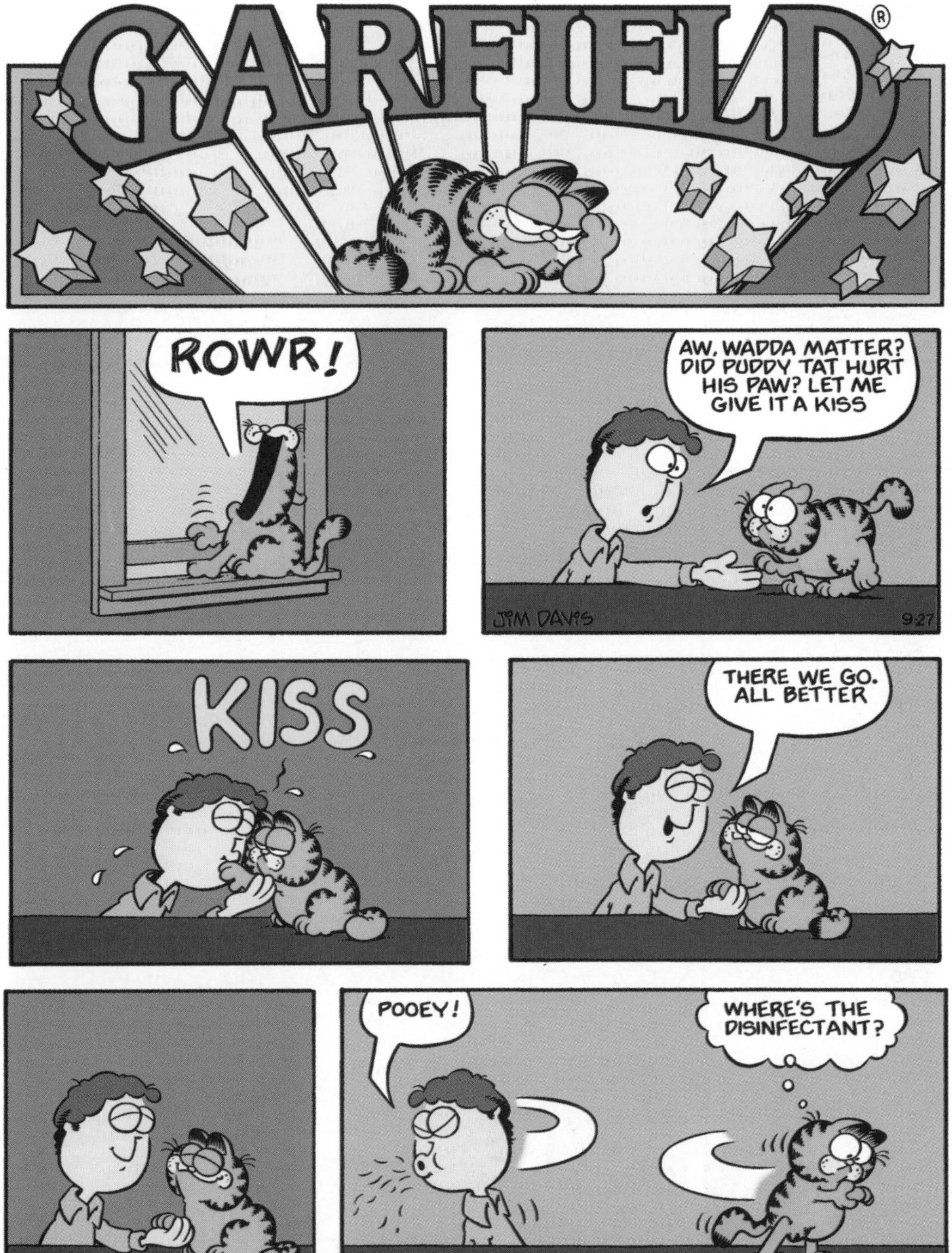
GARFIELD®
ROWR!
AW, WADDA MATTER? DID PUDDY TAT HURT HIS PAW? LET ME GIVE IT A KISS
JIM DAVIS 9-27
KISS
THERE WE GO. ALL BETTER
POOEY!
WHERE'S THE DISINFECTANT?
© 1981 PAWS, INC. All Rights Reserved.

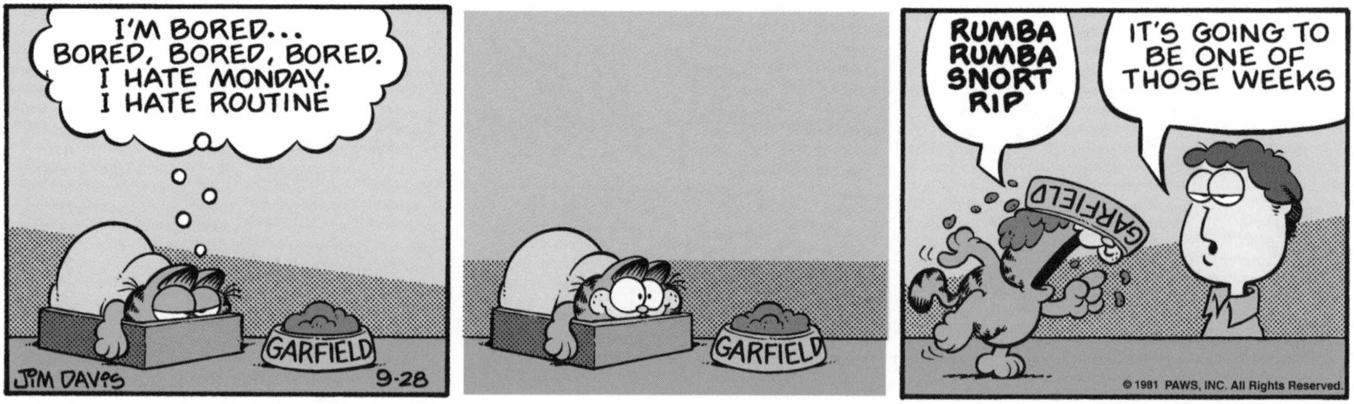
I'M BORED... BORED, BORED, BORED. I HATE MONDAY. I HATE ROUTINE
GARFIELD
JIM DAVIS
9-28
GARFIELD
RUMBA RUMBA SNORT RIP
IT'S GOING TO BE ONE OF THOSE WEEKS
GARFIELD
© 1981 PAWS, INC. All Rights Reserved.

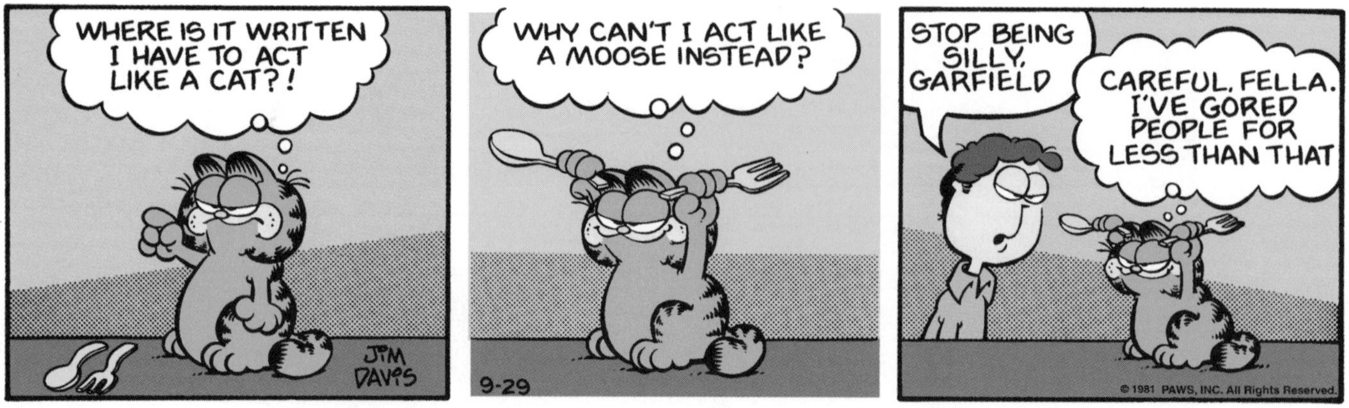
WHERE IS IT WRITTEN I HAVE TO ACT LIKE A CAT?!
JIM DAVIS
WHY CAN'T I ACT LIKE A MOOSE INSTEAD?
9-29
STOP BEING SILLY, GARFIELD
CAREFUL, FELLA. I'VE GORED PEOPLE FOR LESS THAN THAT
© 1981 PAWS, INC. All Rights Reserved.

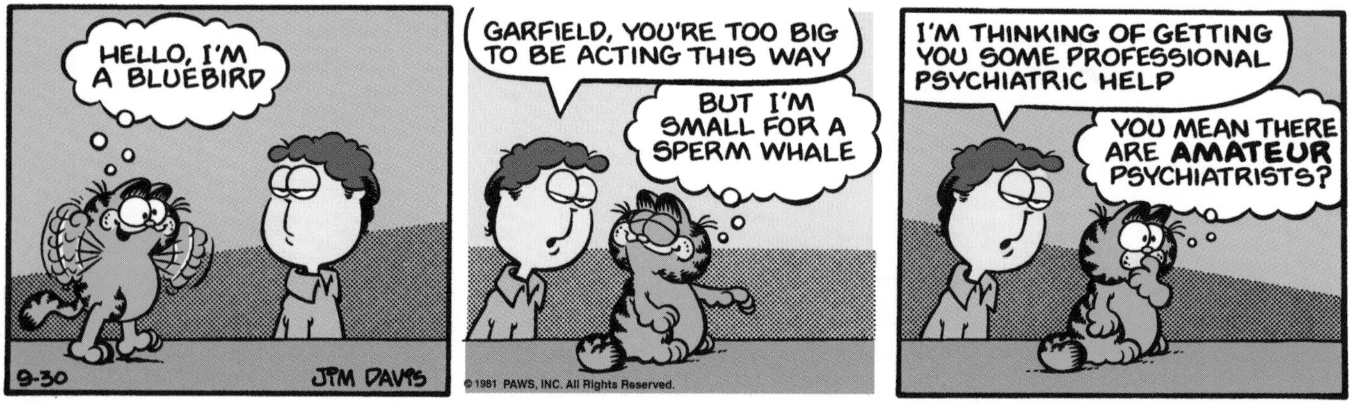
HELLO, I'M A BLUEBIRD
9-30
JIM DAVIS
GARFIELD, YOU'RE TOO BIG TO BE ACTING THIS WAY
BUT I'M SMALL FOR A SPERM WHALE
© 1981 PAWS, INC. All Rights Reserved.
I'M THINKING OF GETTING YOU SOME PROFESSIONAL PSYCHIATRIC HELP
YOU MEAN THERE ARE AMATEUR PSYCHIATRISTS?

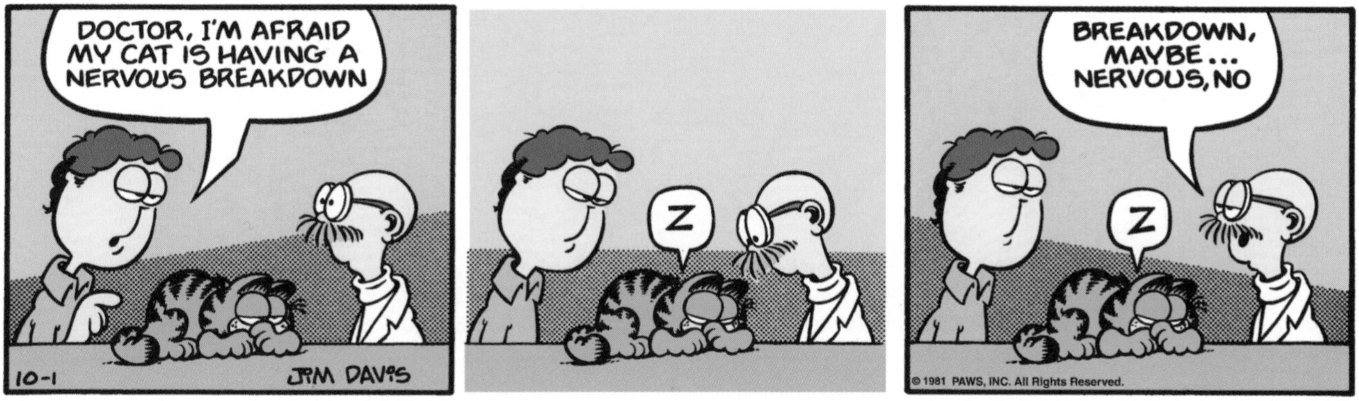
DOCTOR, I'M AFRAID MY CAT IS HAVING A NERVOUS BREAKDOWN
10-1
JIM DAVIS
Z
Z
BREAKDOWN, MAYBE... NERVOUS, NO
© 1981 PAWS, INC. All Rights Reserved.

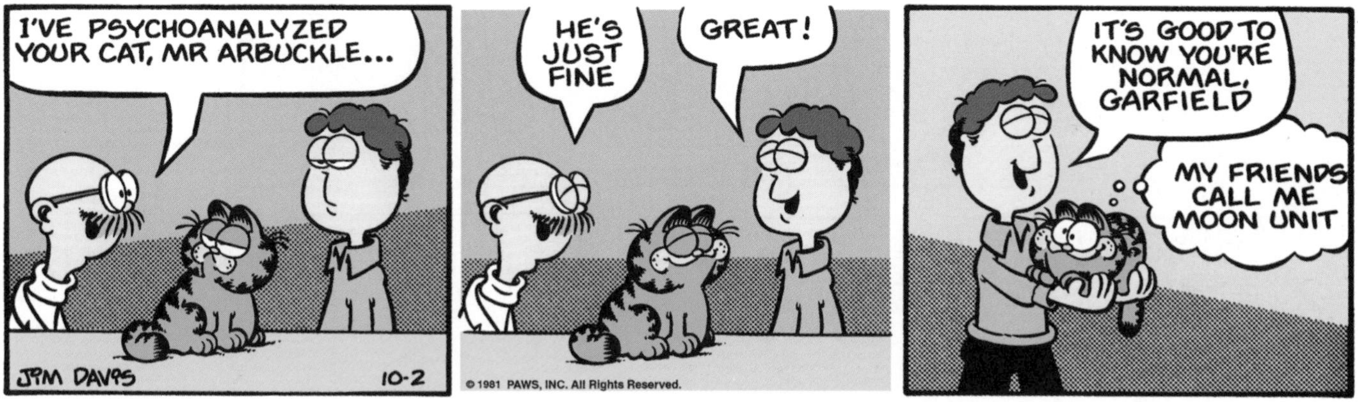
I'VE PSYCHOANALYZED YOUR CAT, MR ARBUCKLE...
JIM DAVIS
10-2
HE'S JUST FINE
GREAT!
© 1981 PAWS, INC. All Rights Reserved.
IT'S GOOD TO KNOW YOU'RE NORMAL, GARFIELD
MY FRIENDS CALL ME MOON UNIT

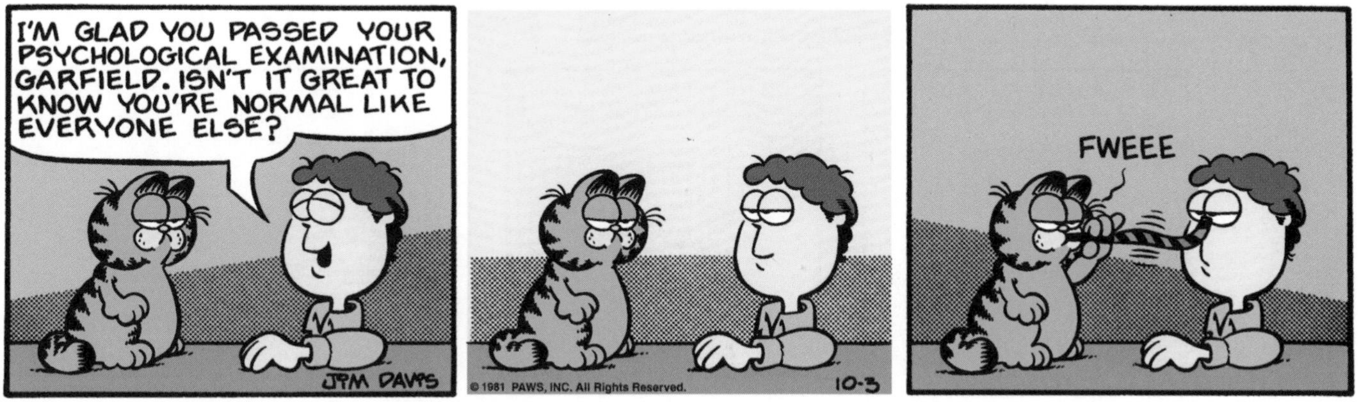
I'M GLAD YOU PASSED YOUR PSYCHOLOGICAL EXAMINATION, GARFIELD. ISN'T IT GREAT TO KNOW YOU'RE NORMAL LIKE EVERYONE ELSE?
JIM DAVIS
© 1981 PAWS, INC. All Rights Reserved.
10-3
FWEEE

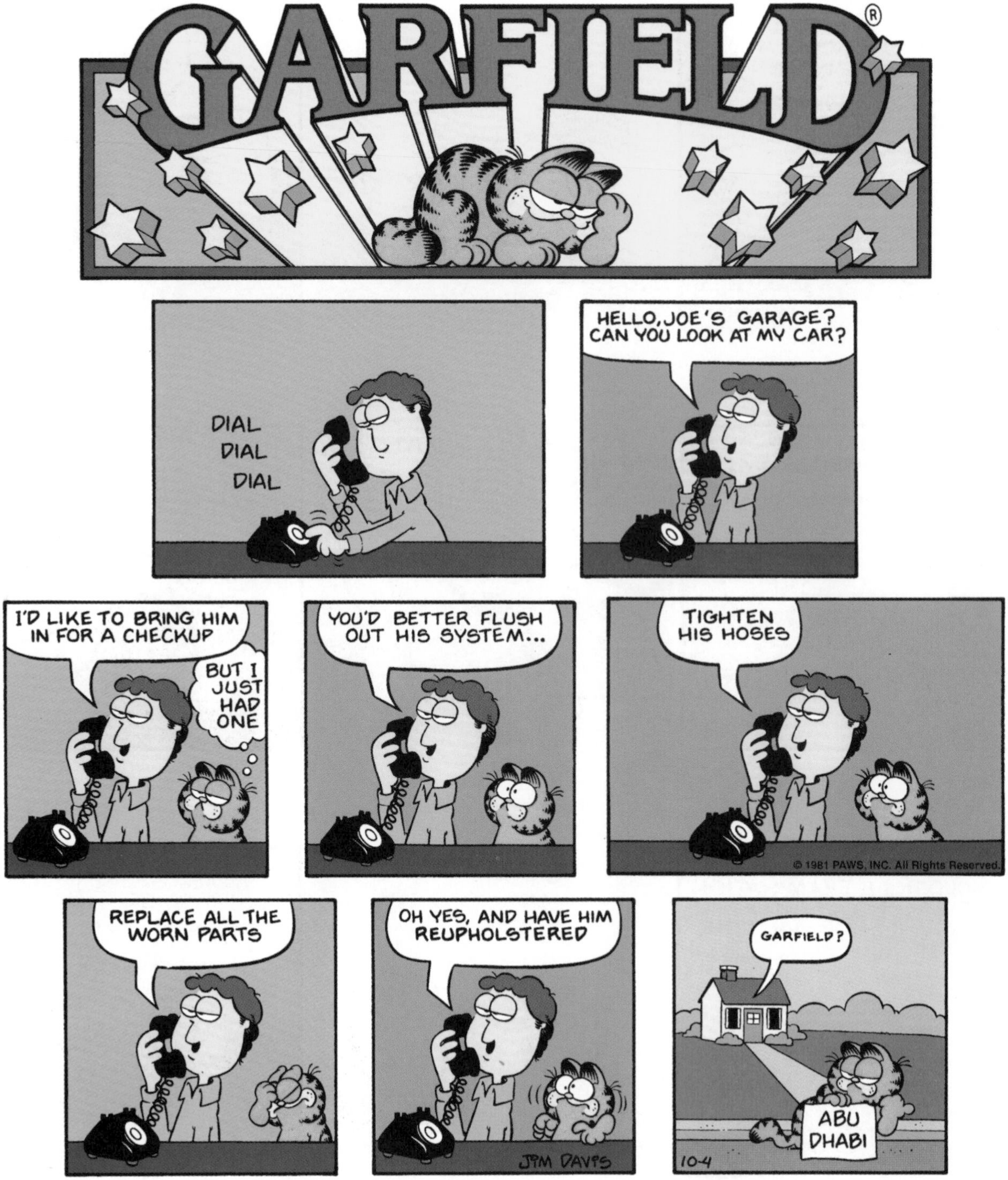
GARFIELD®
DIAL
DIAL
DIAL
HELLO, JOE'S GARAGE? CAN YOU LOOK AT MY CAR?
I'D LIKE TO BRING HIM IN FOR A CHECKUP
BUT I JUST HAD ONE
YOU'D BETTER FLUSH OUT HIS SYSTEM...
TIGHTEN HIS HOSES
© 1981 PAWS, INC. All Rights Reserved.
REPLACE ALL THE WORN PARTS
OH YES, AND HAVE HIM REUPHOLSTERED
JIM DAVIS
GARFIELD?
ABU DHABI
10-4

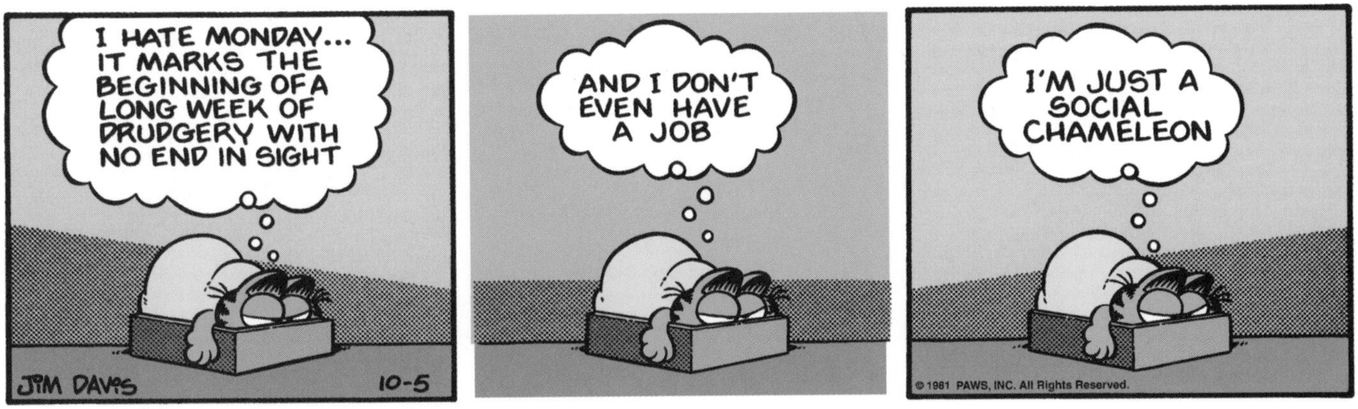
I HATE MONDAY... IT MARKS THE BEGINNING OF A LONG WEEK OF DRUDGERY WITH NO END IN SIGHT
JIM DAVIS
10-5
AND I DON'T EVEN HAVE A JOB
I'M JUST A SOCIAL CHAMELEON
© 1981 PAWS, INC. All Rights Reserved.

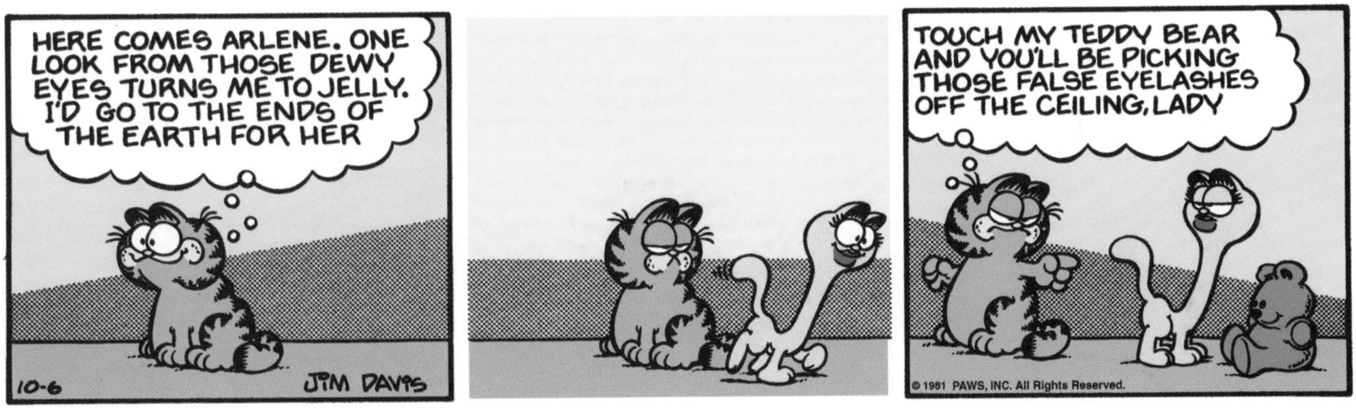
HERE COMES ARLENE. ONE LOOK FROM THOSE DEWY EYES TURNS ME TO JELLY. I'D GO TO THE ENDS OF THE EARTH FOR HER
10-6
JIM DAVIS
TOUCH MY TEDDY BEAR AND YOU'LL BE PICKING THOSE FALSE EYELASHES OFF THE CEILING, LADY
© 1981 PAWS, INC. All Rights Reserved.

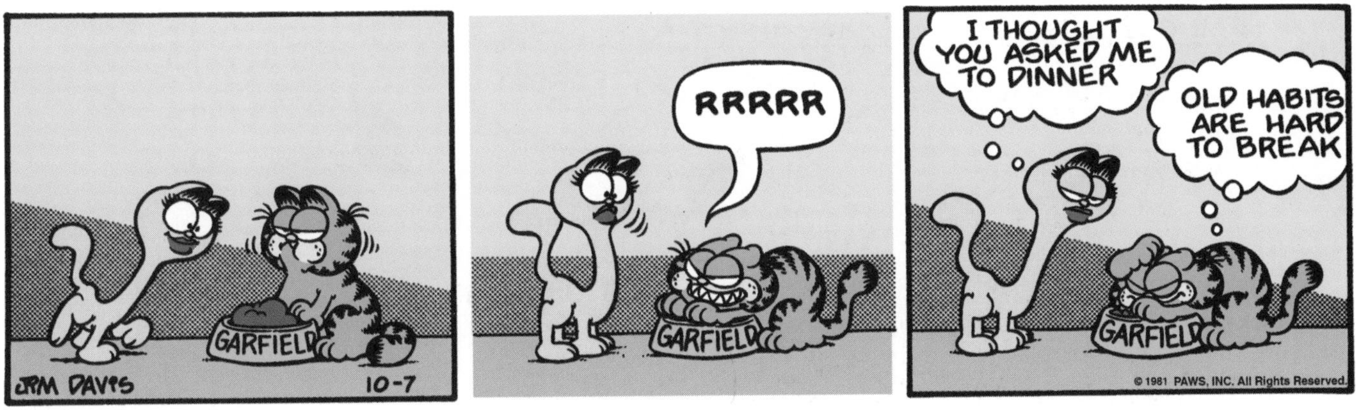
GARFIELD
JIM DAVIS
10-7
RRRRR
GARFIELD
I THOUGHT YOU ASKED ME TO DINNER
OLD HABITS ARE HARD TO BREAK
GARFIELD
© 1981 PAWS, INC. All Rights Reserved.

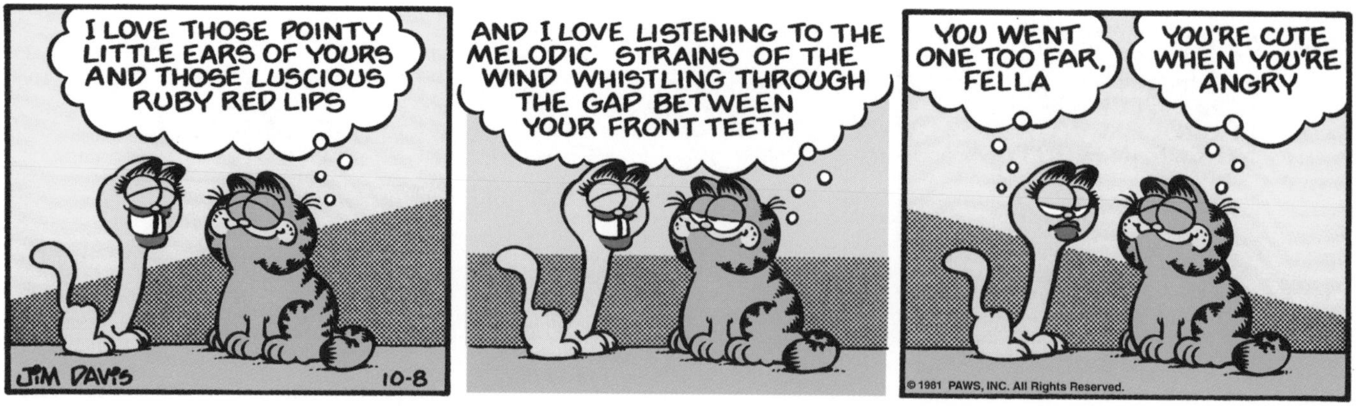
I LOVE THOSE POINTY LITTLE EARS OF YOURS AND THOSE LUSCIOUS RUBY RED LIPS
JIM DAVIS
10-8
AND I LOVE LISTENING TO THE MELODIC STRAINS OF THE WIND WHISTLING THROUGH THE GAP BETWEEN YOUR FRONT TEETH
YOU WENT ONE TOO FAR, FELLA
YOU'RE CUTE WHEN YOU'RE ANGRY
© 1981 PAWS, INC. All Rights Reserved.

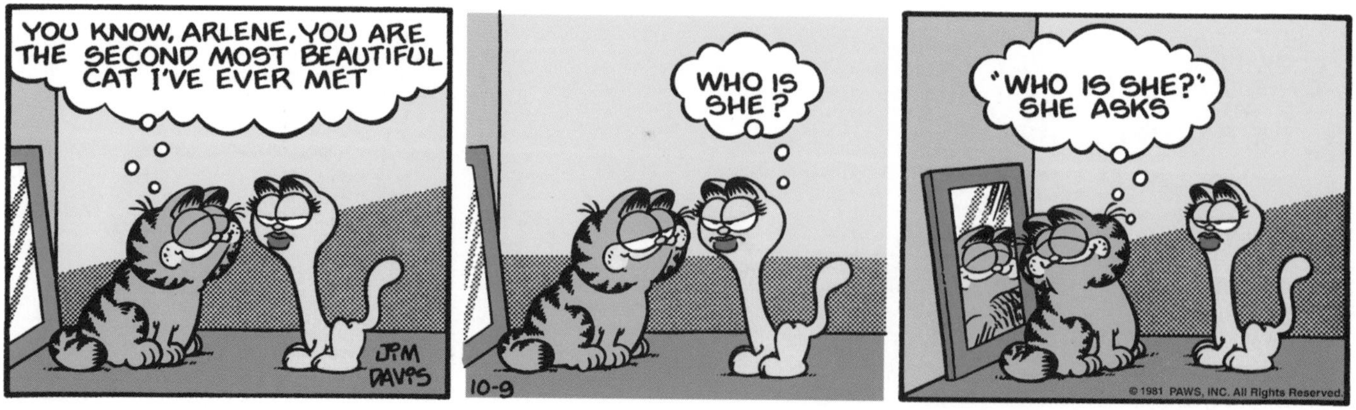
YOU KNOW, ARLENE, YOU ARE THE SECOND MOST BEAUTIFUL CAT I'VE EVER MET
JIM DAVIS
WHO IS SHE?
10-9
"WHO IS SHE?" SHE ASKS
© 1981 PAWS, INC. All Rights Reserved.

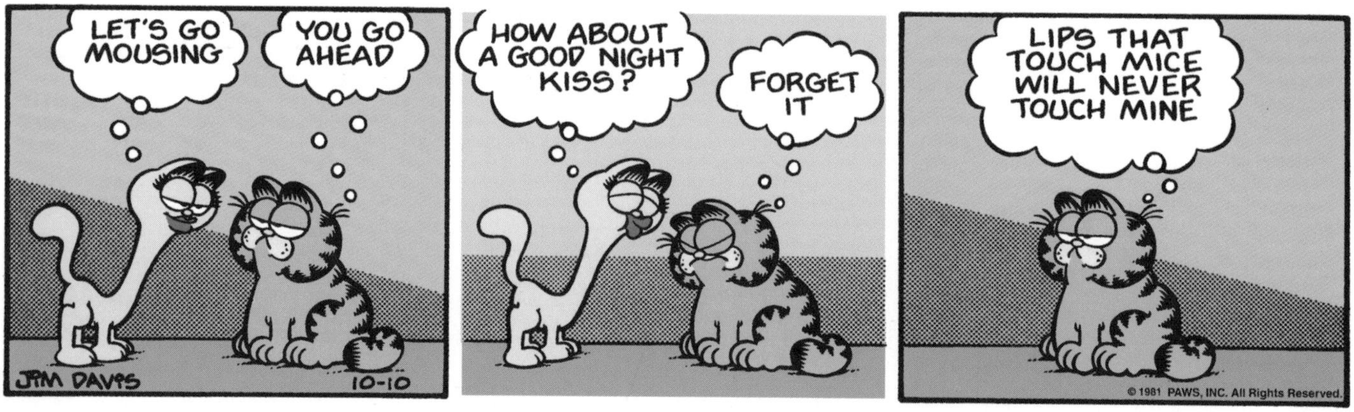
LET'S GO MOUSING
YOU GO AHEAD
JIM DAVIS
10-10
HOW ABOUT A GOOD NIGHT KISS?
FORGET IT
LIPS THAT TOUCH MICE WILL NEVER TOUCH MINE
© 1981 PAWS, INC. All Rights Reserved.

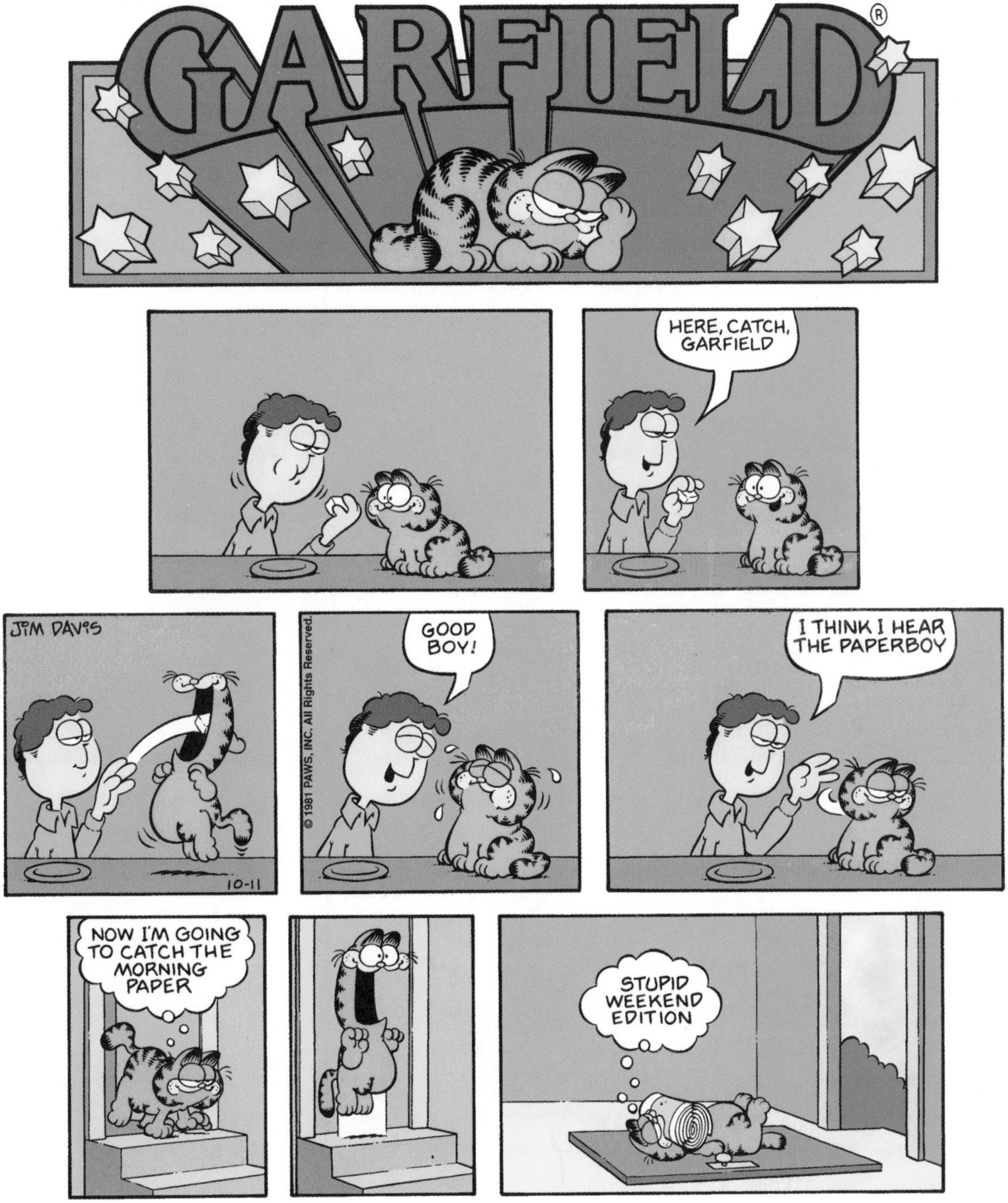
GARFIELD®
HERE, CATCH, GARFIELD
JIM DAVIS
10-11
© 1981 PAWS, INC. All Rights Reserved.
GOOD BOY!
I THINK I HEAR THE PAPERBOY
NOW I'M GOING TO CATCH THE MORNING PAPER
STUPID WEEKEND EDITION

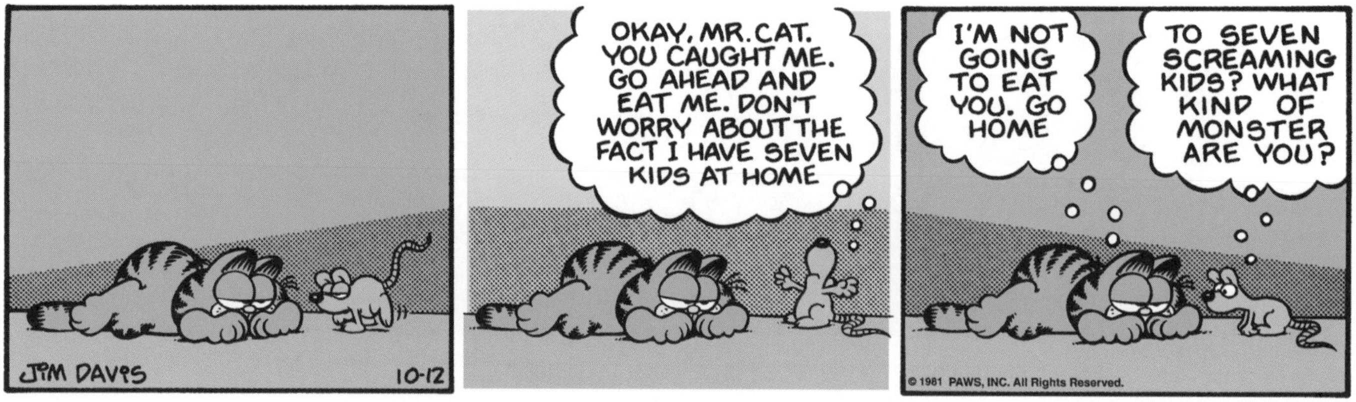
JIM DAVIS
10-12
OKAY, MR. CAT. YOU CAUGHT ME. GO AHEAD AND EAT ME. DON'T WORRY ABOUT THE FACT I HAVE SEVEN KIDS AT HOME
I'M NOT GOING TO EAT YOU. GO HOME
TO SEVEN SCREAMING KIDS? WHAT KIND OF MONSTER ARE YOU?
© 1981 PAWS, INC. All Rights Reserved.

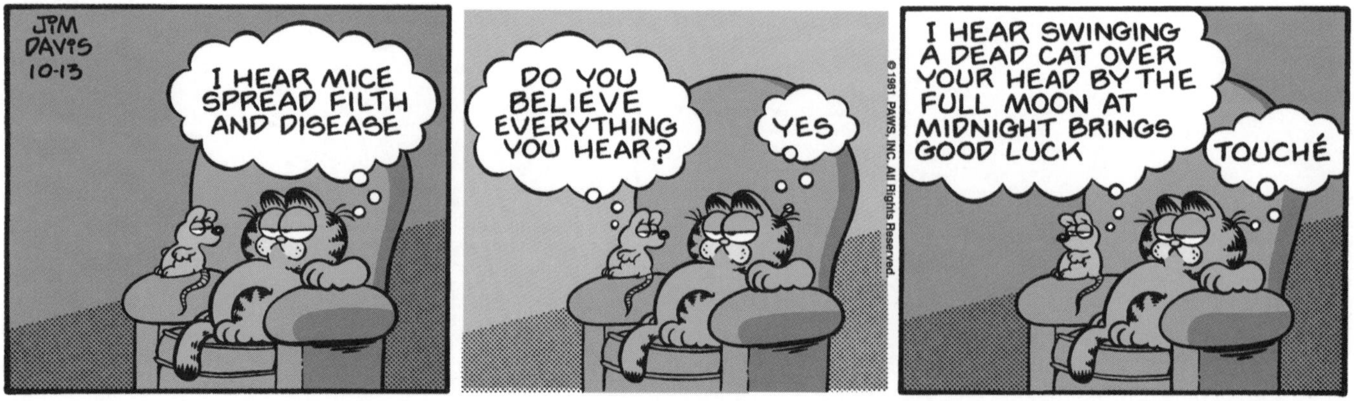
JIM DAVIS 10-13
I HEAR MICE SPREAD FILTH AND DISEASE
DO YOU BELIEVE EVERYTHING YOU HEAR?
YES
© 1981 PAWS, INC. All Rights Reserved.
I HEAR SWINGING A DEAD CAT OVER YOUR HEAD BY THE FULL MOON AT MIDNIGHT BRINGS GOOD LUCK
TOUCHÉ

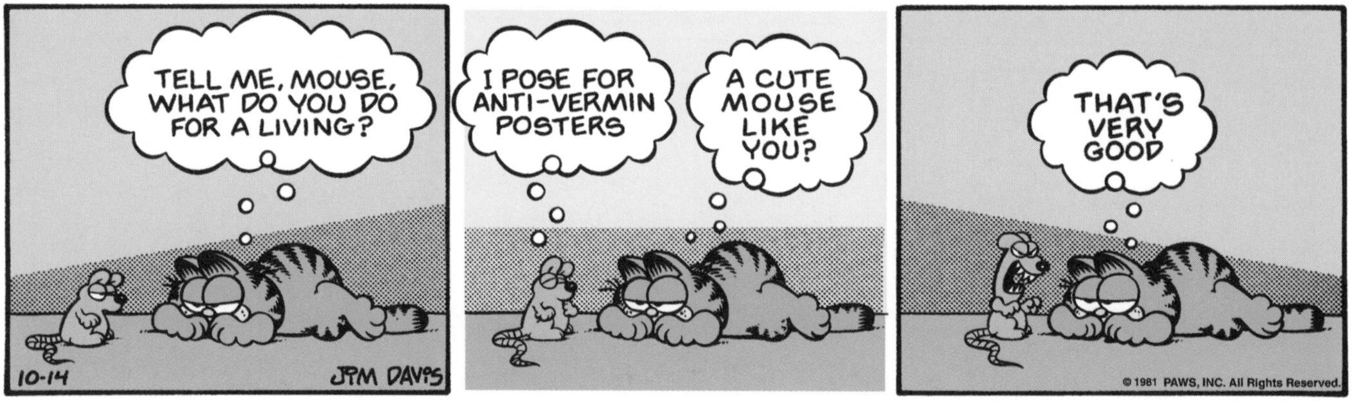
TELL ME, MOUSE, WHAT DO YOU DO FOR A LIVING?
10-14
JIM DAVIS
I POSE FOR ANTI-VERMIN POSTERS
A CUTE MOUSE LIKE YOU?
THAT'S VERY GOOD
© 1981 PAWS, INC. All Rights Reserved.

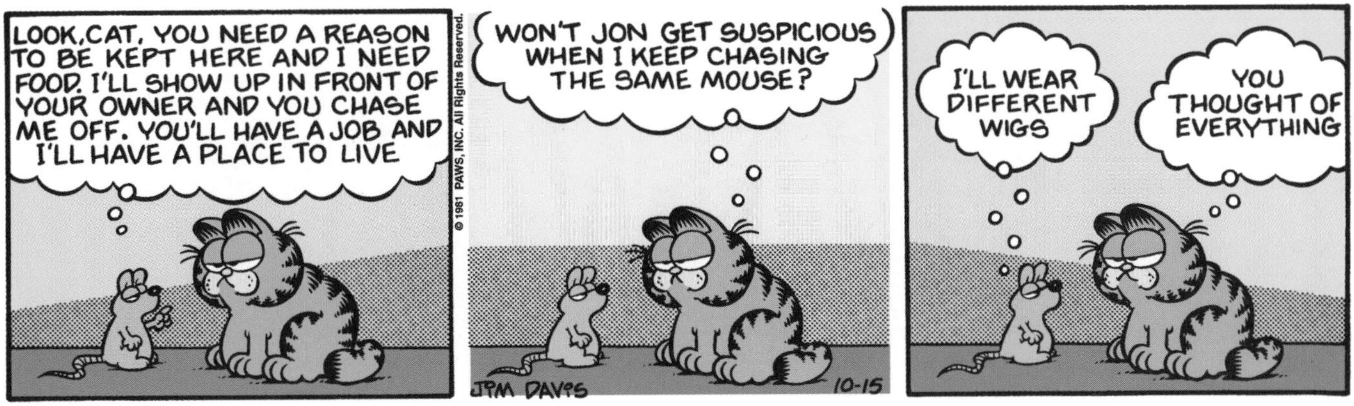
LOOK, CAT. YOU NEED A REASON TO BE KEPT HERE AND I NEED FOOD. I'LL SHOW UP IN FRONT OF YOUR OWNER AND YOU CHASE ME OFF. YOU'LL HAVE A JOB AND I'LL HAVE A PLACE TO LIVE
© 1981 PAWS, INC. All Rights Reserved.
WON'T JON GET SUSPICIOUS WHEN I KEEP CHASING THE SAME MOUSE?
JIM DAVIS
10-15
I'LL WEAR DIFFERENT WIGS
YOU THOUGHT OF EVERYTHING

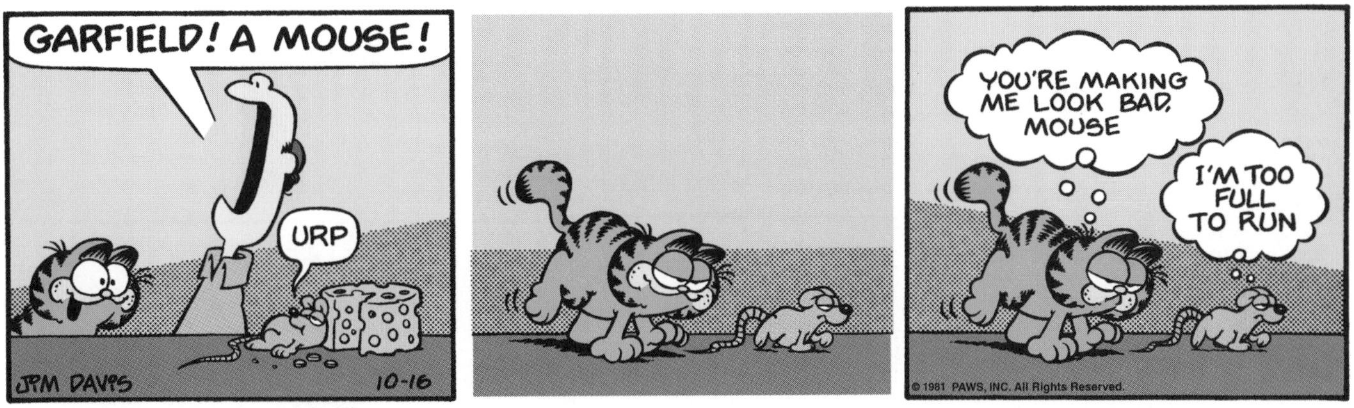
GARFIELD! A MOUSE!
URP
JIM DAVIS
10-16
YOU'RE MAKING ME LOOK BAD, MOUSE
I'M TOO FULL TO RUN
© 1981 PAWS, INC. All Rights Reserved.

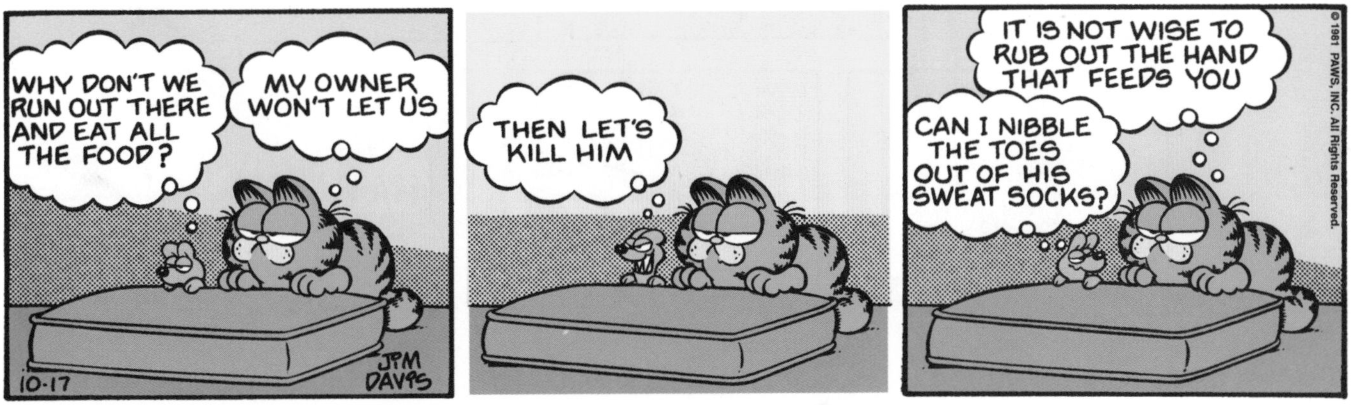
WHY DON'T WE RUN OUT THERE AND EAT ALL THE FOOD?
MY OWNER WON'T LET US
10-17
JIM DAVIS
THEN LET'S KILL HIM
IT IS NOT WISE TO RUB OUT THE HAND THAT FEEDS YOU
CAN I NIBBLE THE TOES OUT OF HIS SWEAT SOCKS?
© 1981 PAWS, INC. All Rights Reserved.

GARFIELD®
YOU KNOW, SOME FOODS ARE FUNNIER THAN OTHERS
10-18
JIM DAVIS
BEETS ARE FUNNY
LIVER... NOT FUNNY
PRUNES ARE FUNNY, POTATOES AREN'T
CHICKEN, NOW THAT'S FUNNY
HOW ABOUT PICKLES AND KUMQUATS FOR LUNCH, GARFIELD?
WAH HA HA!

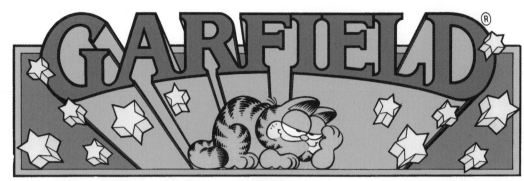

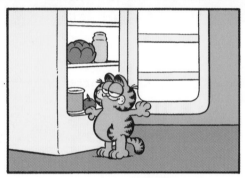

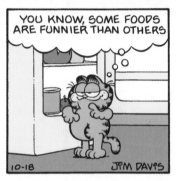

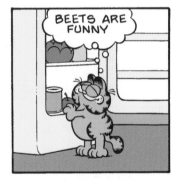

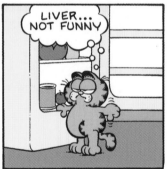

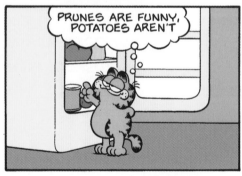

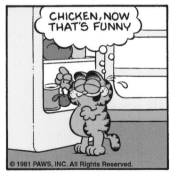

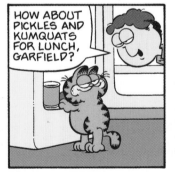

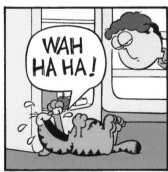

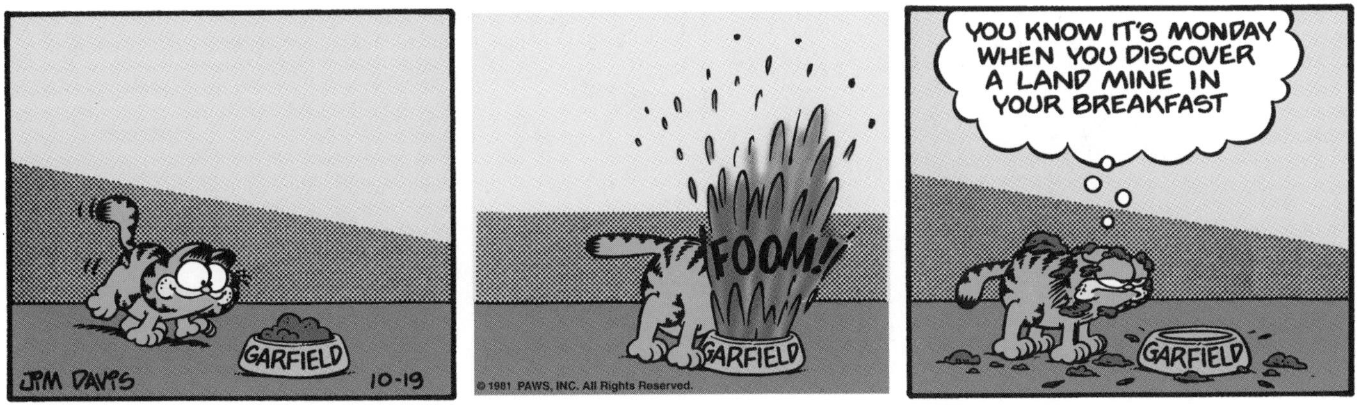
JIM DAVIS
GARFIELD
10-19
FOOM!!
GARFIELD
© 1981 PAWS, INC. All Rights Reserved.
YOU KNOW IT'S MONDAY WHEN YOU DISCOVER A LAND MINE IN YOUR BREAKFAST
GARFIELD

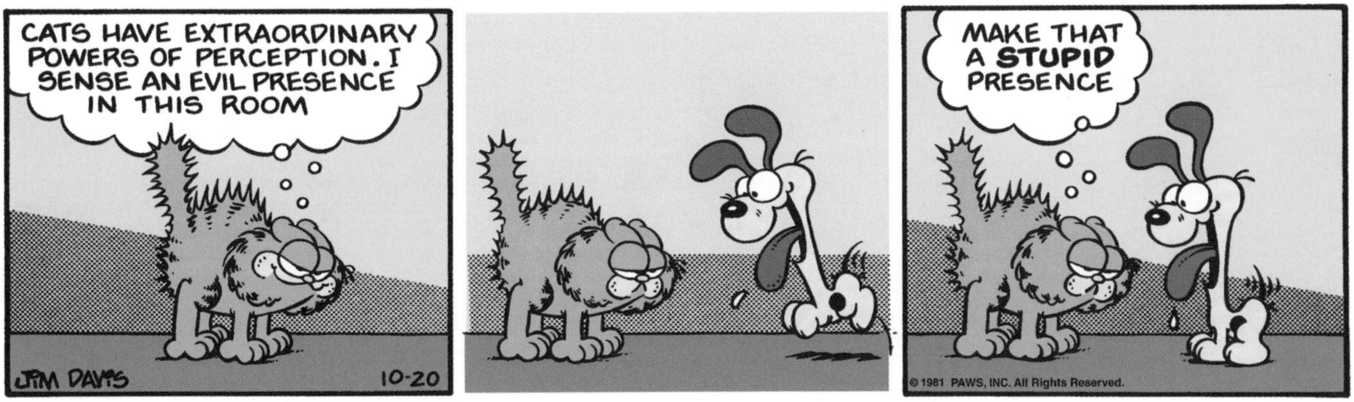
CATS HAVE EXTRAORDINARY POWERS OF PERCEPTION. I SENSE AN EVIL PRESENCE IN THIS ROOM
JIM DAVIS
10-20
MAKE THAT A **STUPID** PRESENCE
© 1981 PAWS, INC. All Rights Reserved.

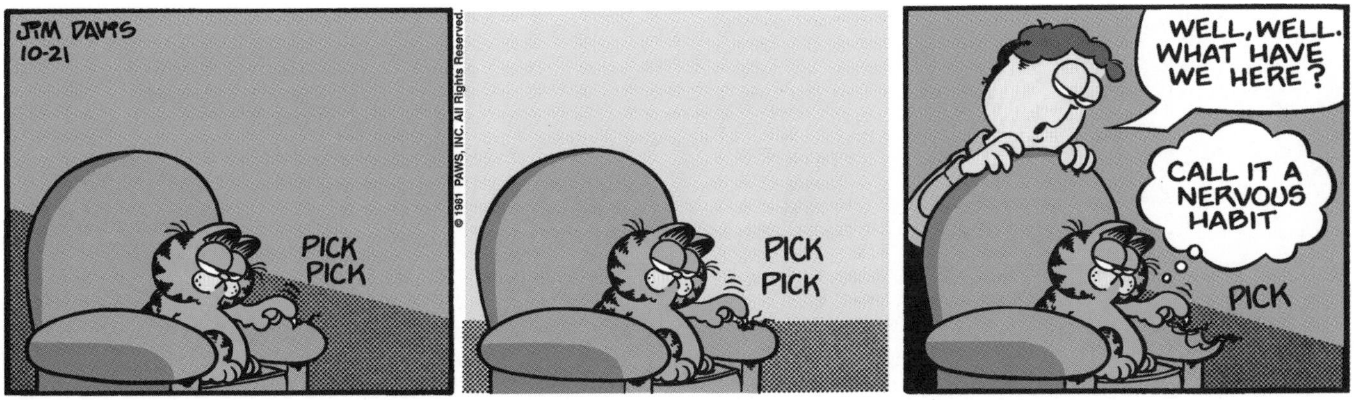
JIM DAVIS
10-21
PICK
PICK
© 1981 PAWS, INC. All Rights Reserved.
PICK
PICK
WELL, WELL. WHAT HAVE WE HERE?
CALL IT A NERVOUS HABIT
PICK

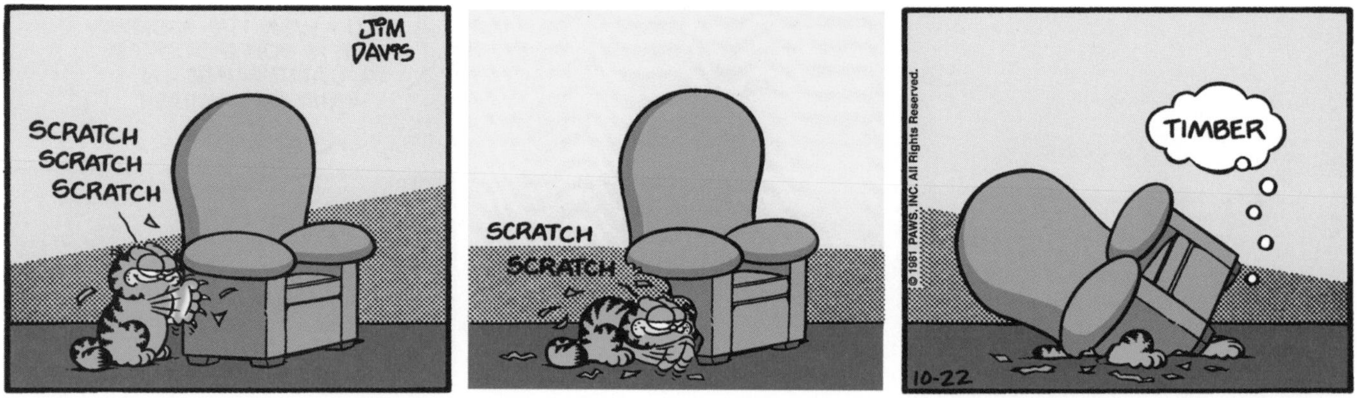
JIM DAVIS
SCRATCH
SCRATCH
SCRATCH
SCRATCH
SCRATCH
© 1981 PAWS, INC. All Rights Reserved.
TIMBER
10-22

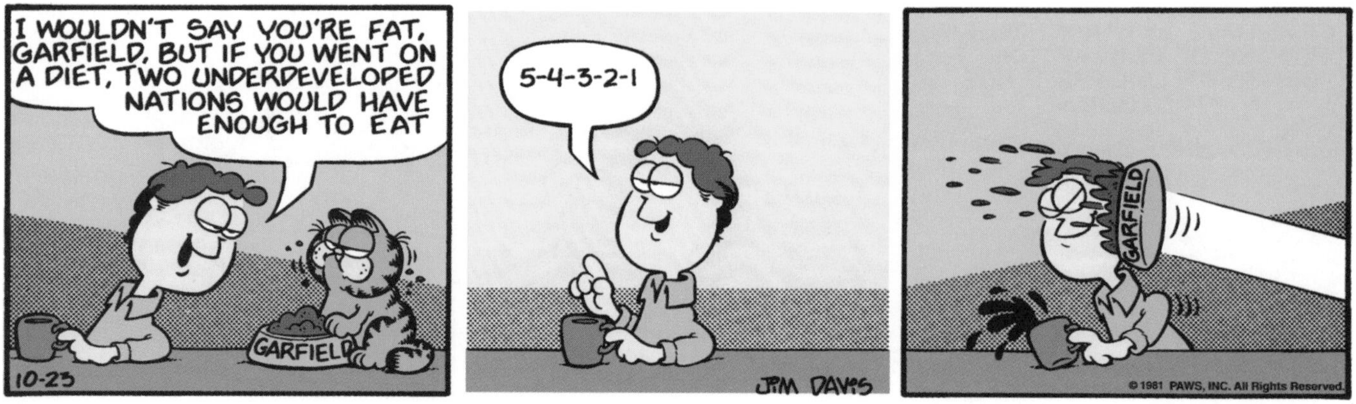
I WOULDN'T SAY YOU'RE FAT, GARFIELD, BUT IF YOU WENT ON A DIET, TWO UNDERDEVELOPED NATIONS WOULD HAVE ENOUGH TO EAT
GARFIELD
10-23
5-4-3-2-1
JIM DAVIS
GARFIELD
© 1981 PAWS, INC. All Rights Reserved.

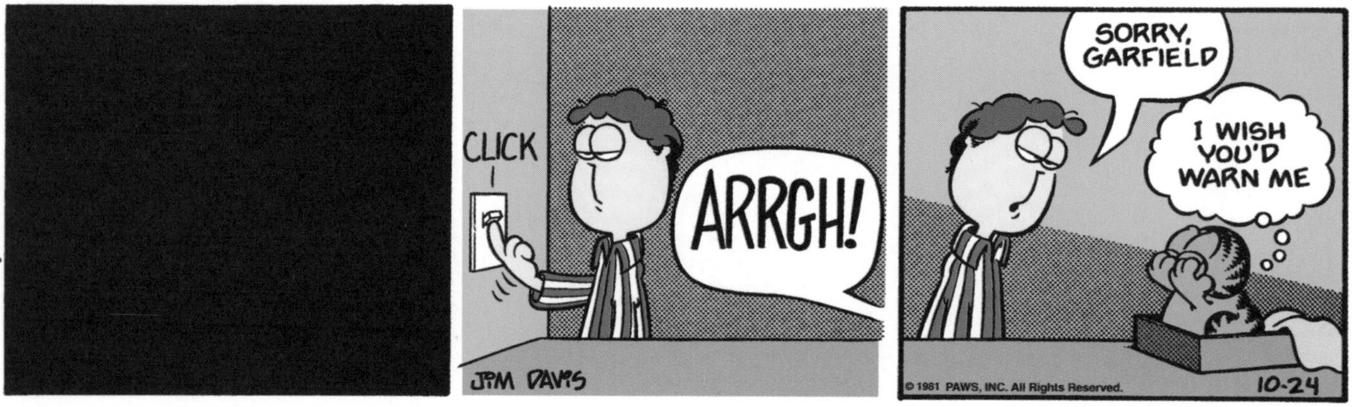
CLICK
ARRGH!
JIM DAVIS
SORRY, GARFIELD
I WISH YOU'D WARN ME
© 1981 PAWS, INC. All Rights Reserved.
10-24

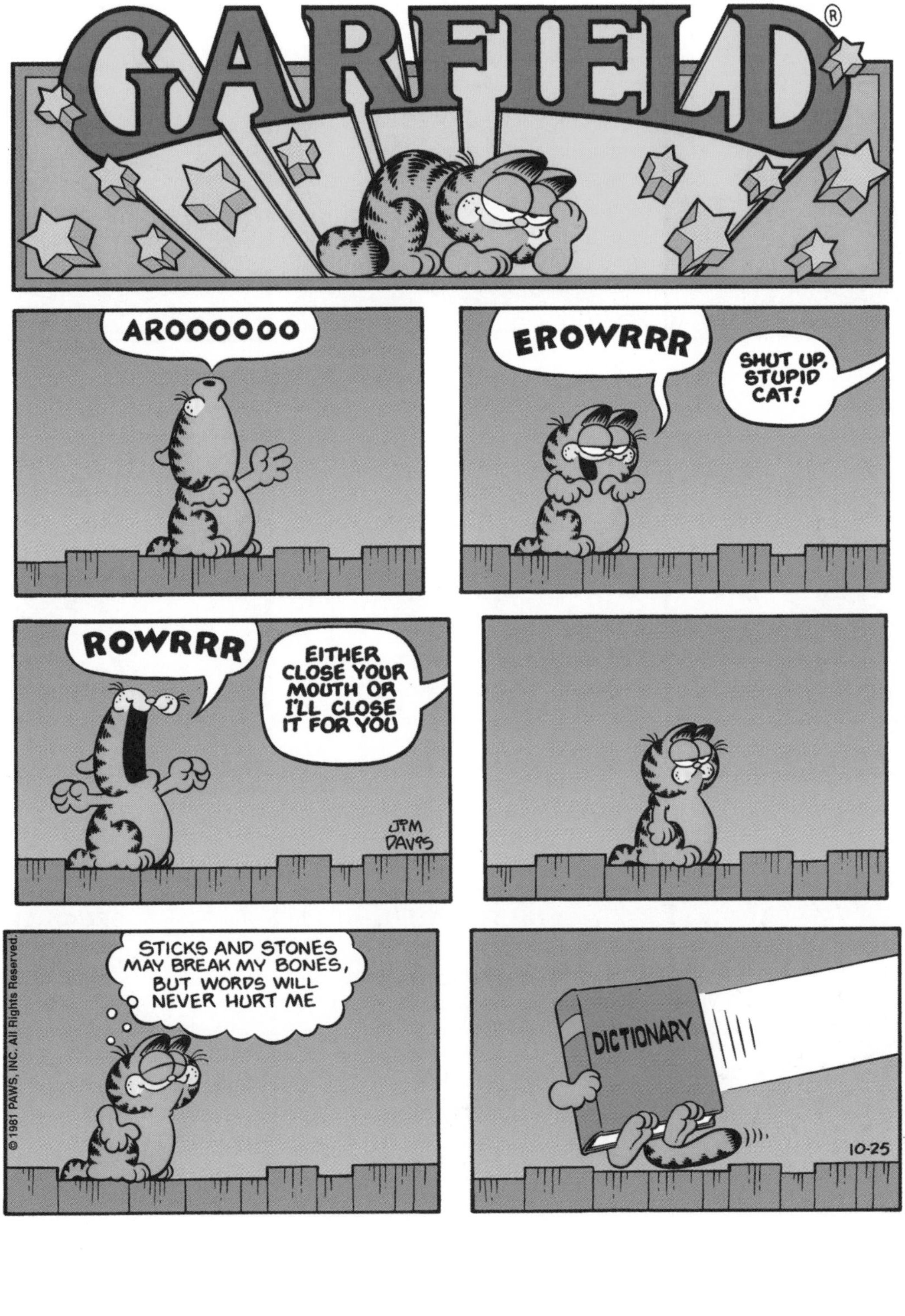
GARFIELD®
AROOOOOO
EROWRRR
SHUT UP, STUPID CAT!
ROWRRR
EITHER CLOSE YOUR MOUTH OR I'LL CLOSE IT FOR YOU
JIM DAVIS
STICKS AND STONES MAY BREAK MY BONES, BUT WORDS WILL NEVER HURT ME
DICTIONARY
10-25

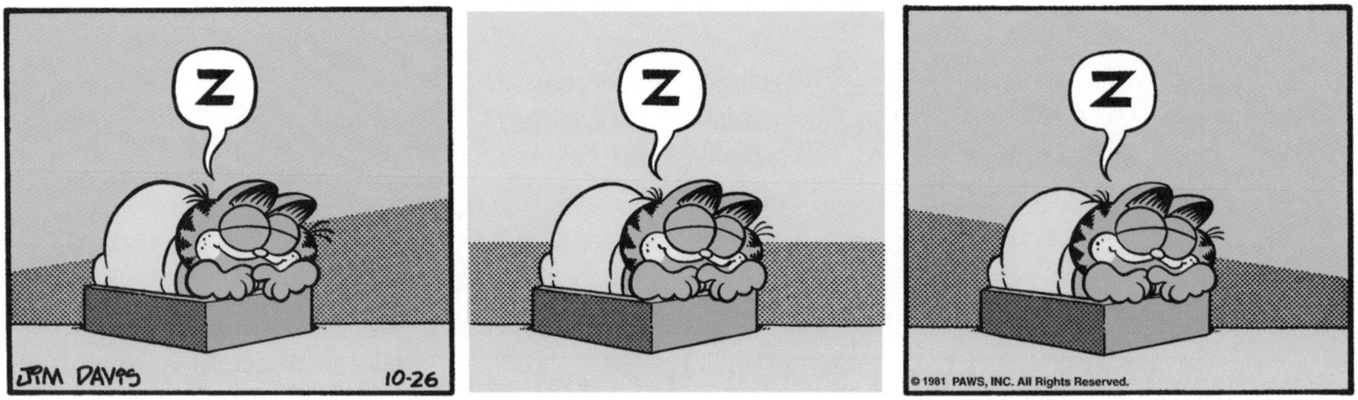
Z
Z
Z
JIM DAVIS
10-26
© 1981 PAWS, INC. All Rights Reserved.

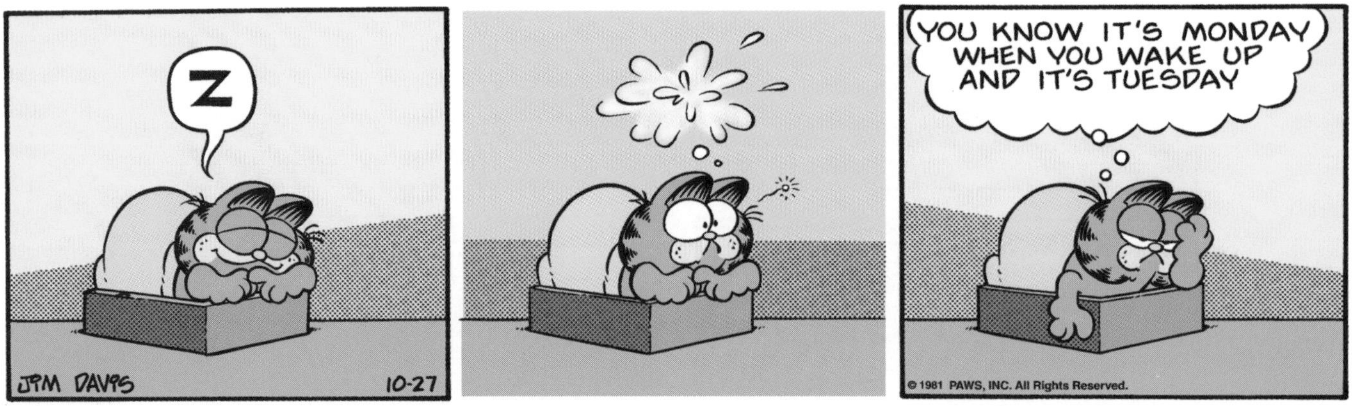
Z
YOU KNOW IT'S MONDAY WHEN YOU WAKE UP AND IT'S TUESDAY
JIM DAVIS
10-27
© 1981 PAWS, INC. All Rights Reserved.

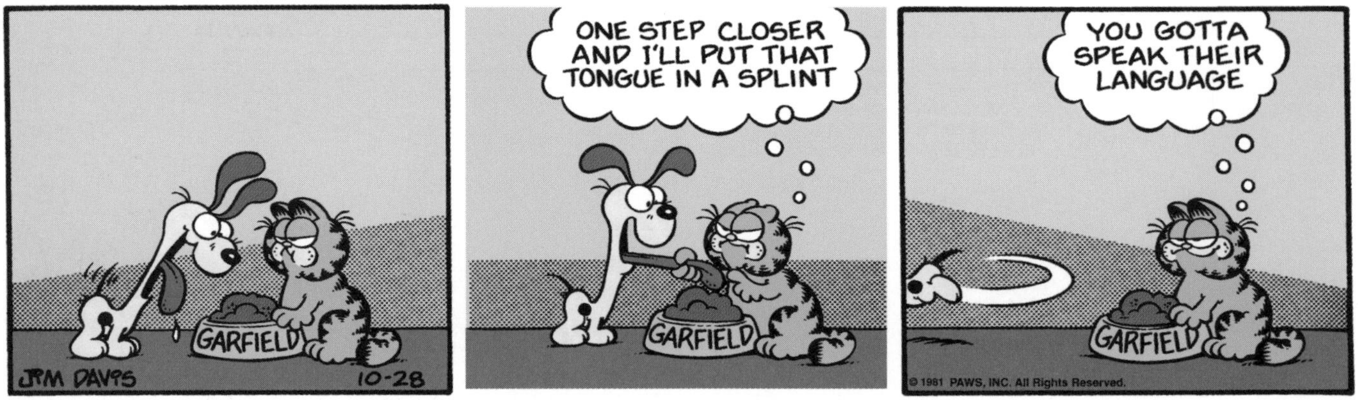
GARFIELD
ONE STEP CLOSER AND I'LL PUT THAT TONGUE IN A SPLINT
GARFIELD
YOU GOTTA SPEAK THEIR LANGUAGE
GARFIELD
JIM DAVIS
10-28
© 1981 PAWS, INC. All Rights Reserved.

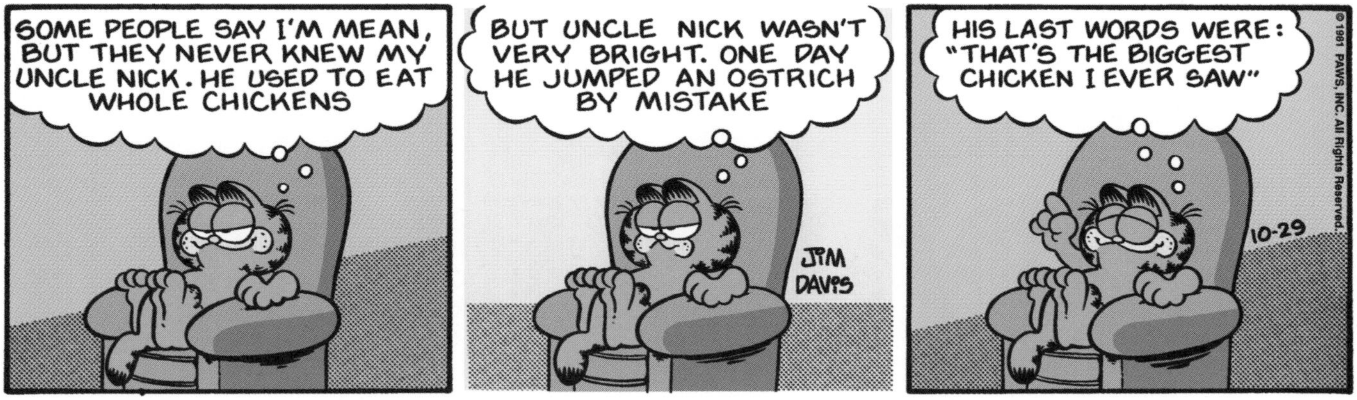

SOME PEOPLE SAY I'M MEAN, BUT THEY NEVER KNEW MY UNCLE NICK. HE USED TO EAT WHOLE CHICKENS
BUT UNCLE NICK WASN'T VERY BRIGHT. ONE DAY HE JUMPED AN OSTRICH BY MISTAKE
JIM DAVIS
HIS LAST WORDS WERE: "THAT'S THE BIGGEST CHICKEN I EVER SAW"
10-29
© 1981 PAWS, INC. All Rights Reserved.

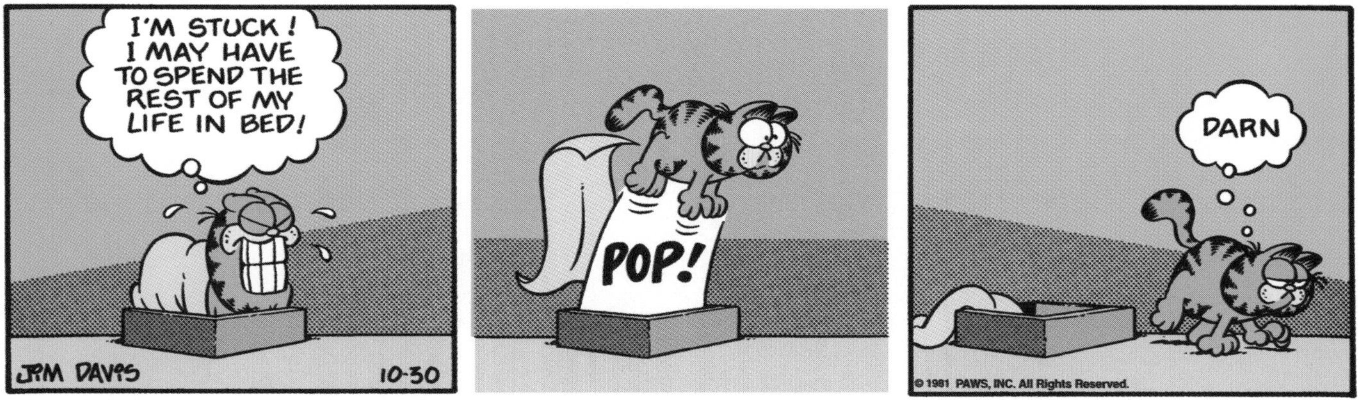

I'M STUCK! I MAY HAVE TO SPEND THE REST OF MY LIFE IN BED!
JIM DAVIS
10-30
POP!
DARN
© 1981 PAWS, INC. All Rights Reserved.

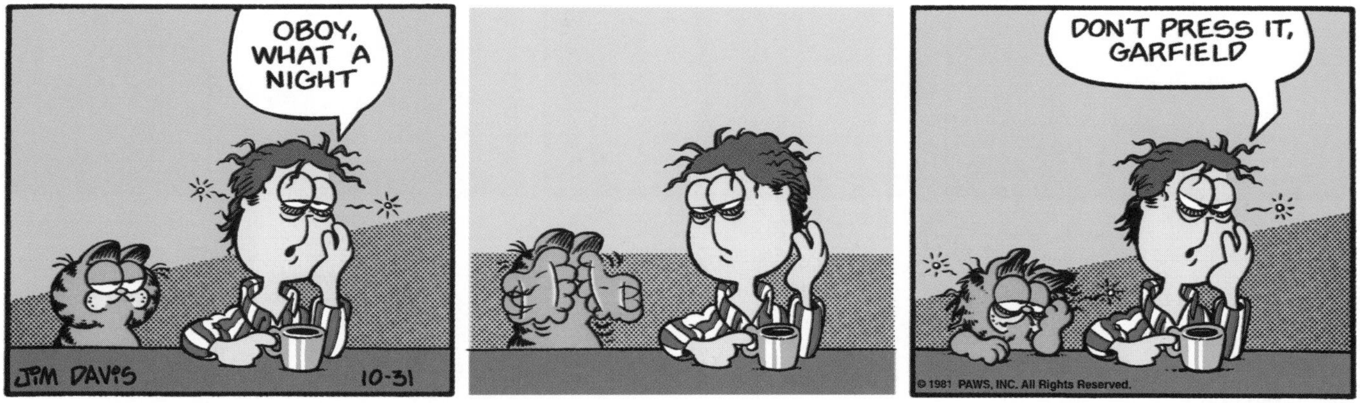

OBOY, WHAT A NIGHT
JIM DAVIS
10-31
DON'T PRESS IT, GARFIELD
© 1981 PAWS, INC. All Rights Reserved.

GARFIELD®
JIM DAVIS
11-1
CHUNG!
© 1981 PAWS, INC. All Rights Reserved.

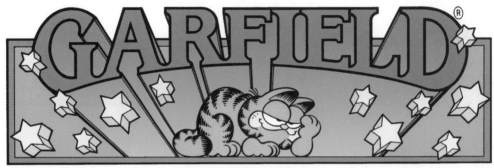

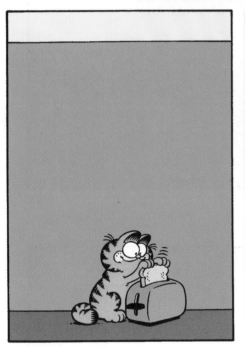

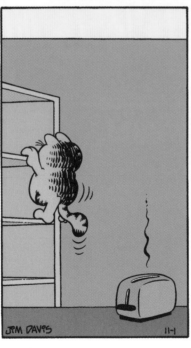

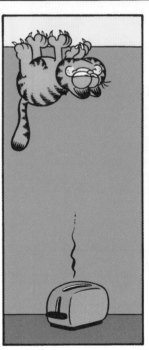

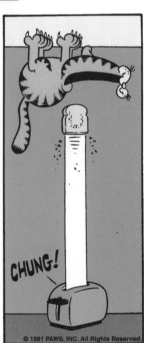

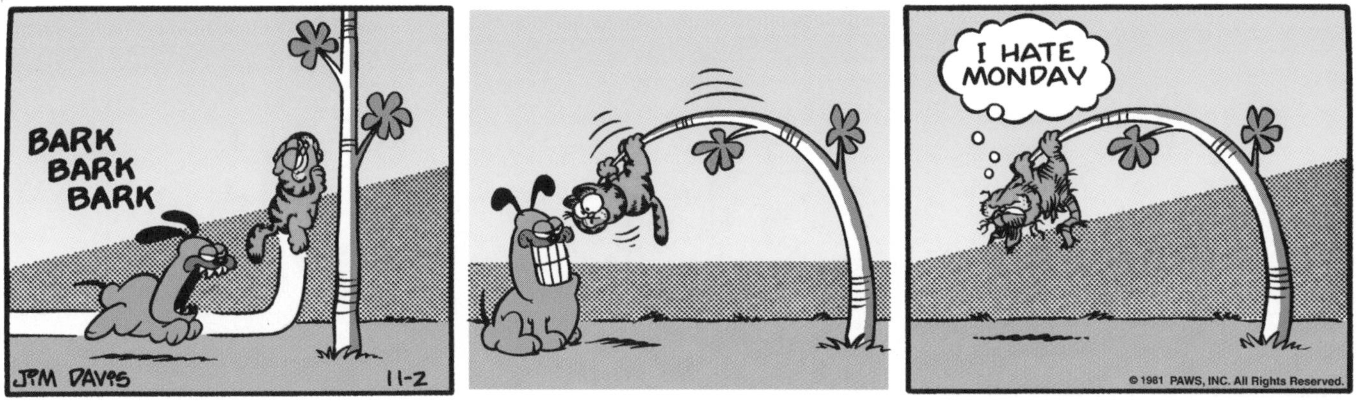
BARK
BARK
BARK
JIM DAVIS
11-2
I HATE MONDAY
© 1981 PAWS, INC. All Rights Reserved.

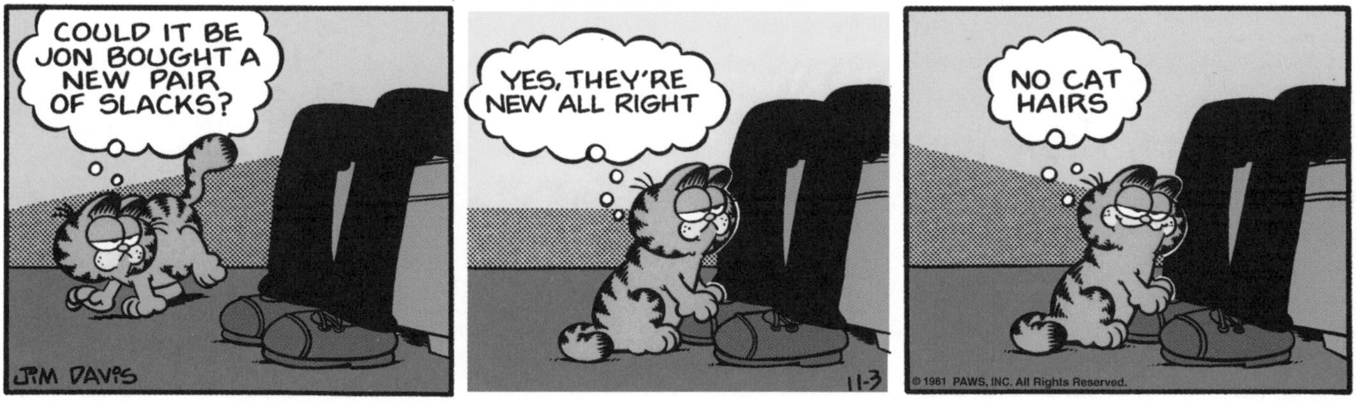
COULD IT BE JON BOUGHT A NEW PAIR OF SLACKS?
JIM DAVIS
YES, THEY'RE NEW ALL RIGHT
11-3
NO CAT HAIRS
© 1981 PAWS, INC. All Rights Reserved.

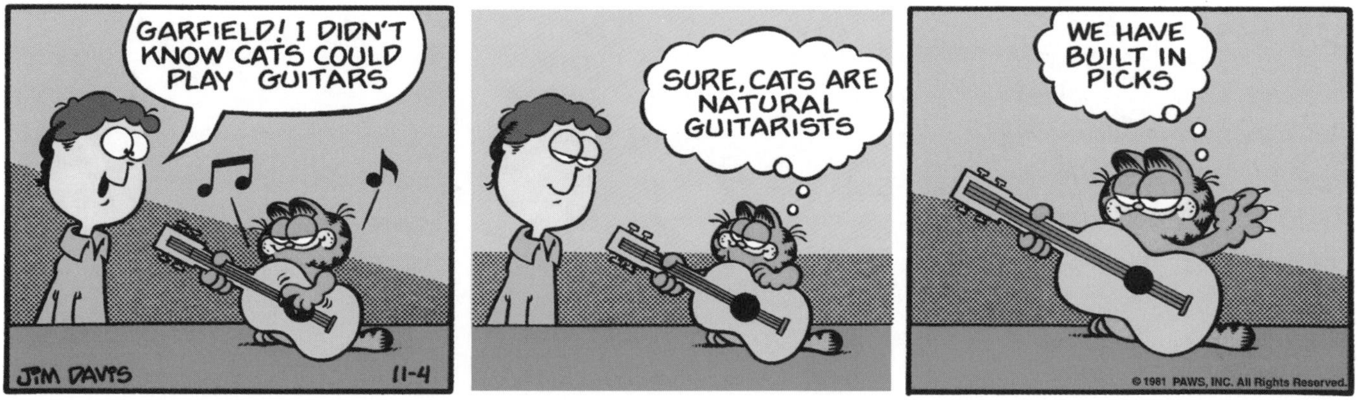
GARFIELD! I DIDN'T KNOW CATS COULD PLAY GUITARS
JIM DAVIS
11-4
SURE, CATS ARE NATURAL GUITARISTS
WE HAVE BUILT IN PICKS
© 1981 PAWS, INC. All Rights Reserved.

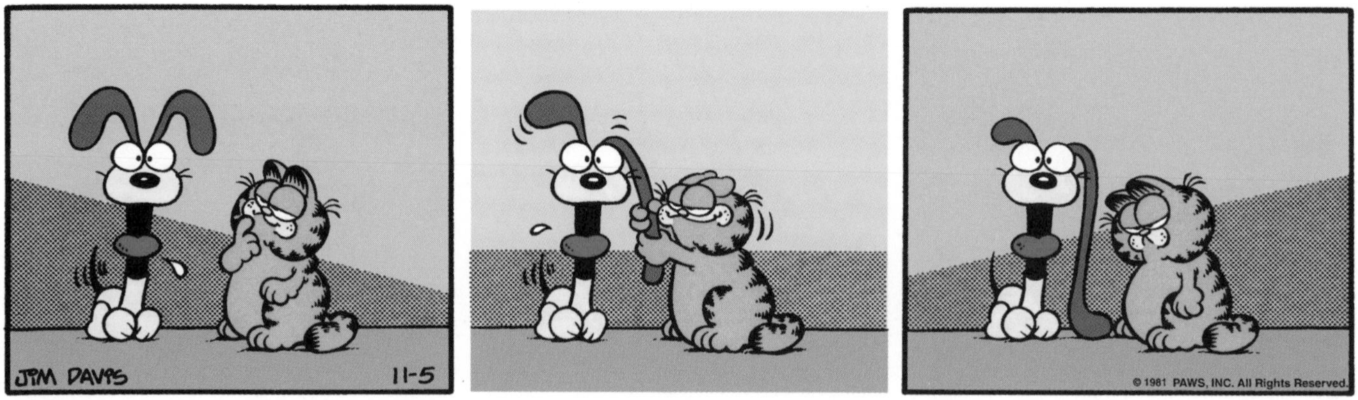
JIM DAVIS
11-5
© 1981 PAWS, INC. All Rights Reserved.

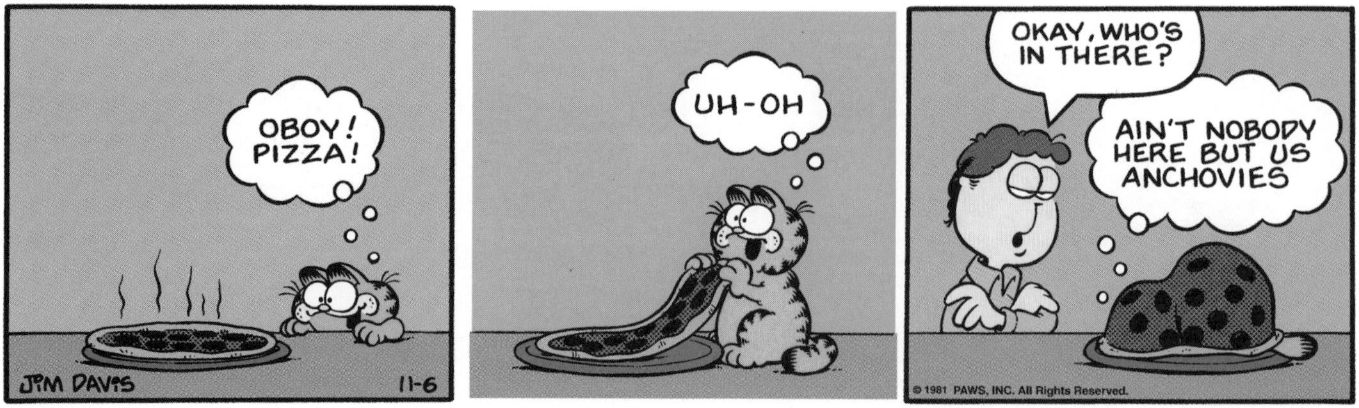
JIM DAVIS
11-6
OBOY! PIZZA!
UH-OH
OKAY, WHO'S IN THERE?
AIN'T NOBODY HERE BUT US ANCHOVIES
© 1981 PAWS, INC. All Rights Reserved.

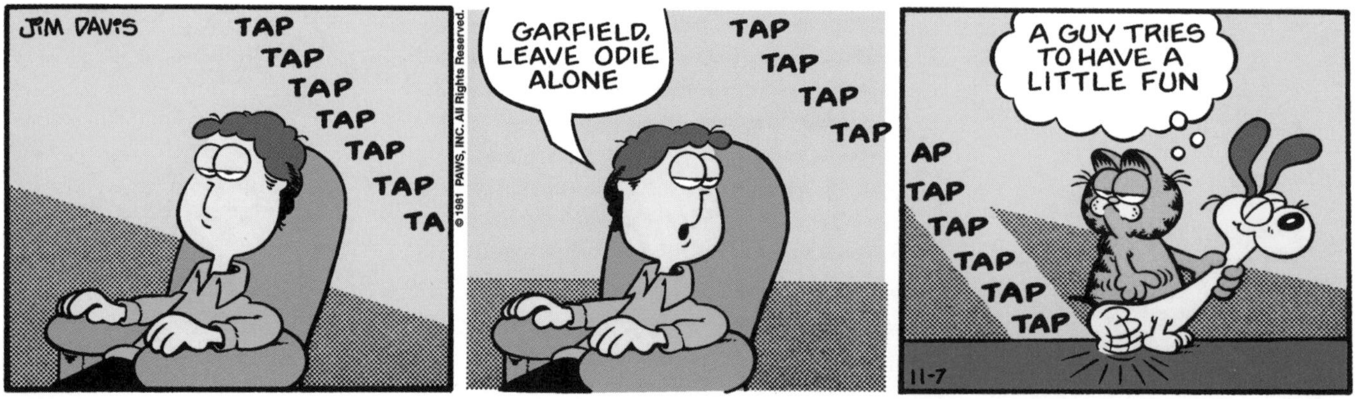
JIM DAVIS
TAP TAP TAP TAP TAP TAP TA
© 1981 PAWS, INC. All Rights Reserved.
GARFIELD, LEAVE ODIE ALONE
TAP TAP TAP TAP
AP TAP TAP TAP TAP TAP
A GUY TRIES TO HAVE A LITTLE FUN
11-7

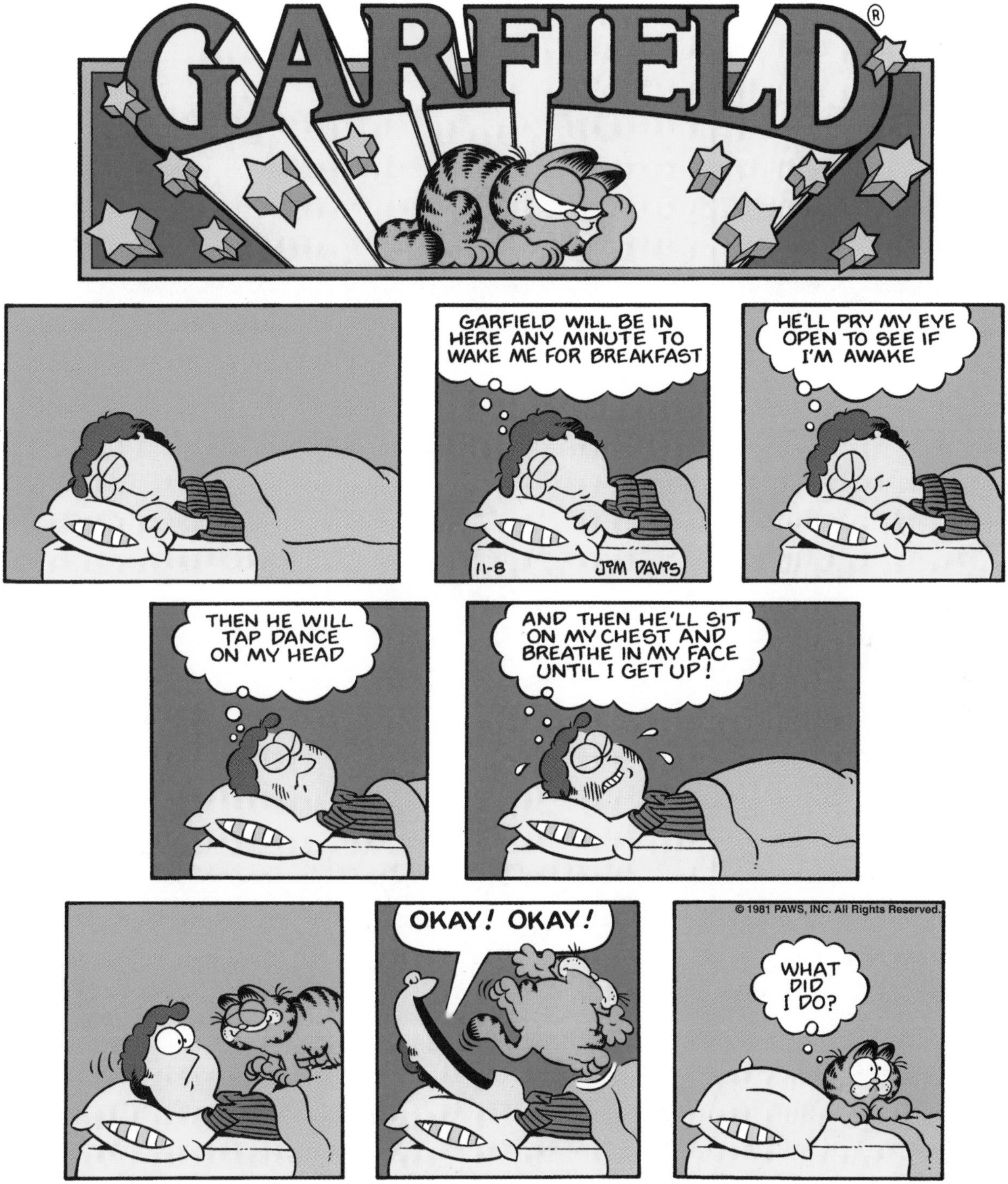
GARFIELD®
GARFIELD WILL BE IN HERE ANY MINUTE TO WAKE ME FOR BREAKFAST
11-8
JIM DAVIS
HE'LL PRY MY EYE OPEN TO SEE IF I'M AWAKE
THEN HE WILL TAP DANCE ON MY HEAD
AND THEN HE'LL SIT ON MY CHEST AND BREATHE IN MY FACE UNTIL I GET UP!
OKAY! OKAY!
© 1981 PAWS, INC. All Rights Reserved.
WHAT DID I DO?

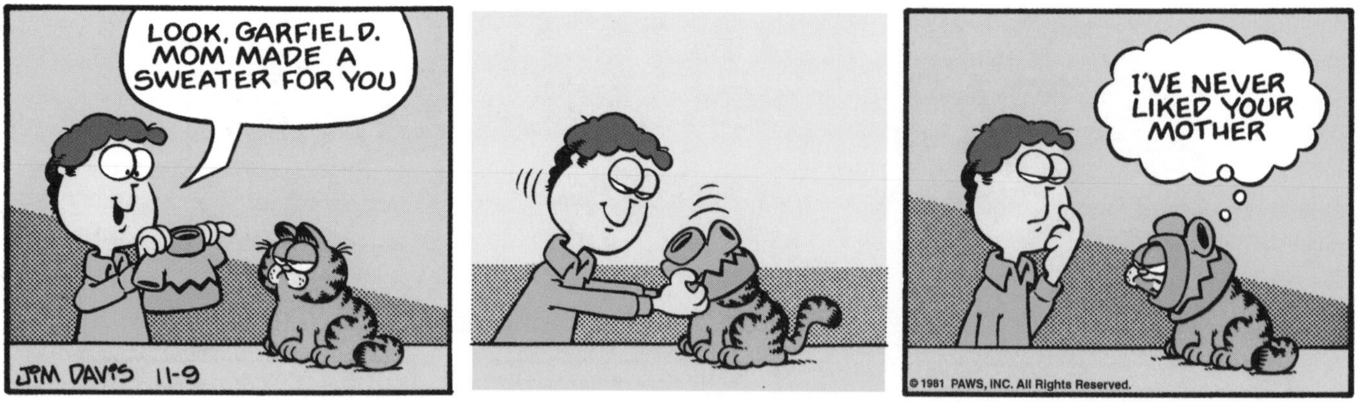
LOOK, GARFIELD. MOM MADE A SWEATER FOR YOU
I'VE NEVER LIKED YOUR MOTHER
JIM DAVIS 11-9
© 1981 PAWS, INC. All Rights Reserved.

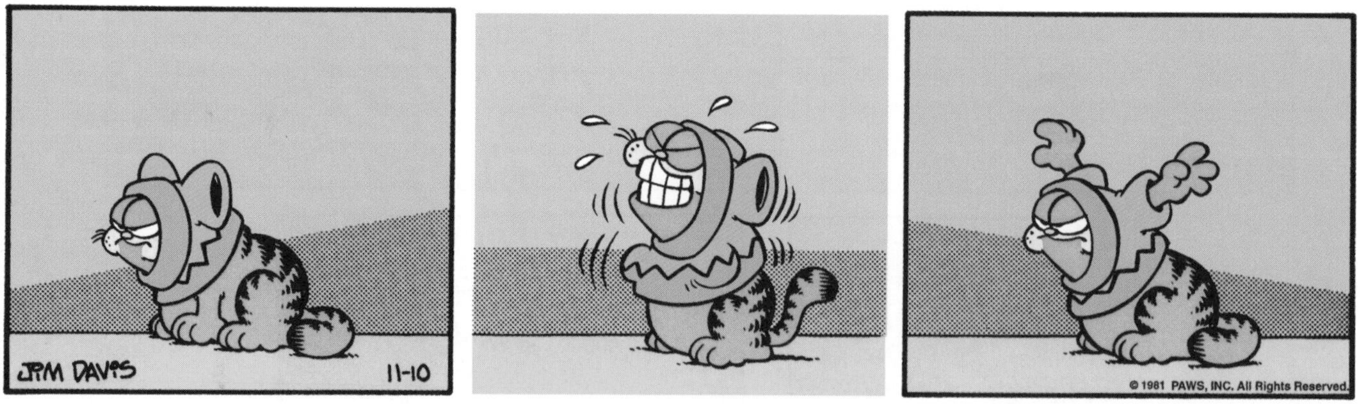
JIM DAVIS 11-10
© 1981 PAWS, INC. All Rights Reserved.

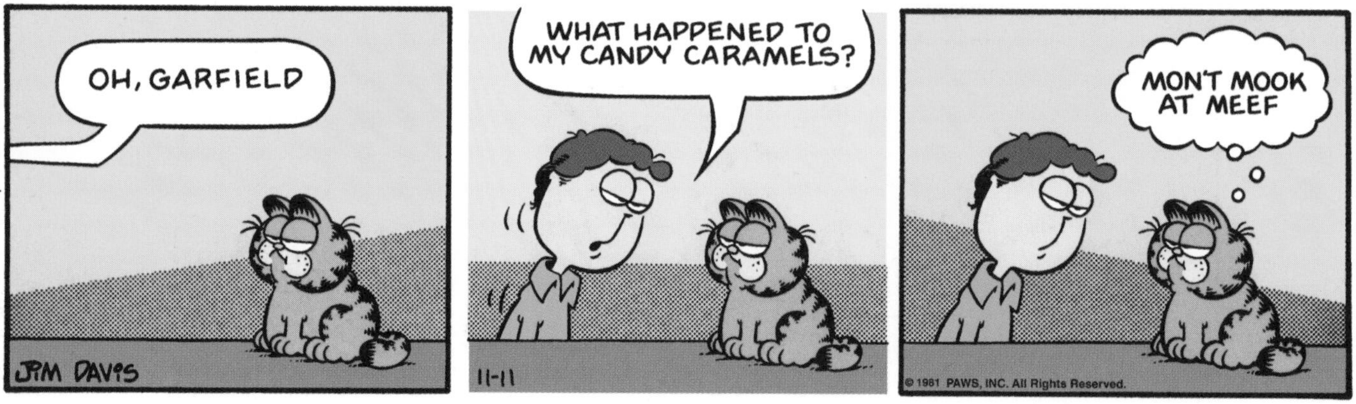
OH, GARFIELD
WHAT HAPPENED TO MY CANDY CARAMELS?
MON'T MOOK AT MEEF
JIM DAVIS 11-11
© 1981 PAWS, INC. All Rights Reserved.

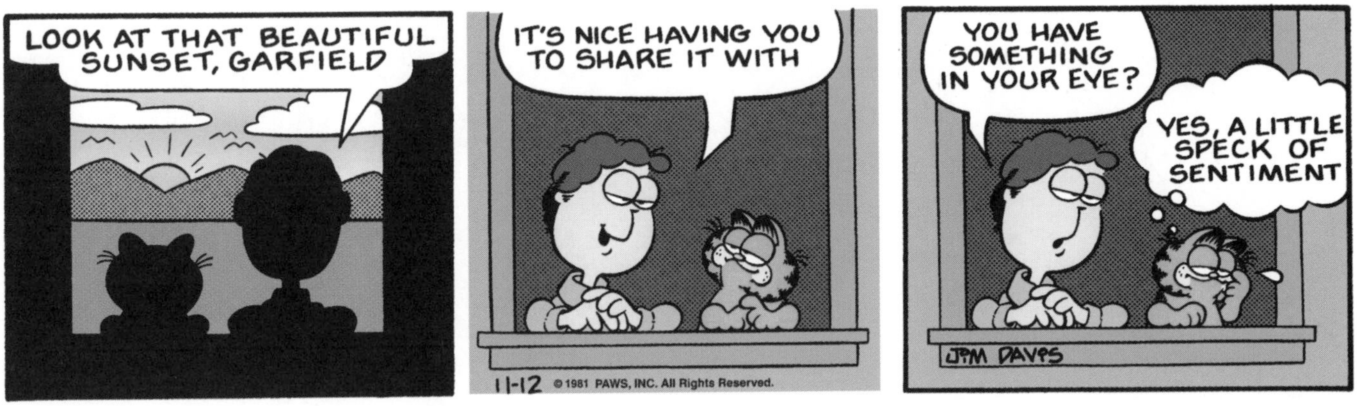
LOOK AT THAT BEAUTIFUL SUNSET, GARFIELD
IT'S NICE HAVING YOU TO SHARE IT WITH
11-12 © 1981 PAWS, INC. All Rights Reserved.
YOU HAVE SOMETHING IN YOUR EYE?
YES, A LITTLE SPECK OF SENTIMENT
JIM DAVIS

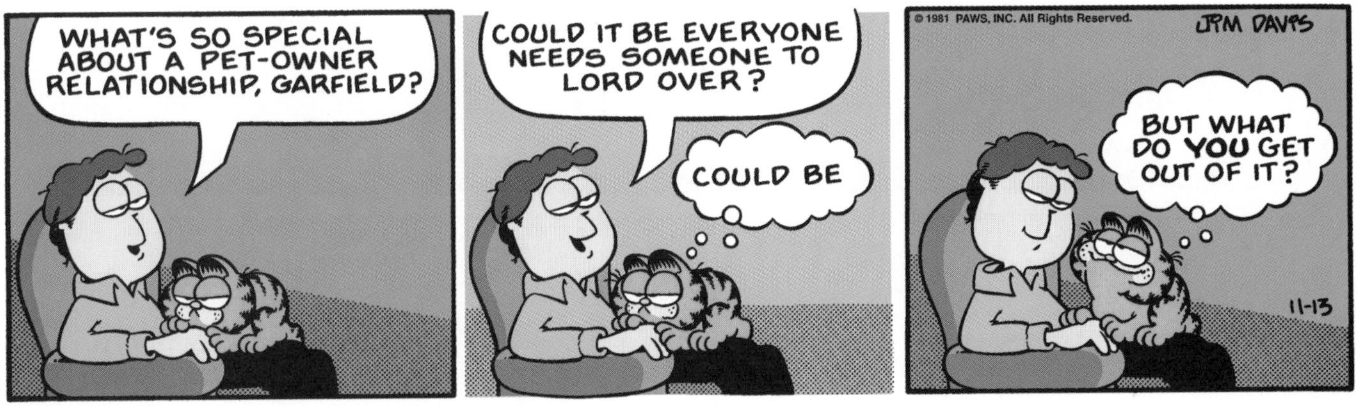
WHAT'S SO SPECIAL ABOUT A PET-OWNER RELATIONSHIP, GARFIELD?
COULD IT BE EVERYONE NEEDS SOMEONE TO LORD OVER?
COULD BE
© 1981 PAWS, INC. All Rights Reserved.
JIM DAVIS
BUT WHAT DO YOU GET OUT OF IT?
11-13

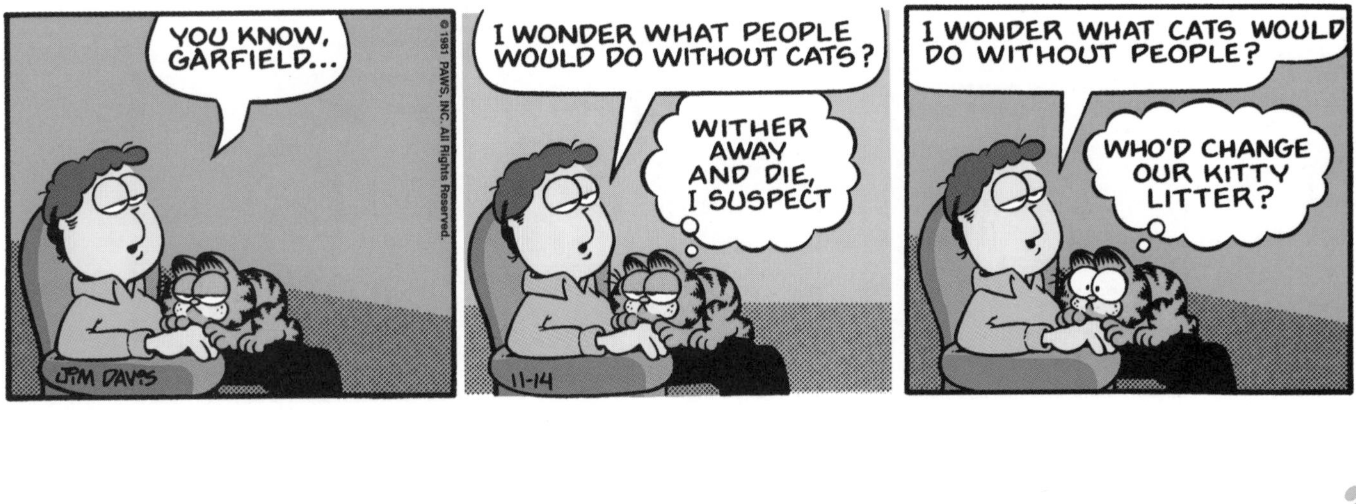
YOU KNOW, GARFIELD...
© 1981 PAWS, INC. All Rights Reserved.
JIM DAVIS
I WONDER WHAT PEOPLE WOULD DO WITHOUT CATS?
WITHER AWAY AND DIE, I SUSPECT
11-14
I WONDER WHAT CATS WOULD DO WITHOUT PEOPLE?
WHO'D CHANGE OUR KITTY LITTER?

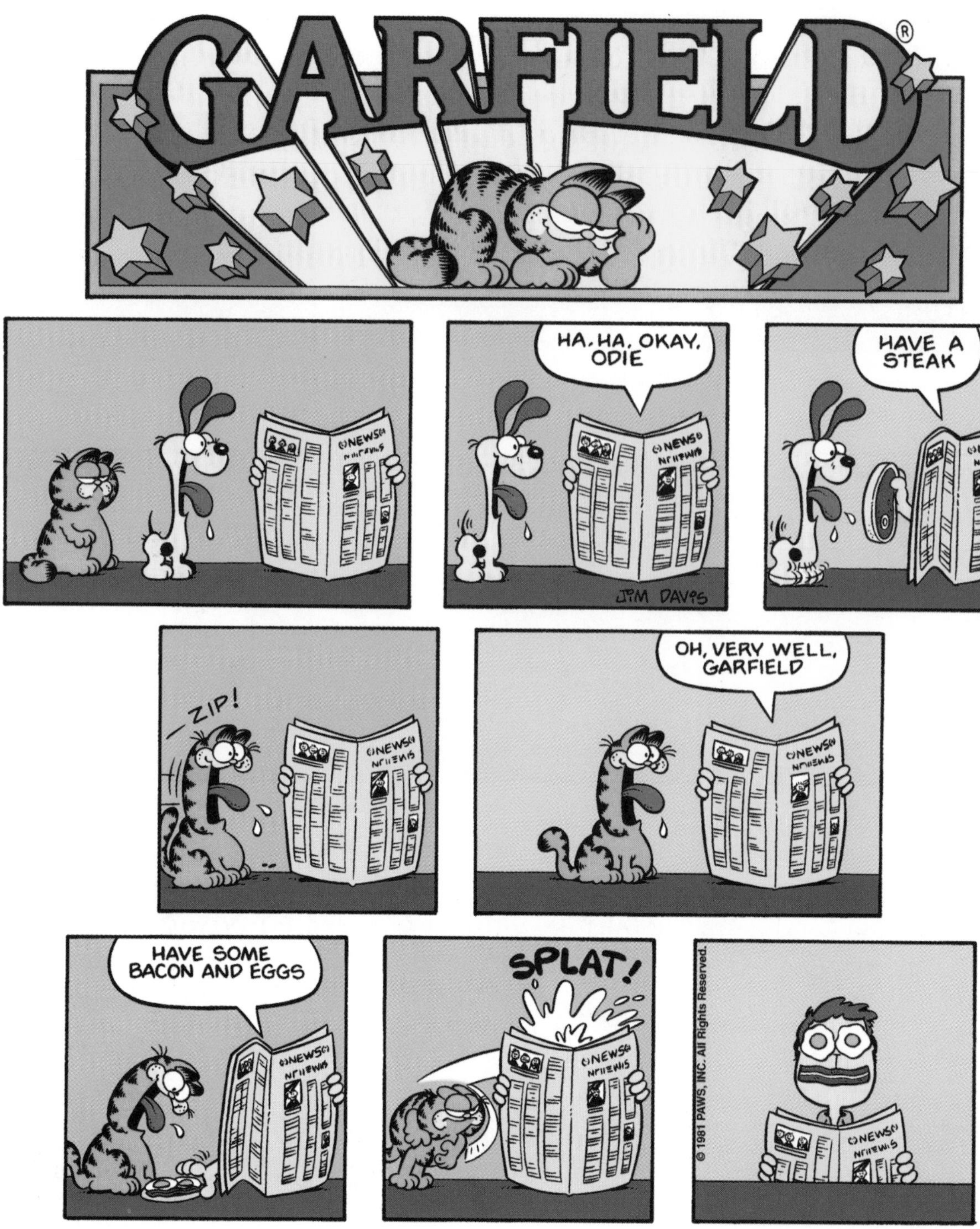
GARFIELD®
HA, HA, OKAY, ODIE
JIM DAVIS
HAVE A STEAK
11-15
ZIP!
OH, VERY WELL, GARFIELD
HAVE SOME BACON AND EGGS
SPLAT!
© 1981 PAWS, INC. All Rights Reserved.

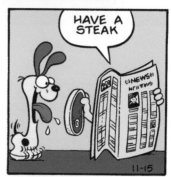

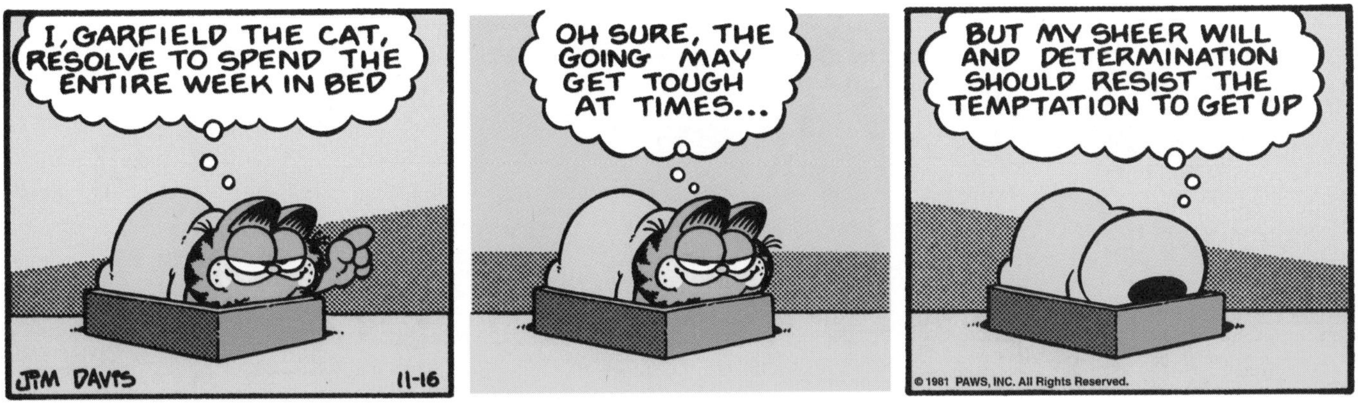
I, GARFIELD THE CAT, RESOLVE TO SPEND THE ENTIRE WEEK IN BED
JIM DAVIS
11-16
OH SURE, THE GOING MAY GET TOUGH AT TIMES...
BUT MY SHEER WILL AND DETERMINATION SHOULD RESIST THE TEMPTATION TO GET UP
© 1981 PAWS, INC. All Rights Reserved.

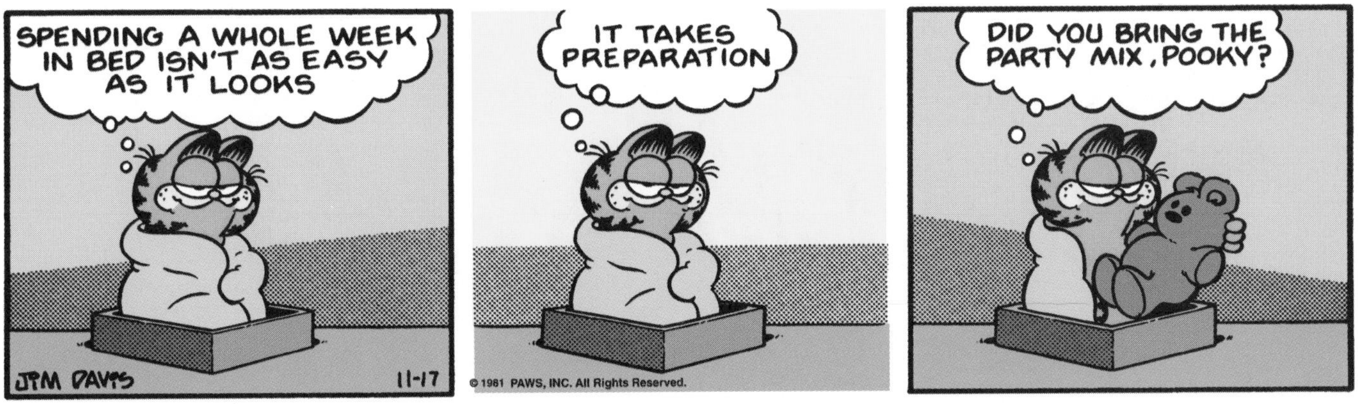
SPENDING A WHOLE WEEK IN BED ISN'T AS EASY AS IT LOOKS
JIM DAVIS
11-17
IT TAKES PREPARATION
© 1981 PAWS, INC. All Rights Reserved.
DID YOU BRING THE PARTY MIX, POOKY?

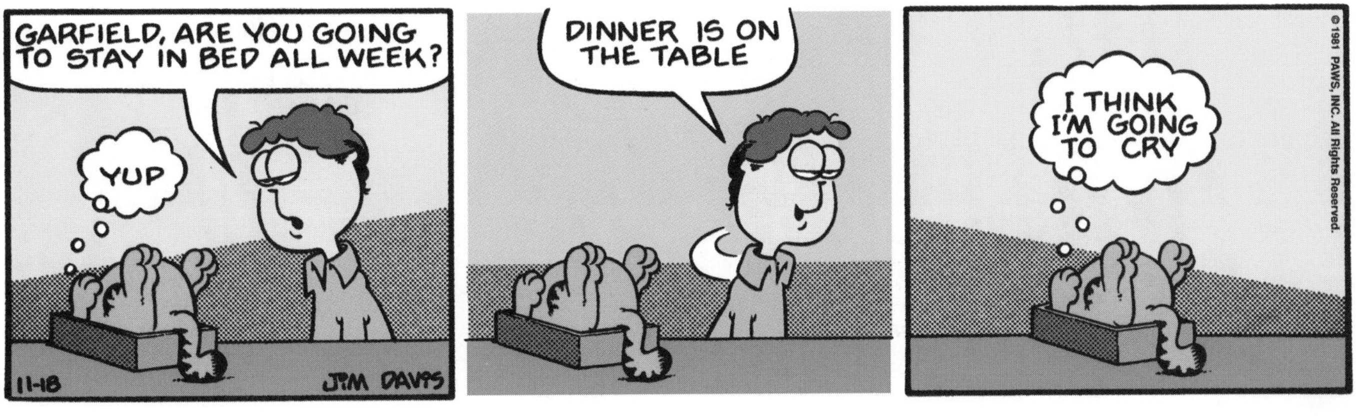
GARFIELD, ARE YOU GOING TO STAY IN BED ALL WEEK?
YUP
11-18
JIM DAVIS
DINNER IS ON THE TABLE
I THINK I'M GOING TO CRY
© 1981 PAWS, INC. All Rights Reserved.

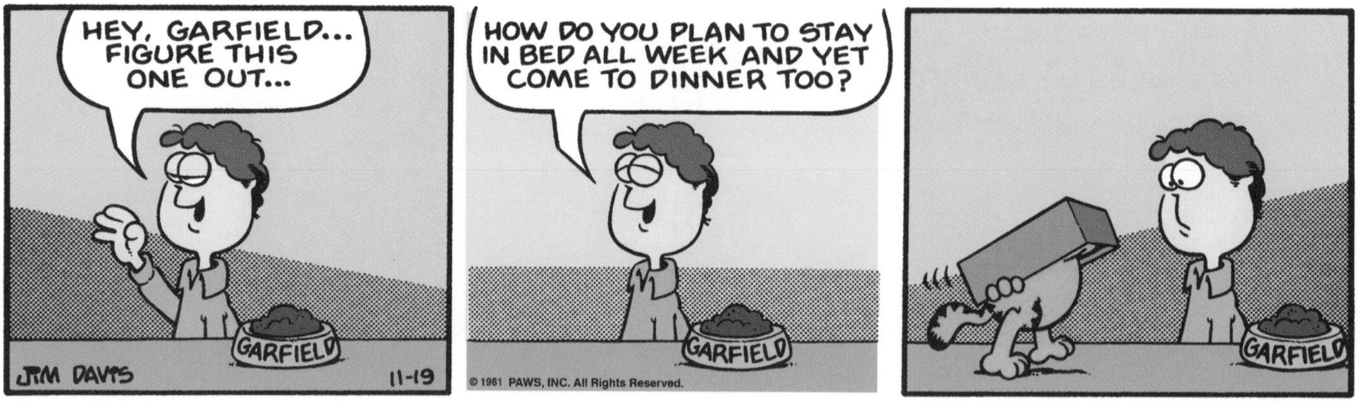
HEY, GARFIELD... FIGURE THIS ONE OUT...
HOW DO YOU PLAN TO STAY IN BED ALL WEEK AND YET COME TO DINNER TOO?
GARFIELD
JIM DAVIS
11-19
© 1981 PAWS, INC. All Rights Reserved.

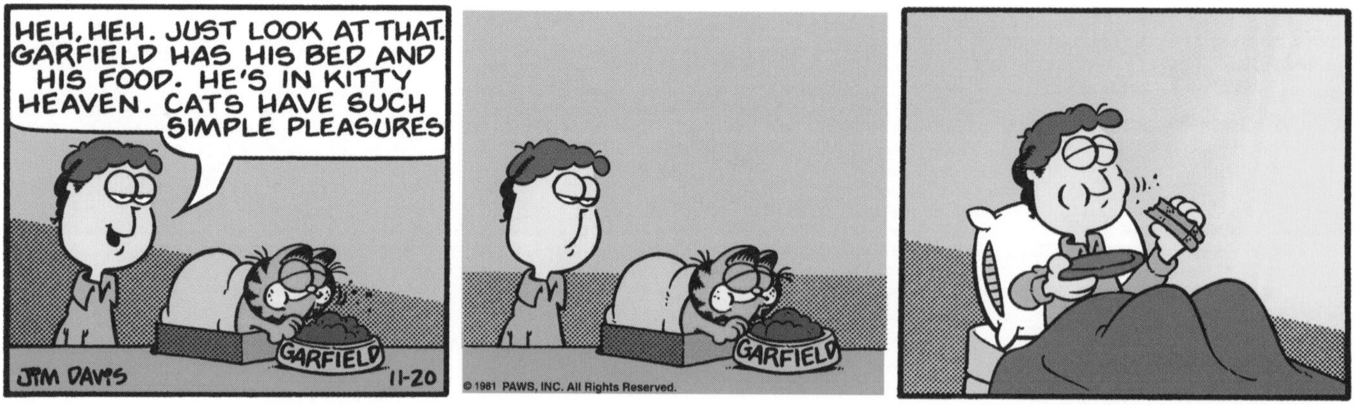
HEH, HEH. JUST LOOK AT THAT. GARFIELD HAS HIS BED AND HIS FOOD. HE'S IN KITTY HEAVEN. CATS HAVE SUCH SIMPLE PLEASURES
GARFIELD
JIM DAVIS
11-20
© 1981 PAWS, INC. All Rights Reserved.

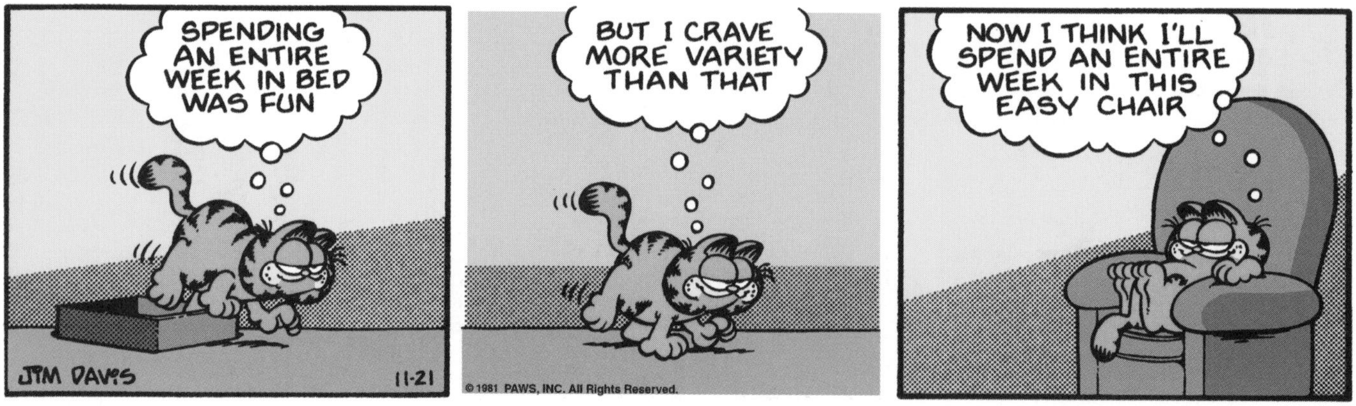
SPENDING AN ENTIRE WEEK IN BED WAS FUN
BUT I CRAVE MORE VARIETY THAN THAT
NOW I THINK I'LL SPEND AN ENTIRE WEEK IN THIS EASY CHAIR
JIM DAVIS
11-21
© 1981 PAWS, INC. All Rights Reserved.

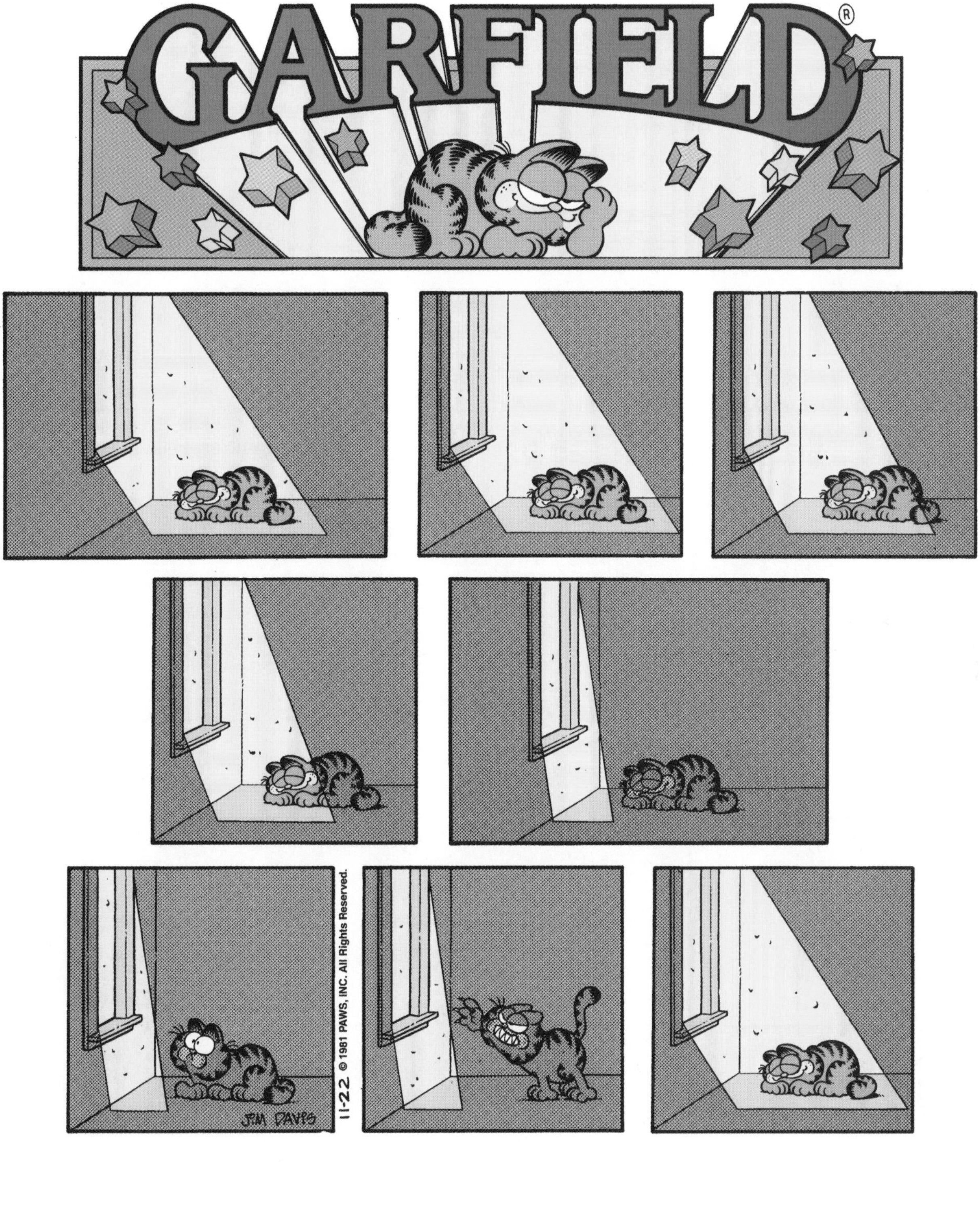
GARFIELD®
JIM DAVIS
11-22 © 1981 PAWS, INC. All Rights Reserved.

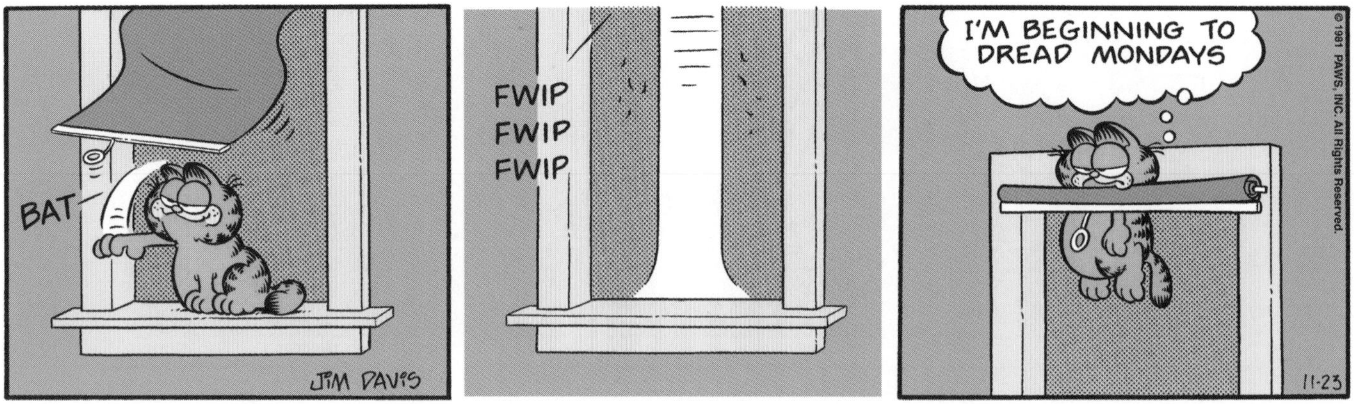
BAT
JIM DAVIS
FWIP
FWIP
FWIP
I'M BEGINNING TO DREAD MONDAYS
© 1981 PAWS, INC. All Rights Reserved.
11-23

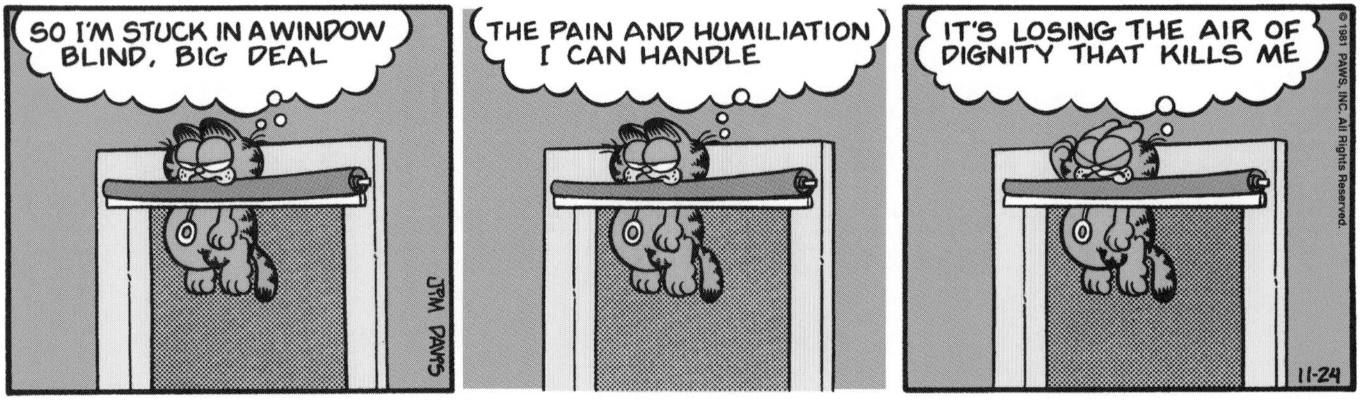
SO I'M STUCK IN A WINDOW BLIND, BIG DEAL
JIM DAVIS
THE PAIN AND HUMILIATION I CAN HANDLE
IT'S LOSING THE AIR OF DIGNITY THAT KILLS ME
© 1981 PAWS, INC. All Rights Reserved.
11-24

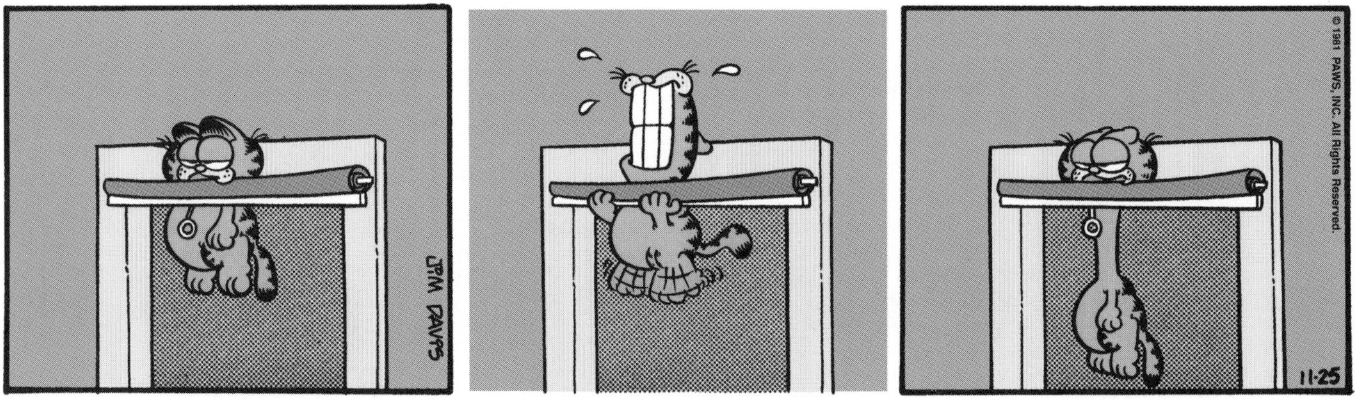
JIM DAVIS
© 1981 PAWS, INC. All Rights Reserved.
11-25

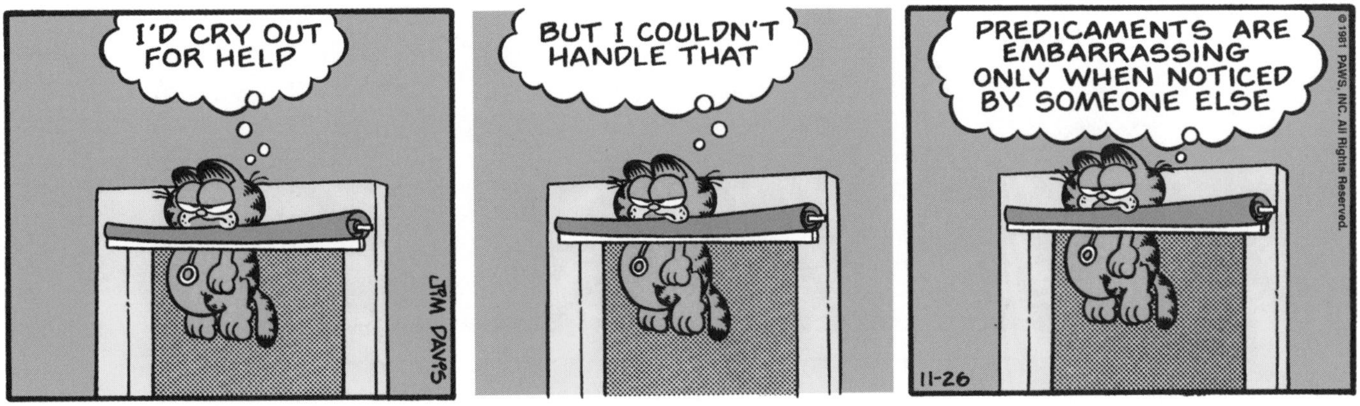
I'D CRY OUT FOR HELP
BUT I COULDN'T HANDLE THAT
PREDICAMENTS ARE EMBARRASSING ONLY WHEN NOTICED BY SOMEONE ELSE
JIM DAVIS
11-26
© 1981 PAWS, INC. All Rights Reserved.

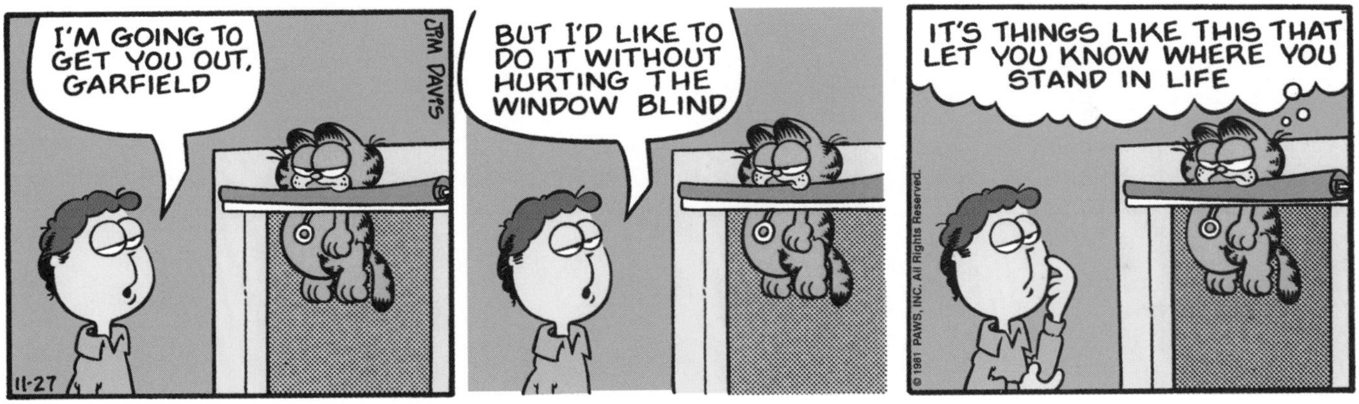
I'M GOING TO GET YOU OUT, GARFIELD
BUT I'D LIKE TO DO IT WITHOUT HURTING THE WINDOW BLIND
IT'S THINGS LIKE THIS THAT LET YOU KNOW WHERE YOU STAND IN LIFE
JIM DAVIS
11-27
© 1981 PAWS, INC. All Rights Reserved.

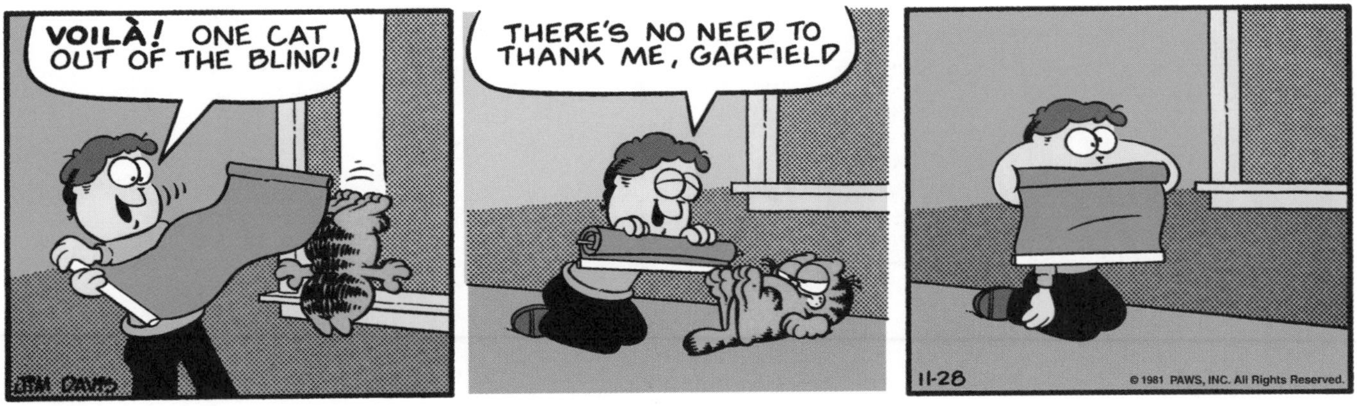
VOILÀ! ONE CAT OUT OF THE BLIND!
THERE'S NO NEED TO THANK ME, GARFIELD
JIM DAVIS
11-28
© 1981 PAWS, INC. All Rights Reserved.

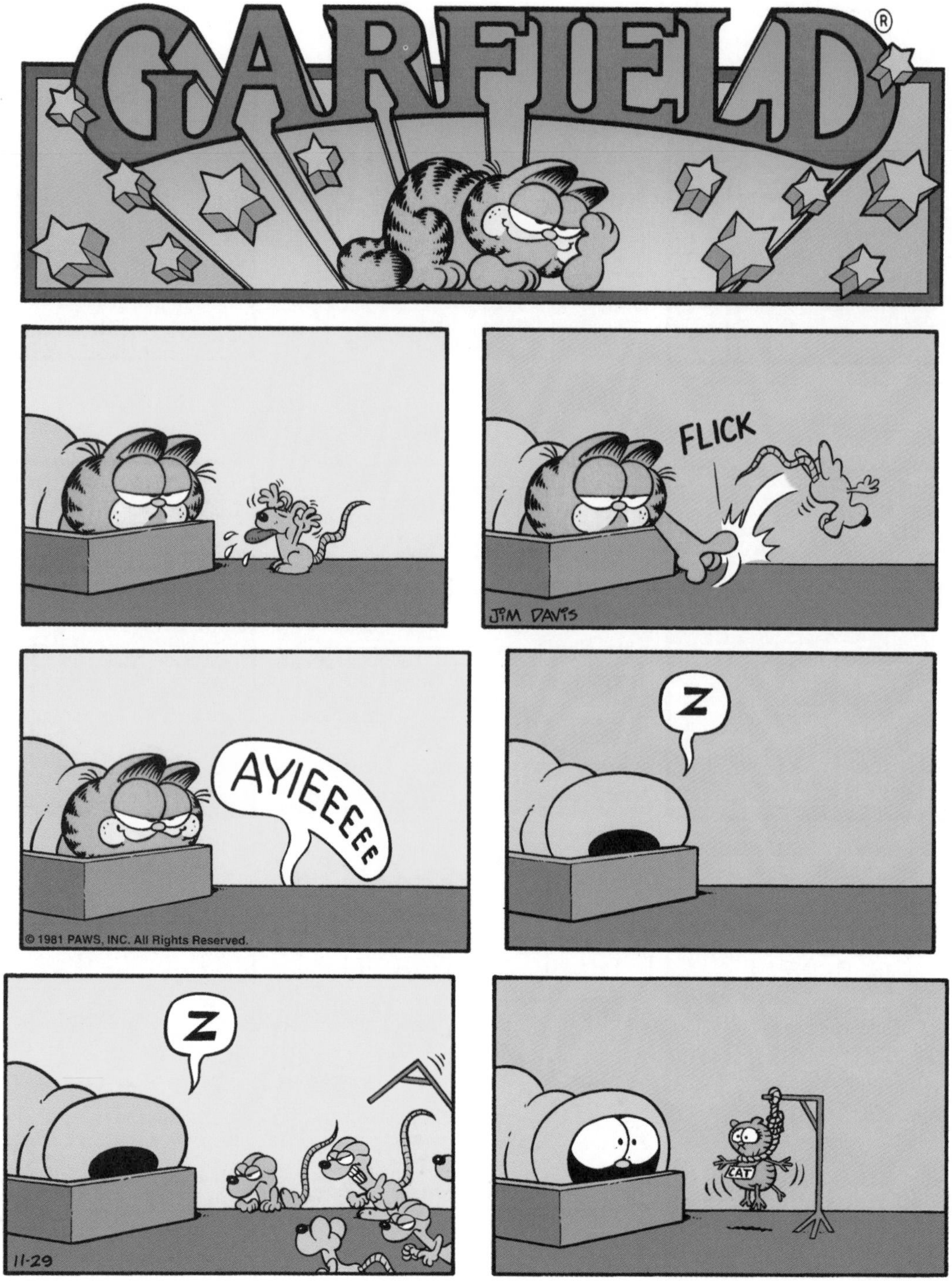
GARFIELD®
FLICK
JIM DAVIS
AYIEEEEEE
© 1981 PAWS, INC. All Rights Reserved.
Z
Z
11-29
CAT

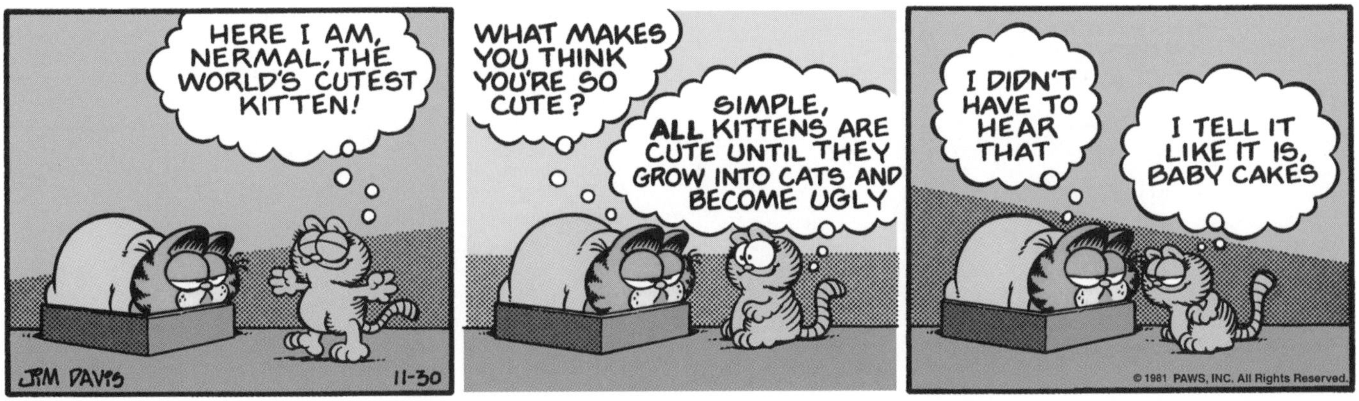
HERE I AM, NERMAL, THE WORLD'S CUTEST KITTEN!
JIM DAVIS
11-30
WHAT MAKES YOU THINK YOU'RE SO CUTE?
SIMPLE, **ALL** KITTENS ARE CUTE UNTIL THEY GROW INTO CATS AND BECOME UGLY
I DIDN'T HAVE TO HEAR THAT
I TELL IT LIKE IT IS, BABY CAKES
© 1981 PAWS, INC. All Rights Reserved.

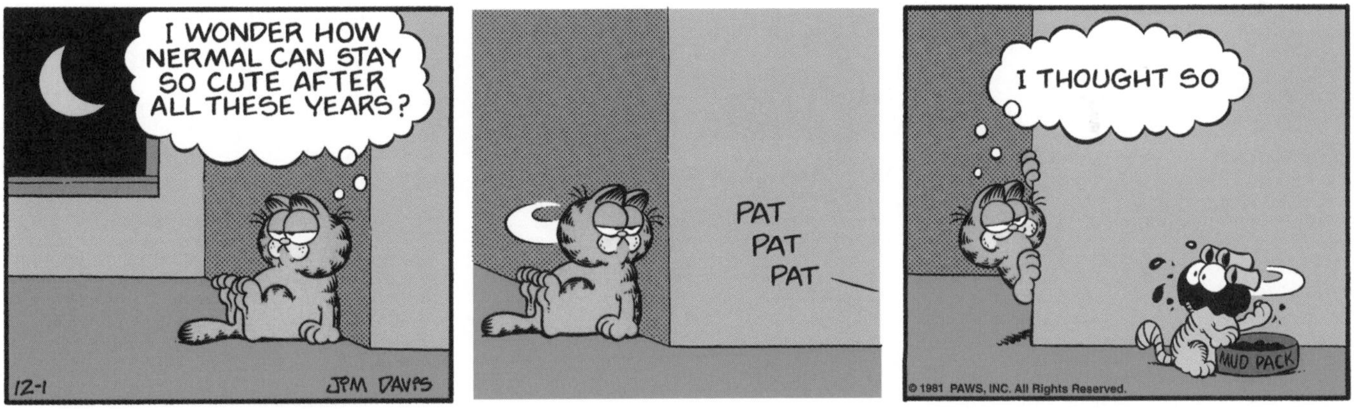
I WONDER HOW NERMAL CAN STAY SO CUTE AFTER ALL THESE YEARS?
12-1
JIM DAVIS
PAT
PAT
PAT
I THOUGHT SO
MUD PACK
© 1981 PAWS, INC. All Rights Reserved.

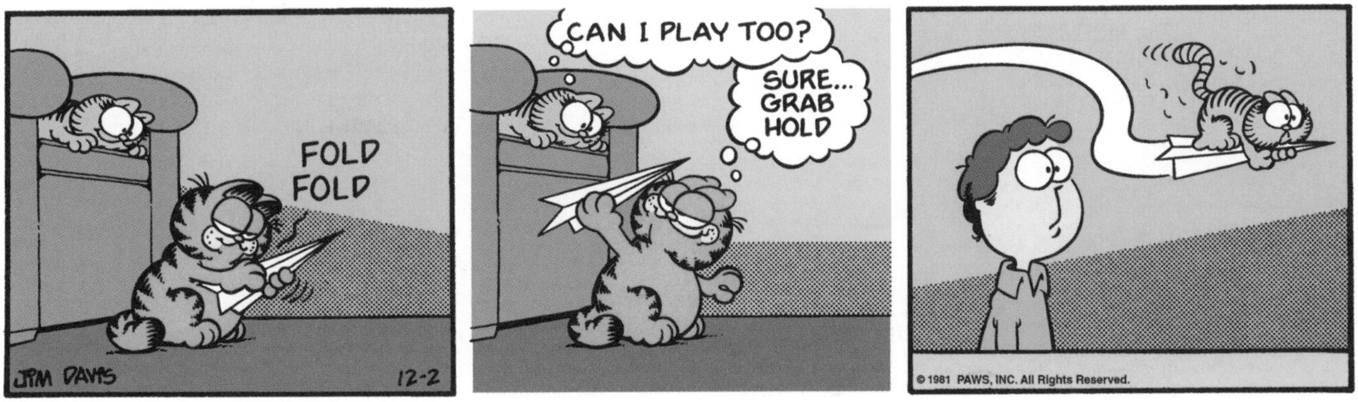
FOLD
FOLD
JIM DAVIS
12-2
CAN I PLAY TOO?
SURE... GRAB HOLD
© 1981 PAWS, INC. All Rights Reserved.

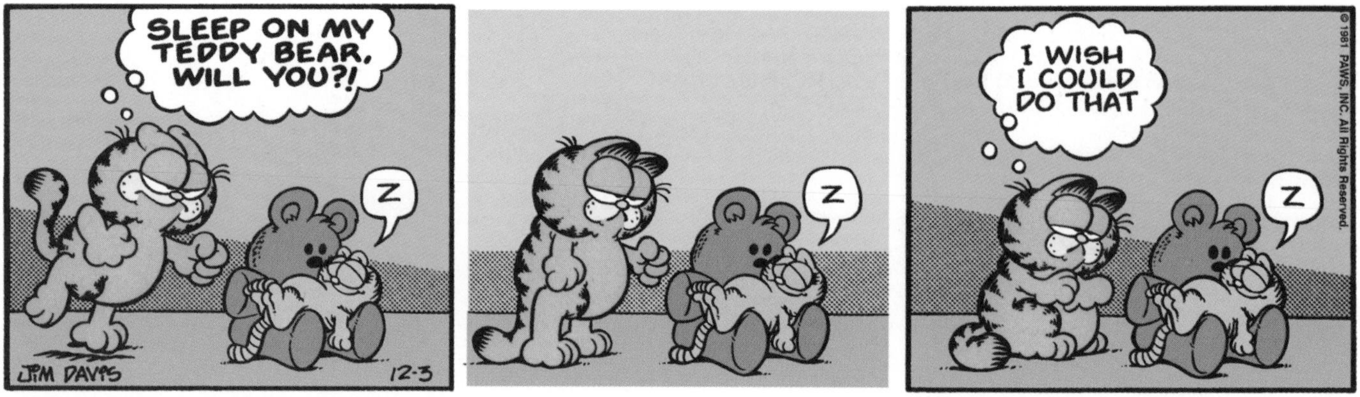
SLEEP ON MY TEDDY BEAR, WILL YOU?!
Z
JIM DAVIS
12-3
Z
I WISH I COULD DO THAT
Z
© 1981 PAWS, INC. All Rights Reserved.

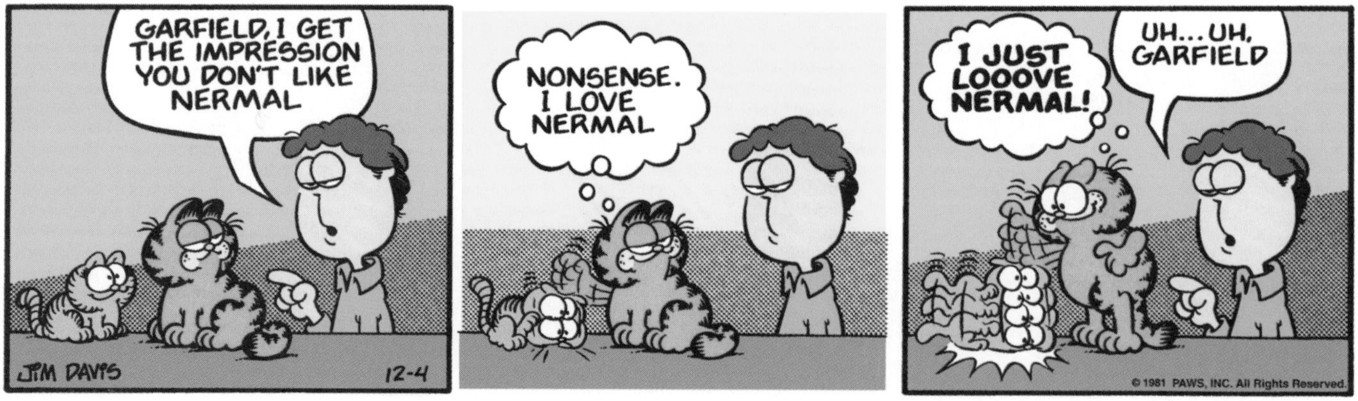
GARFIELD, I GET THE IMPRESSION YOU DON'T LIKE NERMAL
JIM DAVIS
12-4
NONSENSE. I LOVE NERMAL
I JUST LOOOVE NERMAL!
UH... UH, GARFIELD
© 1981 PAWS, INC. All Rights Reserved.

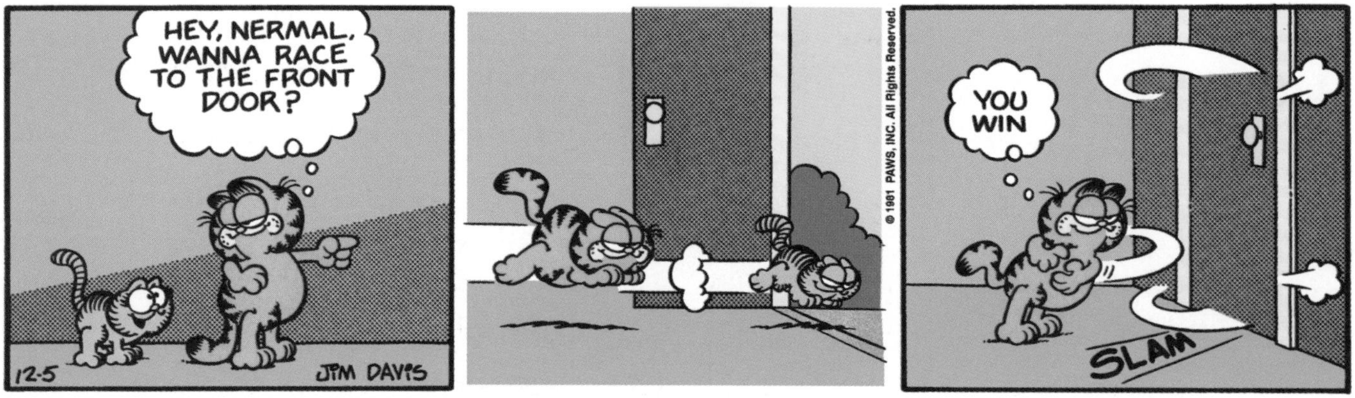
HEY, NERMAL, WANNA RACE TO THE FRONT DOOR?
12-5
JIM DAVIS
© 1981 PAWS, INC. All Rights Reserved.
YOU WIN
SLAM

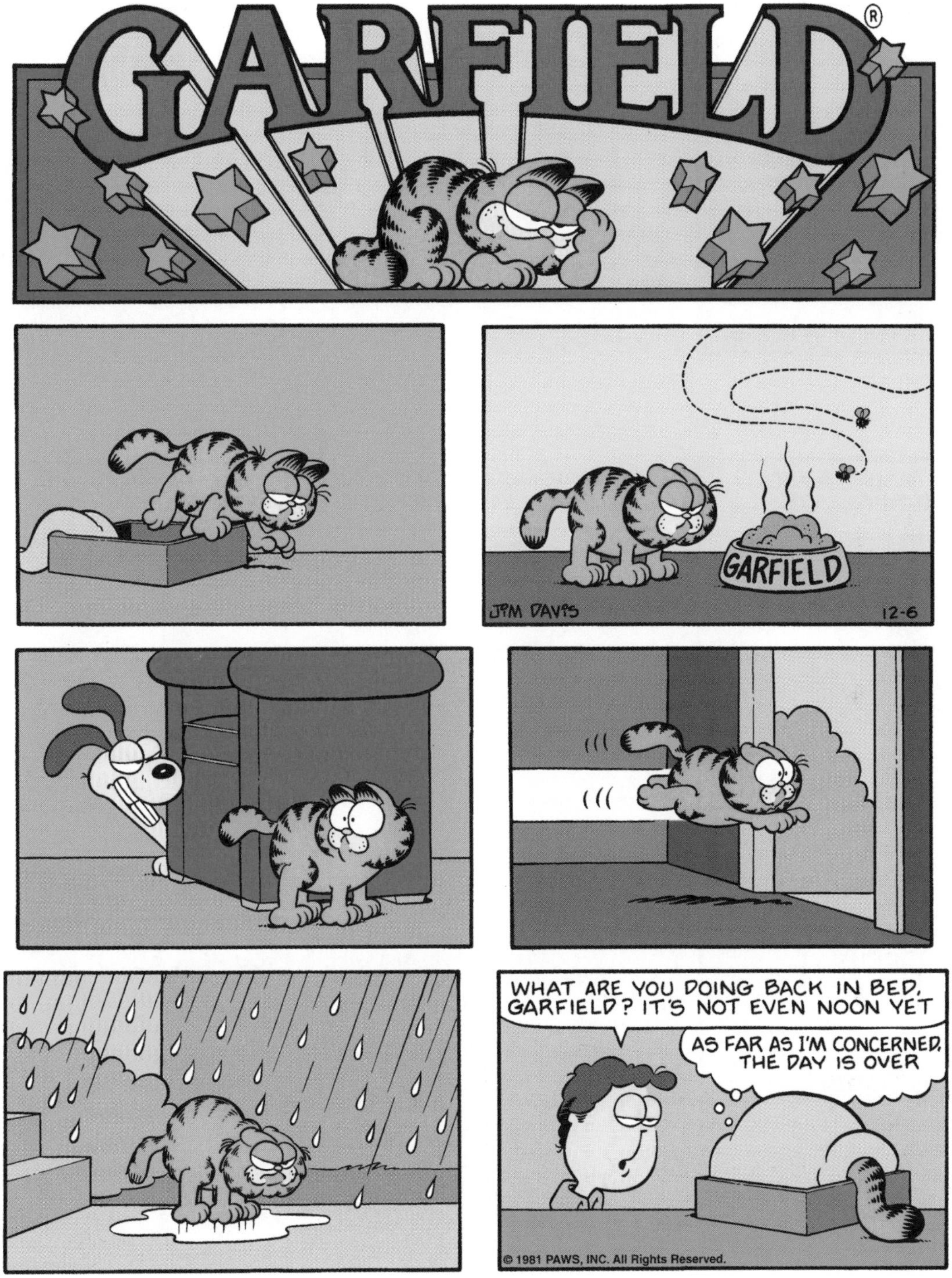
GARFIELD
GARFIELD
JIM DAVIS
12-6
WHAT ARE YOU DOING BACK IN BED, GARFIELD? IT'S NOT EVEN NOON YET
AS FAR AS I'M CONCERNED, THE DAY IS OVER
© 1981 PAWS, INC. All Rights Reserved.

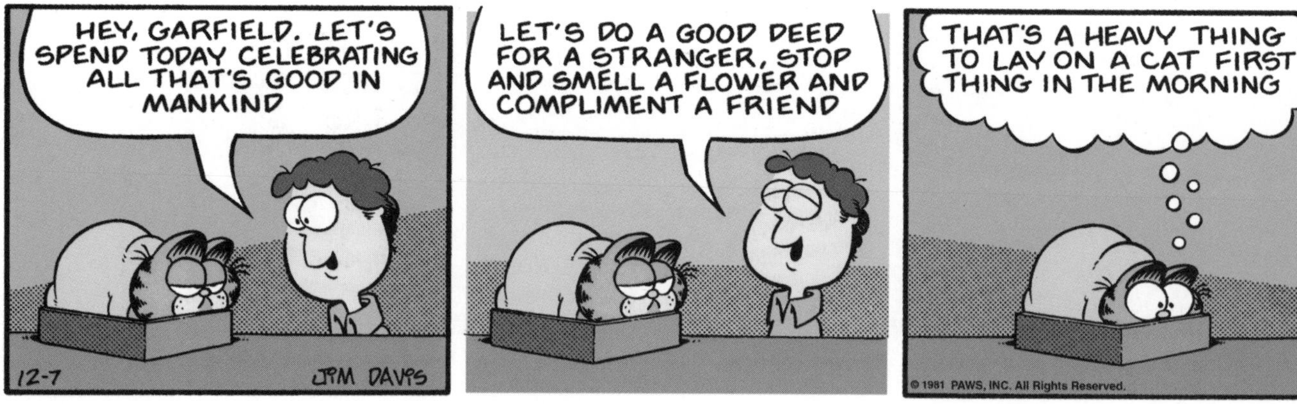
HEY, GARFIELD. LET'S SPEND TODAY CELEBRATING ALL THAT'S GOOD IN MANKIND
12-7
JIM DAVIS
LET'S DO A GOOD DEED FOR A STRANGER, STOP AND SMELL A FLOWER AND COMPLIMENT A FRIEND
THAT'S A HEAVY THING TO LAY ON A CAT FIRST THING IN THE MORNING
© 1981 PAWS, INC. All Rights Reserved.

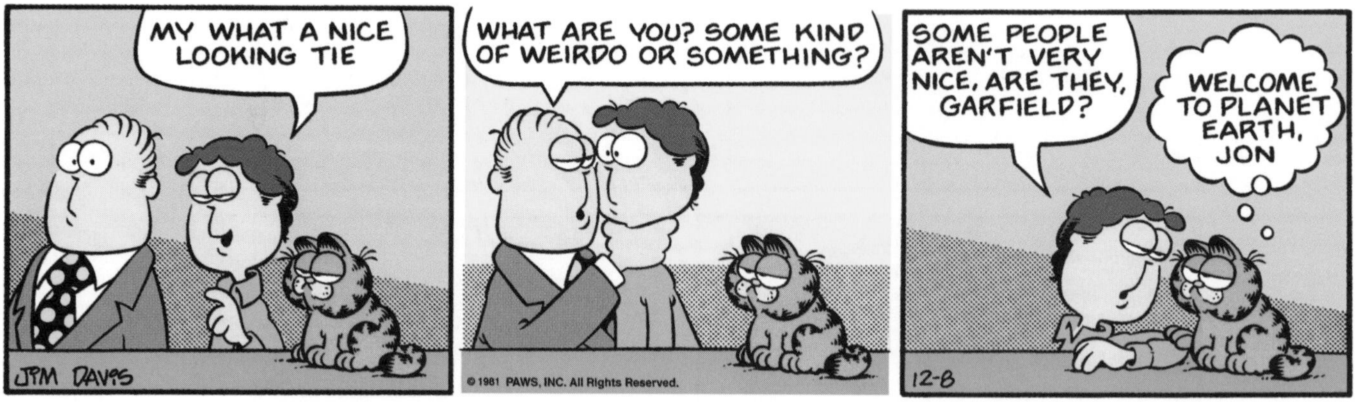
MY WHAT A NICE LOOKING TIE
JIM DAVIS
WHAT ARE YOU? SOME KIND OF WEIRDO OR SOMETHING?
© 1981 PAWS, INC. All Rights Reserved.
SOME PEOPLE AREN'T VERY NICE, ARE THEY, GARFIELD?
WELCOME TO PLANET EARTH, JON
12-8

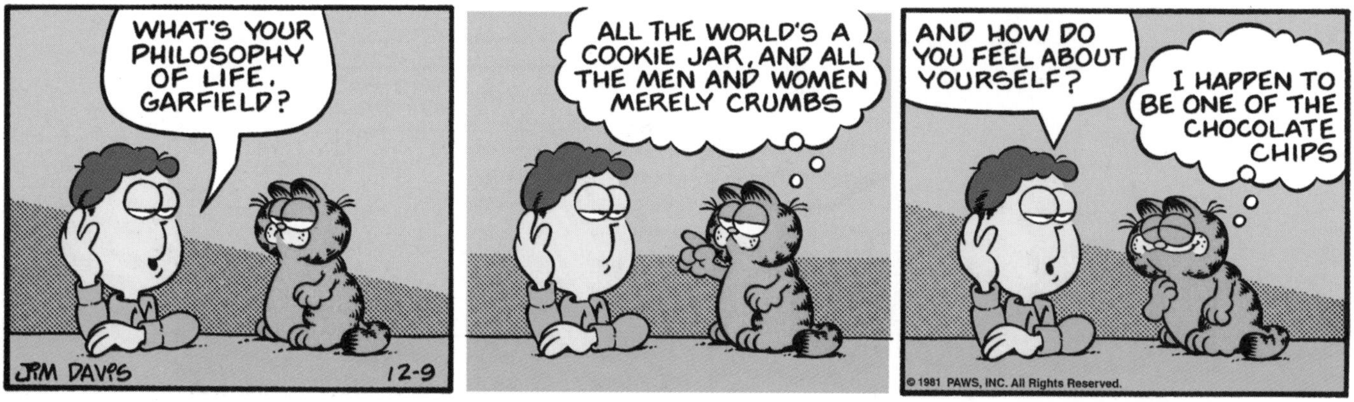
WHAT'S YOUR PHILOSOPHY OF LIFE, GARFIELD?
JIM DAVIS
12-9
ALL THE WORLD'S A COOKIE JAR, AND ALL THE MEN AND WOMEN MERELY CRUMBS
AND HOW DO YOU FEEL ABOUT YOURSELF?
I HAPPEN TO BE ONE OF THE CHOCOLATE CHIPS
© 1981 PAWS, INC. All Rights Reserved.

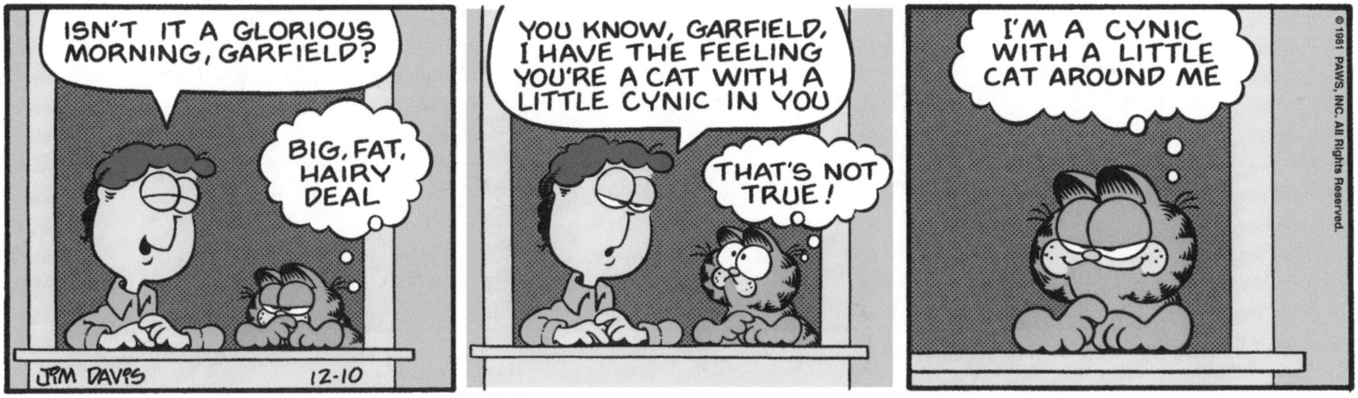
ISN'T IT A GLORIOUS MORNING, GARFIELD?
BIG, FAT, HAIRY DEAL
JIM DAVIS
12-10
YOU KNOW, GARFIELD, I HAVE THE FEELING YOU'RE A CAT WITH A LITTLE CYNIC IN YOU
THAT'S NOT TRUE!
I'M A CYNIC WITH A LITTLE CAT AROUND ME
© 1981 PAWS, INC. All Rights Reserved.

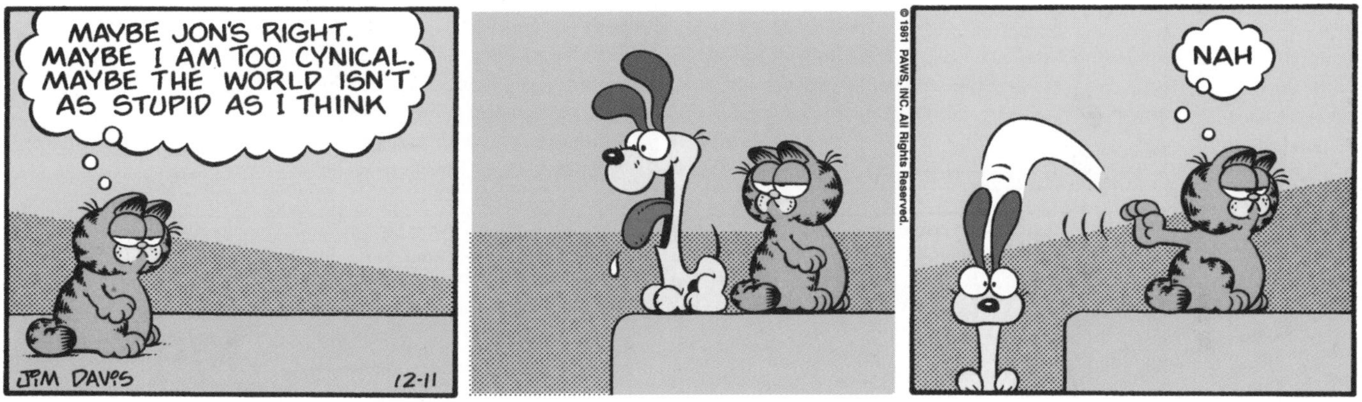
MAYBE JON'S RIGHT. MAYBE I AM TOO CYNICAL. MAYBE THE WORLD ISN'T AS STUPID AS I THINK
JIM DAVIS
12-11
© 1981 PAWS, INC. All Rights Reserved.
NAH

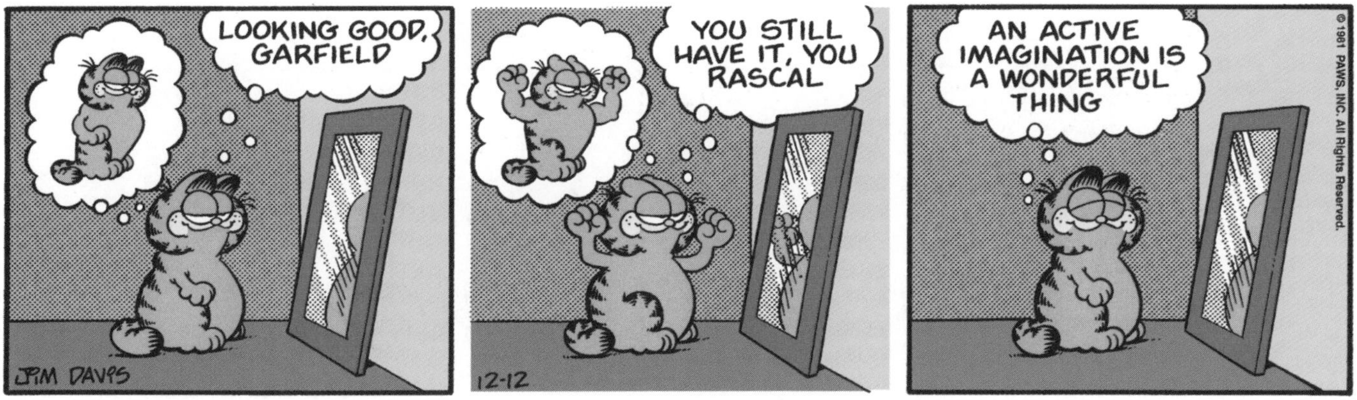
LOOKING GOOD, GARFIELD
JIM DAVIS
YOU STILL HAVE IT, YOU RASCAL
12-12
AN ACTIVE IMAGINATION IS A WONDERFUL THING
© 1981 PAWS, INC. All Rights Reserved.

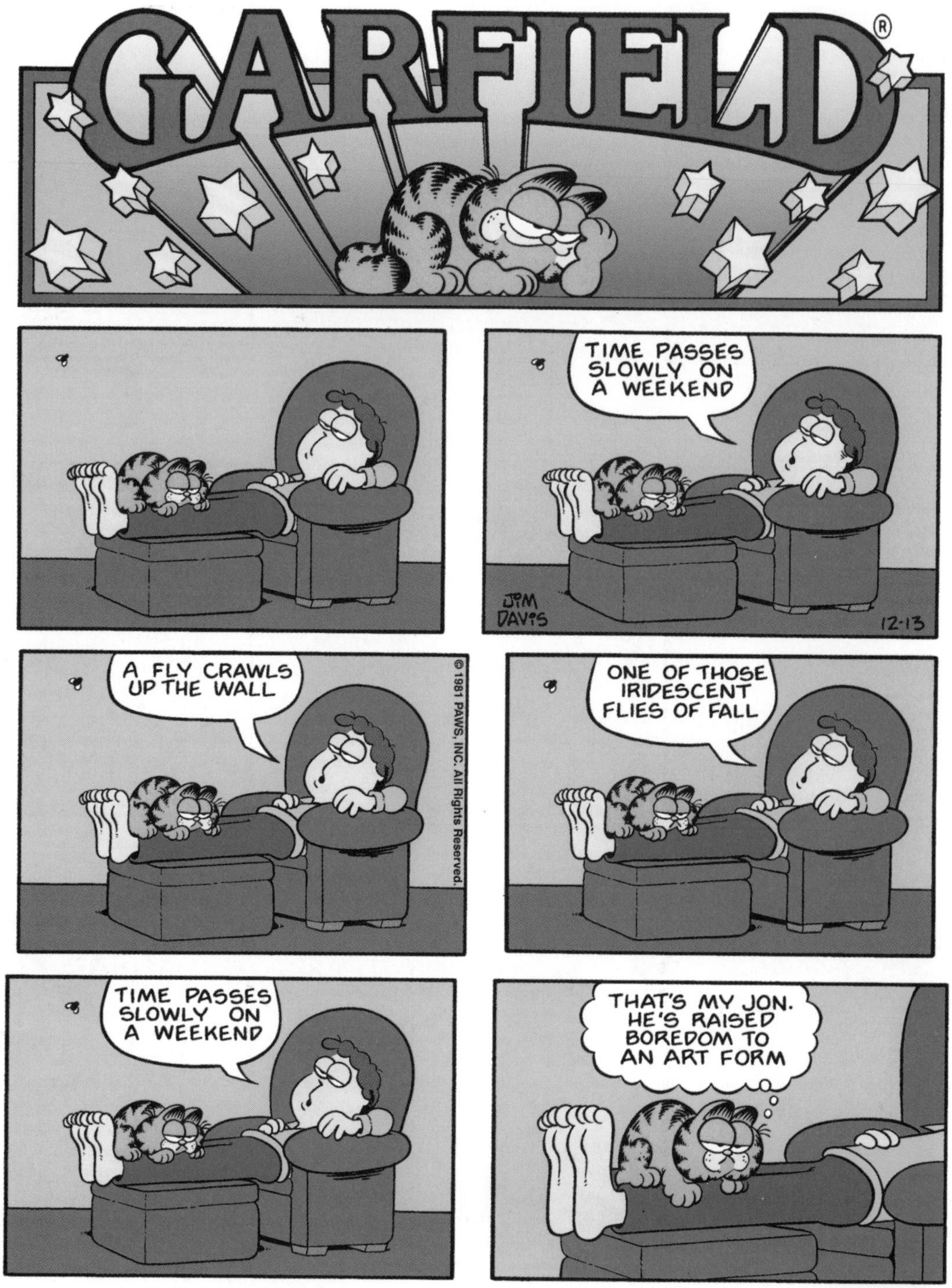
GARFIELD®
TIME PASSES SLOWLY ON A WEEKEND
JIM DAVIS
12-13
© 1981 PAWS, INC. All Rights Reserved.
A FLY CRAWLS UP THE WALL
ONE OF THOSE IRIDESCENT FLIES OF FALL
TIME PASSES SLOWLY ON A WEEKEND
THAT'S MY JON. HE'S RAISED BOREDOM TO AN ART FORM

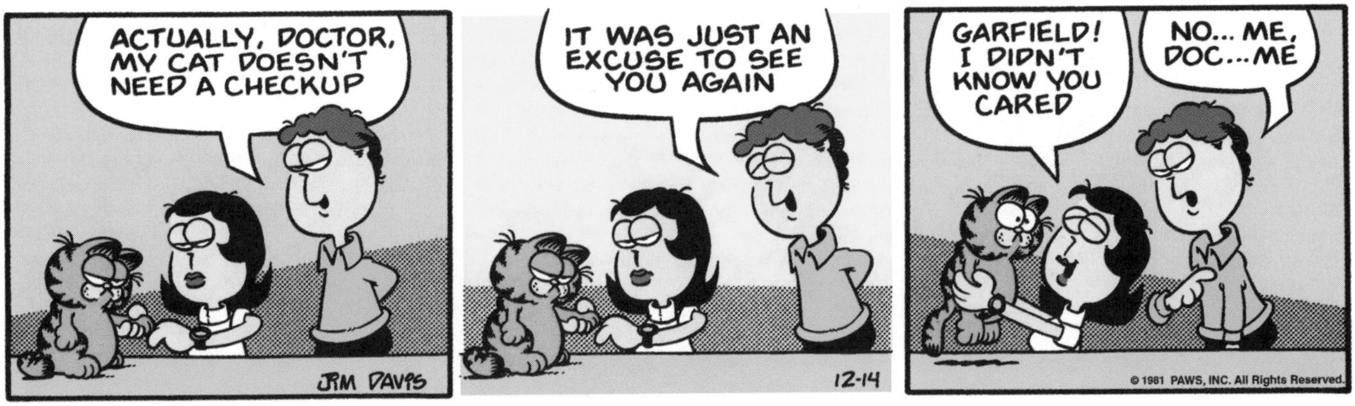
ACTUALLY, DOCTOR, MY CAT DOESN'T NEED A CHECKUP
JIM DAVIS
IT WAS JUST AN EXCUSE TO SEE YOU AGAIN
12-14
GARFIELD! I DIDN'T KNOW YOU CARED
NO... ME, DOC...ME
© 1981 PAWS, INC. All Rights Reserved.

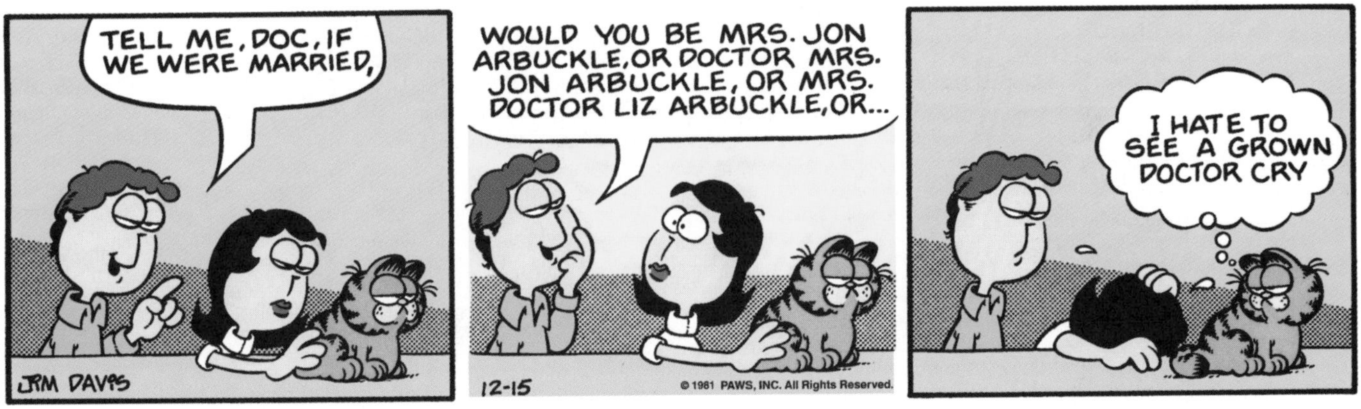
TELL ME, DOC, IF WE WERE MARRIED,
JIM DAVIS
WOULD YOU BE MRS. JON ARBUCKLE, OR DOCTOR MRS. JON ARBUCKLE, OR MRS. DOCTOR LIZ ARBUCKLE, OR...
12-15
© 1981 PAWS, INC. All Rights Reserved.
I HATE TO SEE A GROWN DOCTOR CRY

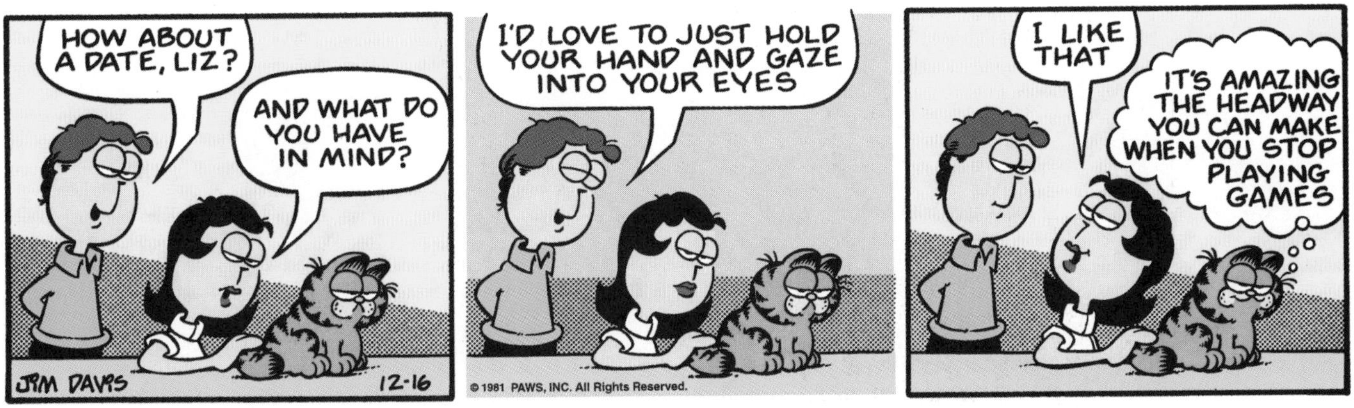
HOW ABOUT A DATE, LIZ?
AND WHAT DO YOU HAVE IN MIND?
JIM DAVIS
12-16
I'D LOVE TO JUST HOLD YOUR HAND AND GAZE INTO YOUR EYES
© 1981 PAWS, INC. All Rights Reserved.
I LIKE THAT
IT'S AMAZING THE HEADWAY YOU CAN MAKE WHEN YOU STOP PLAYING GAMES

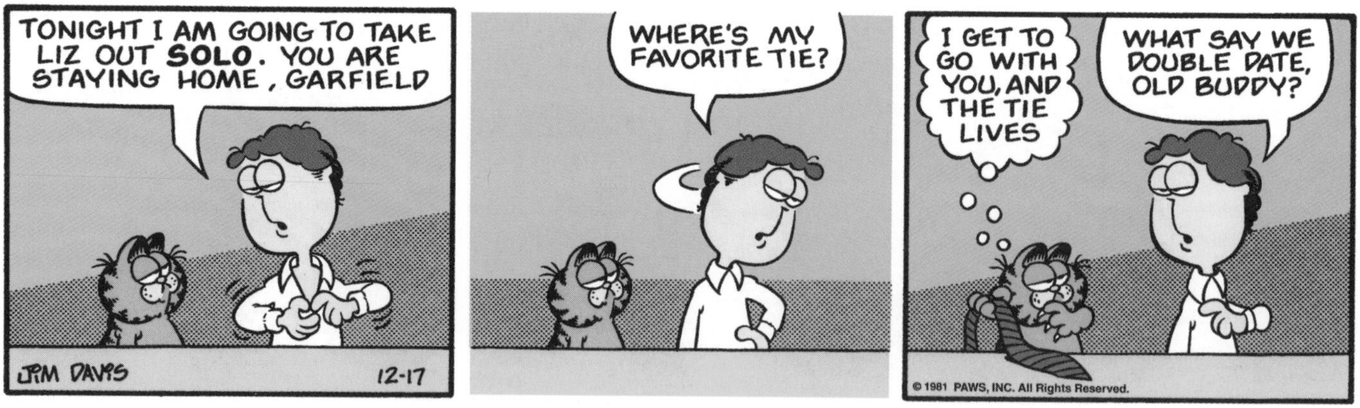
TONIGHT I AM GOING TO TAKE LIZ OUT SOLO. YOU ARE STAYING HOME, GARFIELD
JIM DAVIS
12-17
WHERE'S MY FAVORITE TIE?
I GET TO GO WITH YOU, AND THE TIE LIVES
WHAT SAY WE DOUBLE DATE, OLD BUDDY?
© 1981 PAWS, INC. All Rights Reserved.

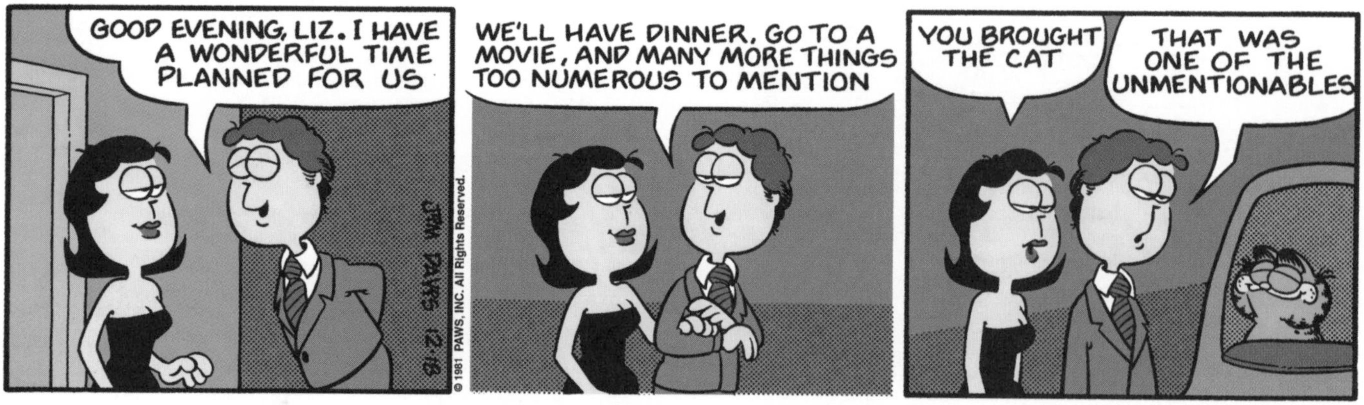
GOOD EVENING, LIZ. I HAVE A WONDERFUL TIME PLANNED FOR US
JIM DAVIS 12-18
© 1981 PAWS, INC. All Rights Reserved.
WE'LL HAVE DINNER, GO TO A MOVIE, AND MANY MORE THINGS TOO NUMEROUS TO MENTION
YOU BROUGHT THE CAT
THAT WAS ONE OF THE UNMENTIONABLES

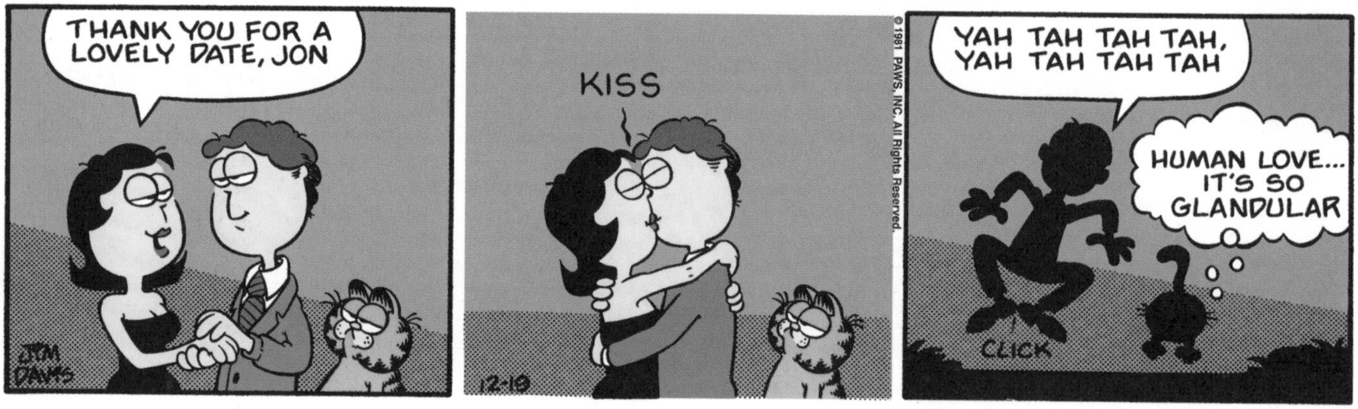
THANK YOU FOR A LOVELY DATE, JON
JIM DAVIS
KISS
12-19
© 1981 PAWS, INC. All Rights Reserved.
YAH TAH TAH TAH, YAH TAH TAH TAH
HUMAN LOVE... IT'S SO GLANDULAR
CLICK

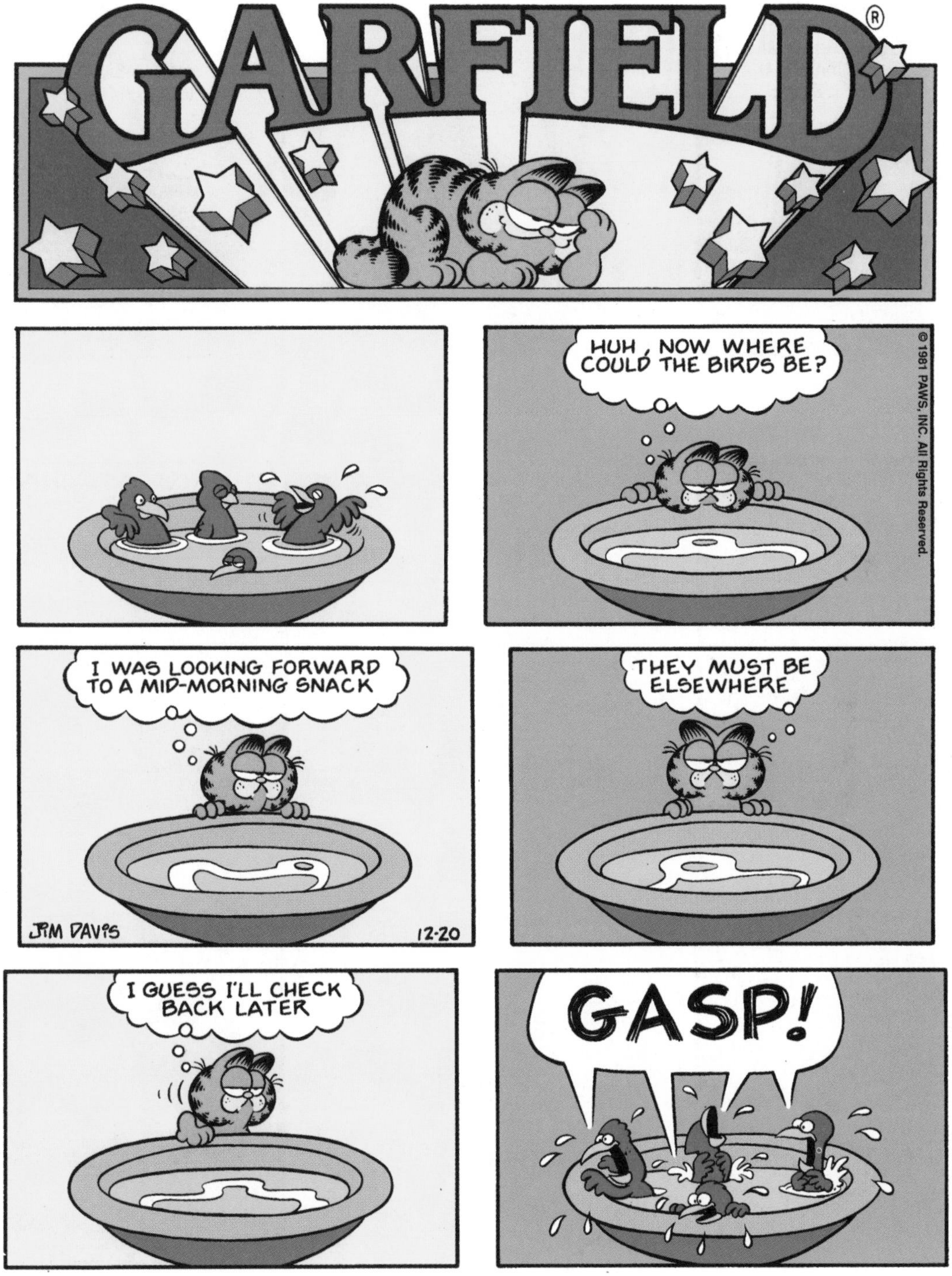
GARFIELD®
HUH, NOW WHERE COULD THE BIRDS BE?
© 1981 PAWS, INC. All Rights Reserved.
I WAS LOOKING FORWARD TO A MID-MORNING SNACK
JIM DAVIS
12-20
THEY MUST BE ELSEWHERE
I GUESS I'LL CHECK BACK LATER
GASP!

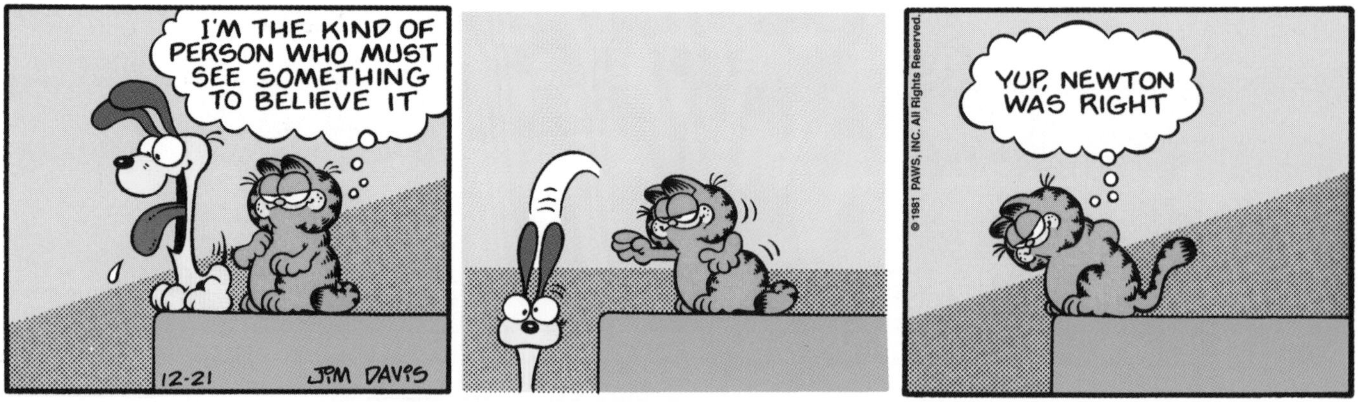
I'M THE KIND OF PERSON WHO MUST SEE SOMETHING TO BELIEVE IT
12-21
JIM DAVIS
© 1981 PAWS, INC. All Rights Reserved.
YUP, NEWTON WAS RIGHT

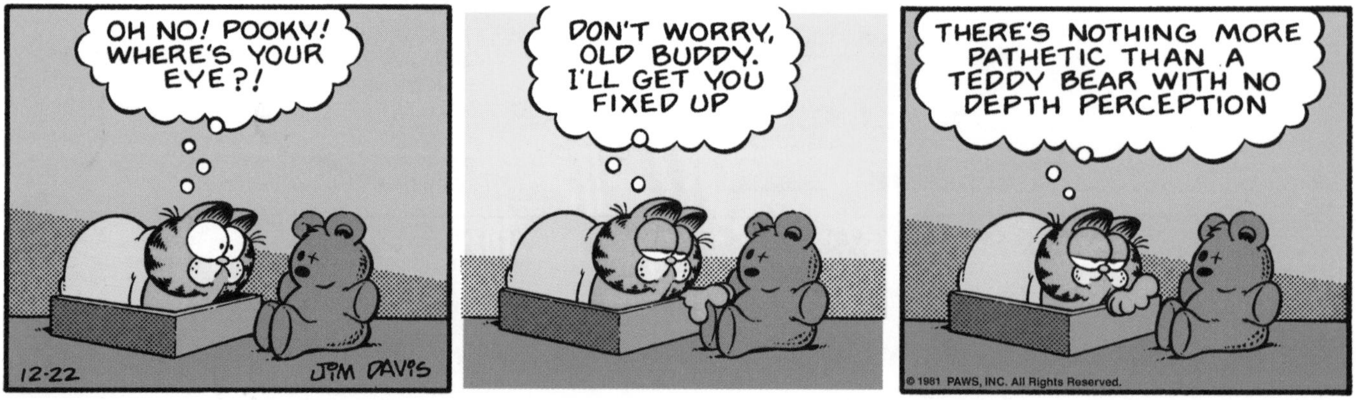
OH NO! POOKY! WHERE'S YOUR EYE?!
12-22
JIM DAVIS
DON'T WORRY, OLD BUDDY. I'LL GET YOU FIXED UP
THERE'S NOTHING MORE PATHETIC THAN A TEDDY BEAR WITH NO DEPTH PERCEPTION
© 1981 PAWS, INC. All Rights Reserved.

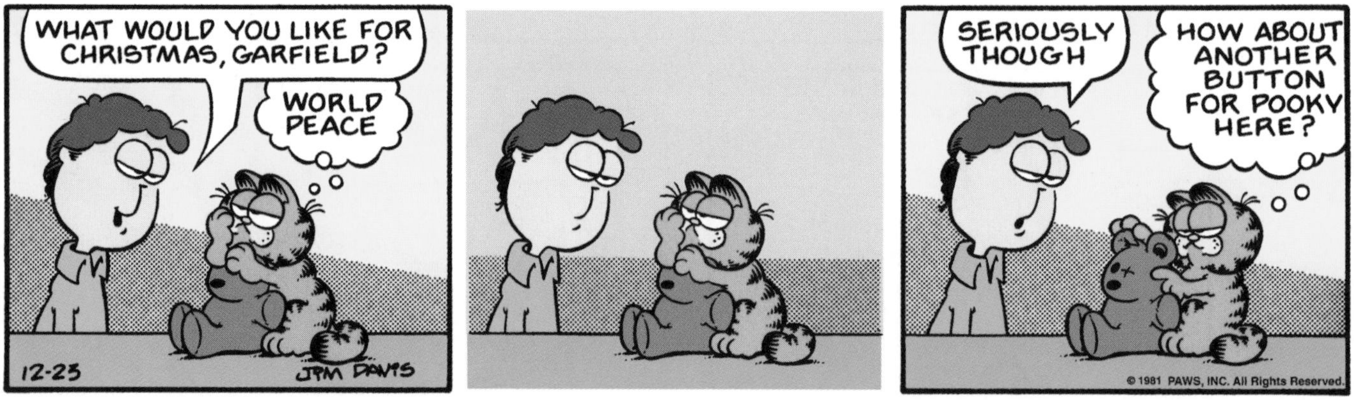
WHAT WOULD YOU LIKE FOR CHRISTMAS, GARFIELD?
WORLD PEACE
12-23
JIM DAVIS
SERIOUSLY THOUGH
HOW ABOUT ANOTHER BUTTON FOR POOKY HERE?
© 1981 PAWS, INC. All Rights Reserved.

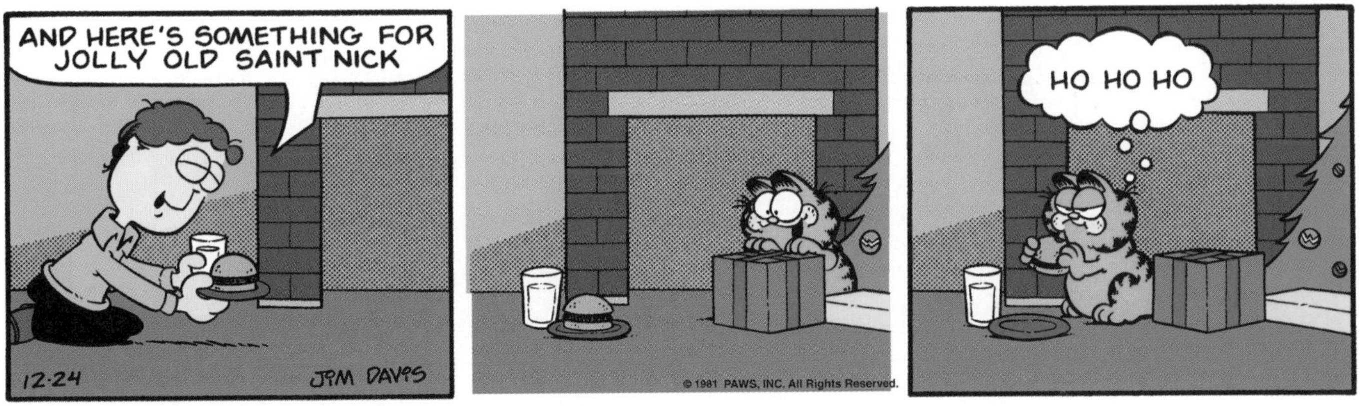
AND HERE'S SOMETHING FOR JOLLY OLD SAINT NICK
12·24
JIM DAVIS
© 1981 PAWS, INC. All Rights Reserved.
HO HO HO

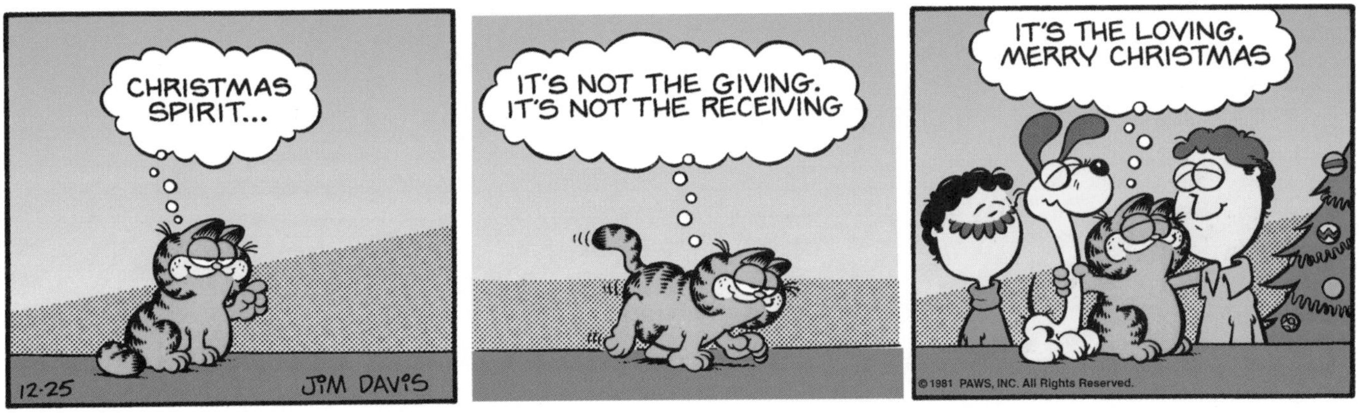
CHRISTMAS SPIRIT...
12·25
JIM DAVIS
IT'S NOT THE GIVING. IT'S NOT THE RECEIVING
IT'S THE LOVING. MERRY CHRISTMAS
© 1981 PAWS, INC. All Rights Reserved.

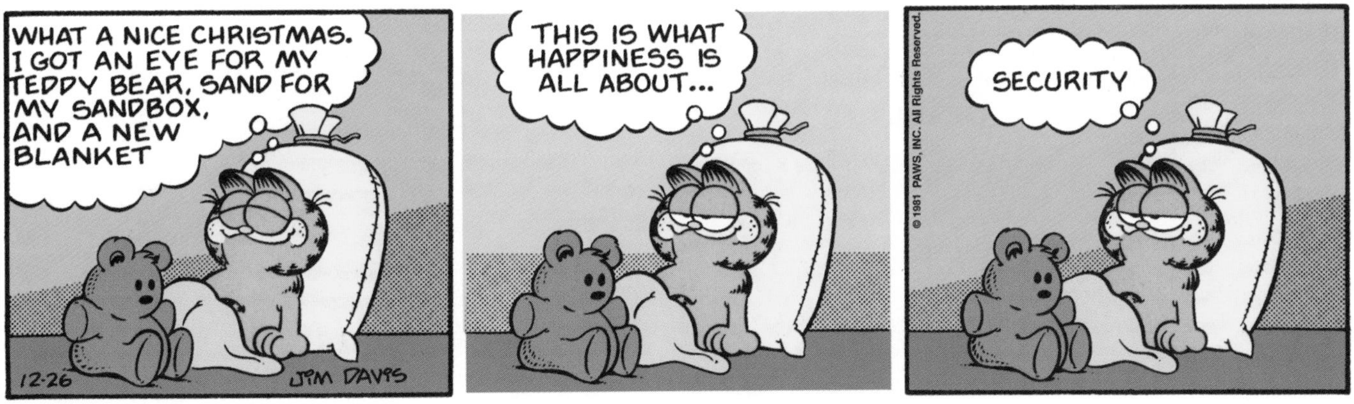
WHAT A NICE CHRISTMAS. I GOT AN EYE FOR MY TEDDY BEAR, SAND FOR MY SANDBOX, AND A NEW BLANKET
12·26
JIM DAVIS
THIS IS WHAT HAPPINESS IS ALL ABOUT...
© 1981 PAWS, INC. All Rights Reserved.
SECURITY

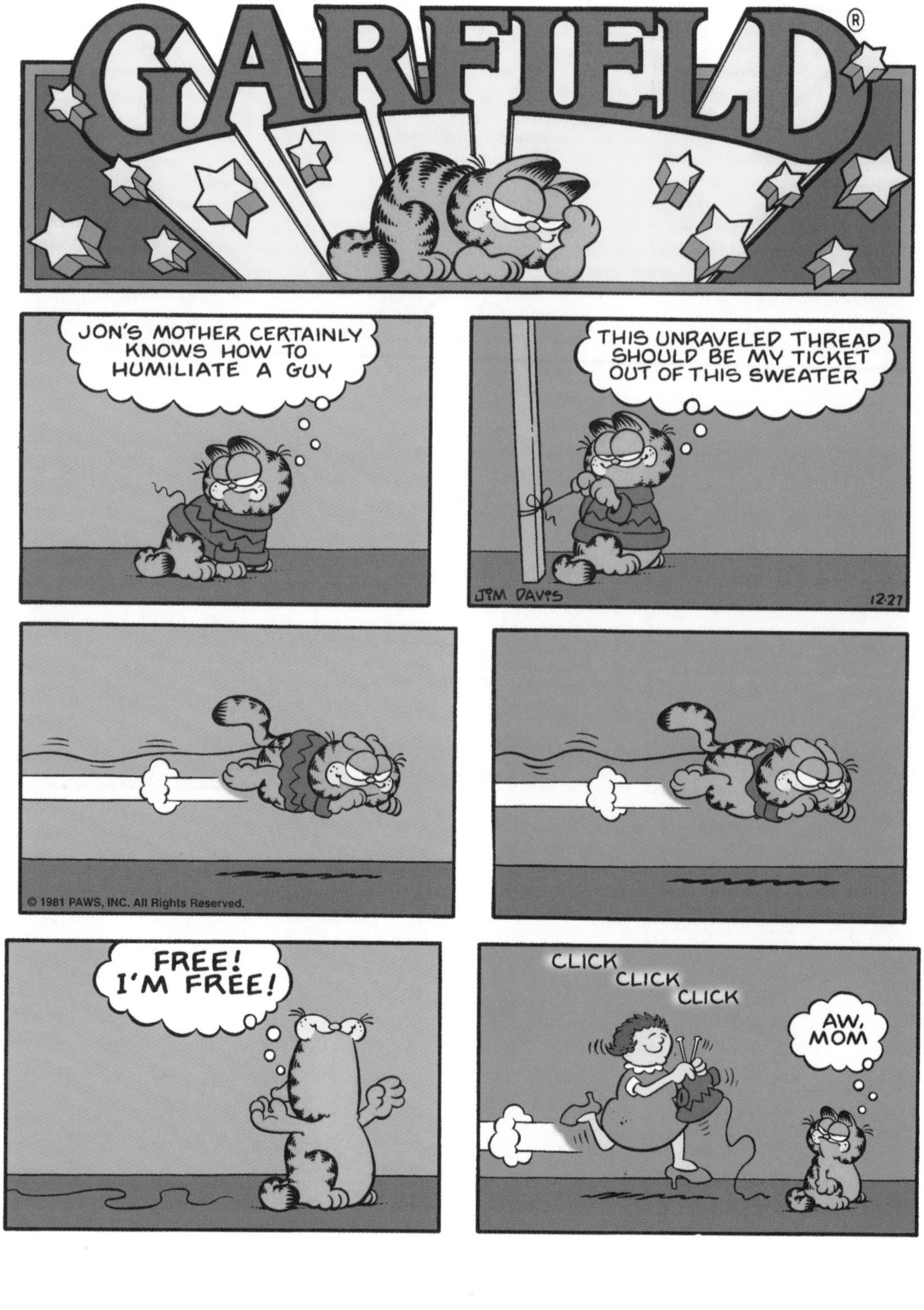
GARFIELD®
JON'S MOTHER CERTAINLY KNOWS HOW TO HUMILIATE A GUY
THIS UNRAVELED THREAD SHOULD BE MY TICKET OUT OF THIS SWEATER
JIM DAVIS
12·27
© 1981 PAWS, INC. All Rights Reserved.
FREE! I'M FREE!
CLICK CLICK CLICK
AW, MOM

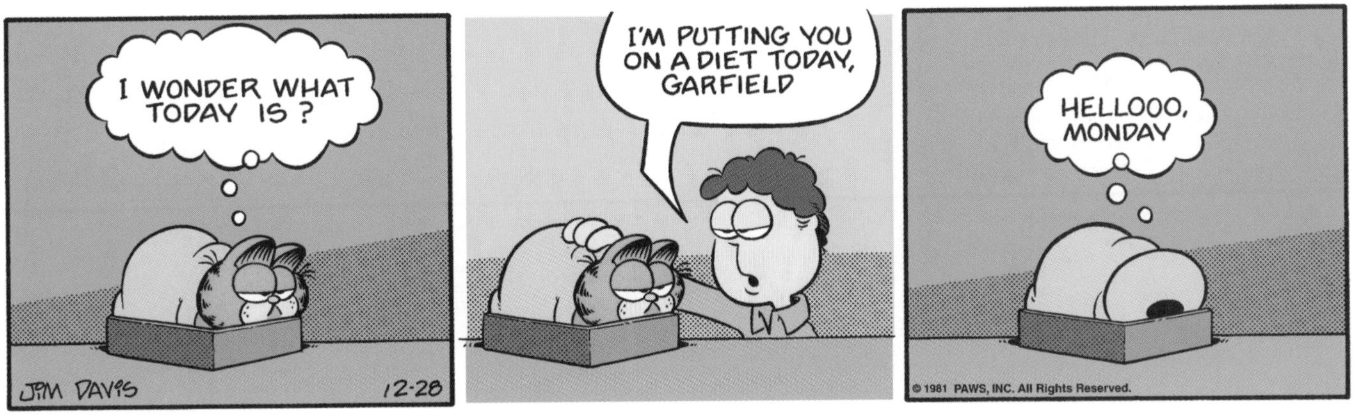
I WONDER WHAT TODAY IS ?
JIM DAVIS
12-28
I'M PUTTING YOU ON A DIET TODAY, GARFIELD
HELLOOO, MONDAY
© 1981 PAWS, INC. All Rights Reserved.

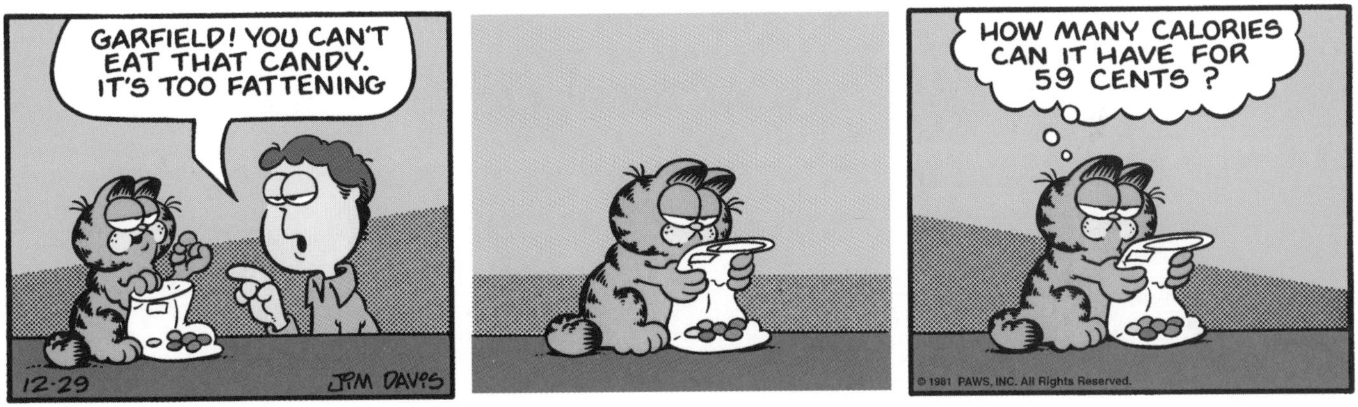
GARFIELD! YOU CAN'T EAT THAT CANDY. IT'S TOO FATTENING
12-29
JIM DAVIS
HOW MANY CALORIES CAN IT HAVE FOR 59 CENTS ?
© 1981 PAWS, INC. All Rights Reserved.

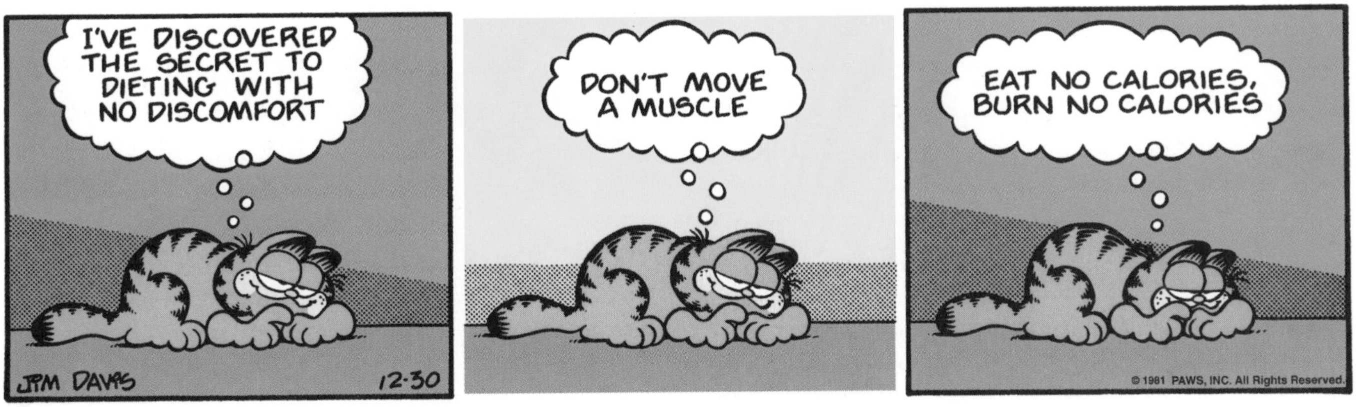
I'VE DISCOVERED THE SECRET TO DIETING WITH NO DISCOMFORT
JIM DAVIS
12-30
DON'T MOVE A MUSCLE
EAT NO CALORIES, BURN NO CALORIES
© 1981 PAWS, INC. All Rights Reserved.

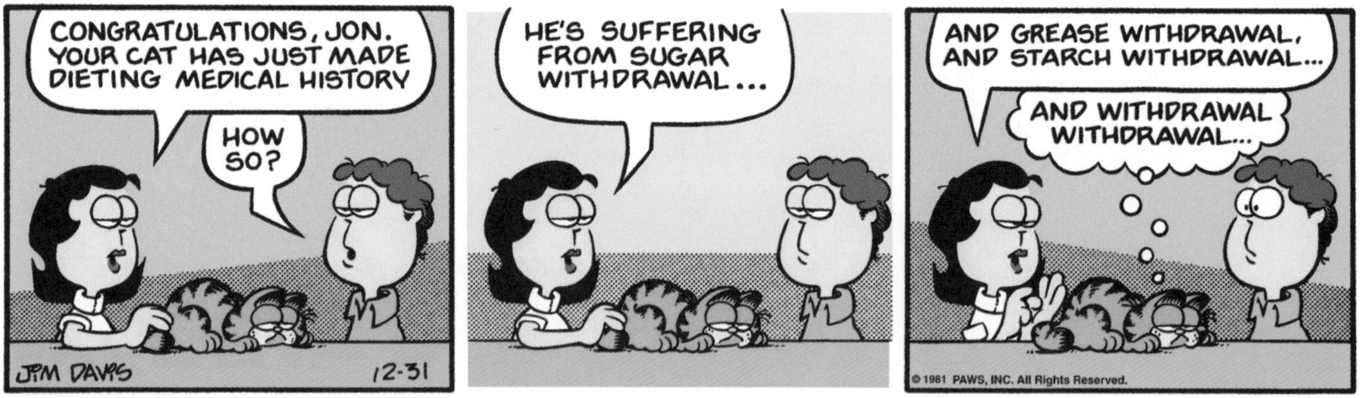
CONGRATULATIONS, JON. YOUR CAT HAS JUST MADE DIETING MEDICAL HISTORY
HOW SO?
JIM DAVIS
12-31
HE'S SUFFERING FROM SUGAR WITHDRAWAL...
AND GREASE WITHDRAWAL, AND STARCH WITHDRAWAL...
AND WITHDRAWAL WITHDRAWAL...
© 1981 PAWS, INC. All Rights Reserved.

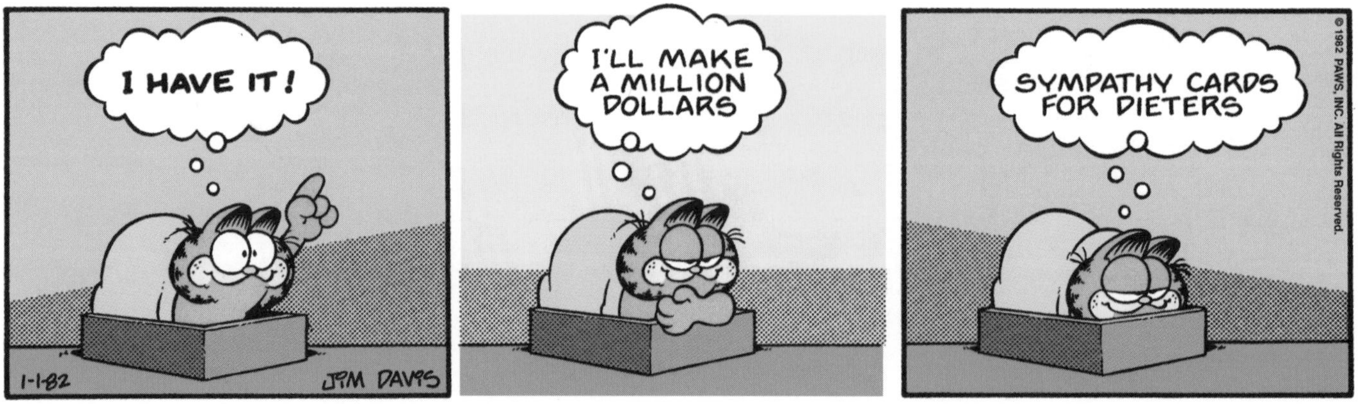
I HAVE IT!
1-1-82
JIM DAVIS
I'LL MAKE A MILLION DOLLARS
SYMPATHY CARDS FOR DIETERS
© 1982 PAWS, INC. All Rights Reserved.

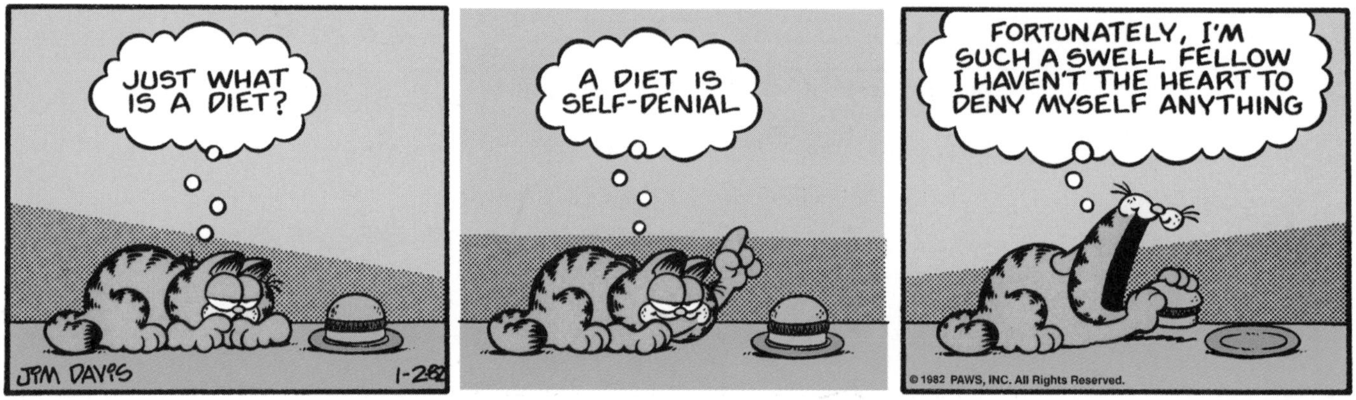
JUST WHAT IS A DIET?
JIM DAVIS
1-2-82
A DIET IS SELF-DENIAL
FORTUNATELY, I'M SUCH A SWELL FELLOW I HAVEN'T THE HEART TO DENY MYSELF ANYTHING
© 1982 PAWS, INC. All Rights Reserved.

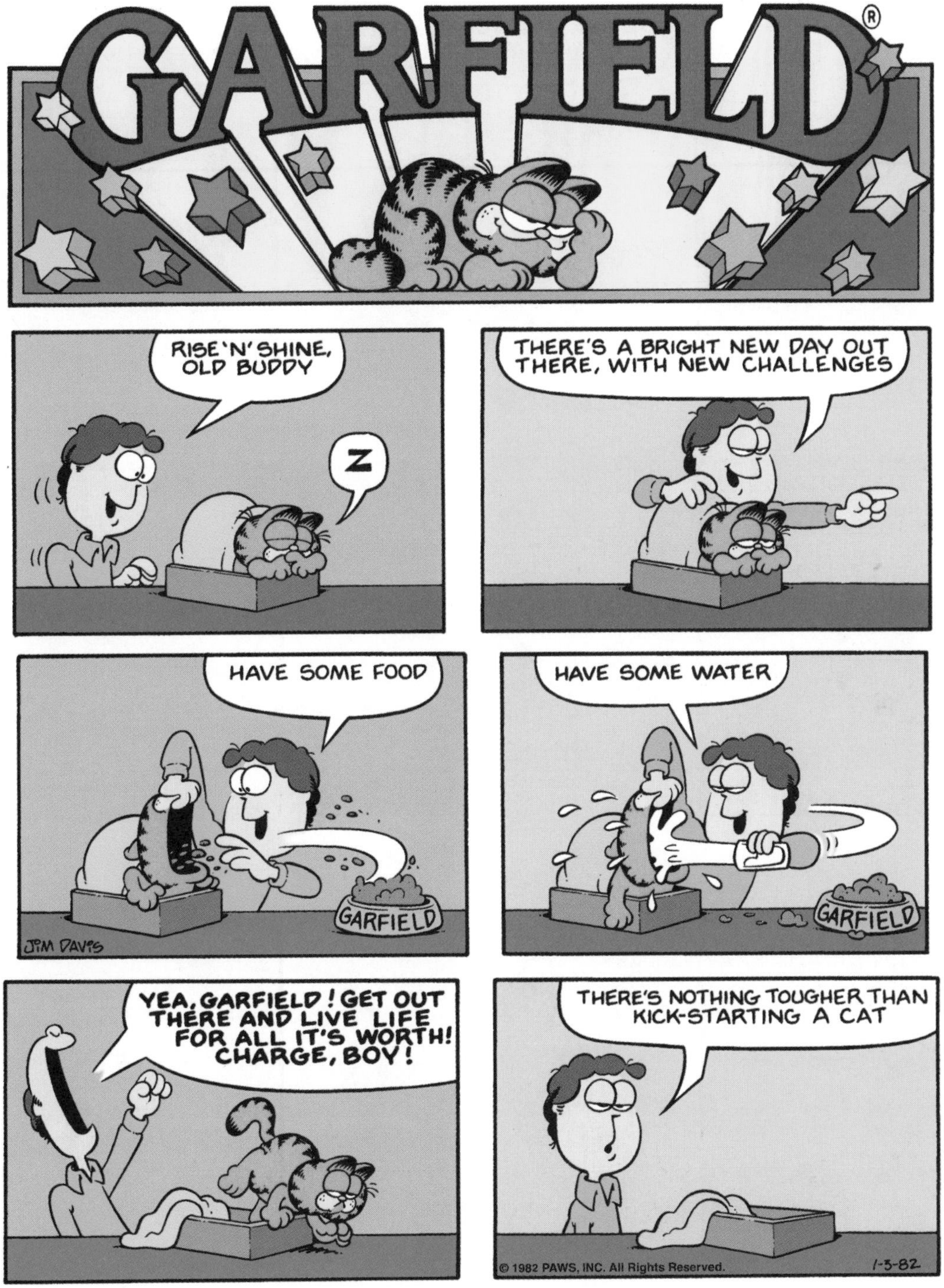
GARFIELD®
RISE 'N' SHINE, OLD BUDDY
Z
THERE'S A BRIGHT NEW DAY OUT THERE, WITH NEW CHALLENGES
HAVE SOME FOOD
GARFIELD
JIM DAVIS
HAVE SOME WATER
GARFIELD
YEA, GARFIELD! GET OUT THERE AND LIVE LIFE FOR ALL IT'S WORTH! CHARGE, BOY!
THERE'S NOTHING TOUGHER THAN KICK-STARTING A CAT
© 1982 PAWS, INC. All Rights Reserved.
1-3-82

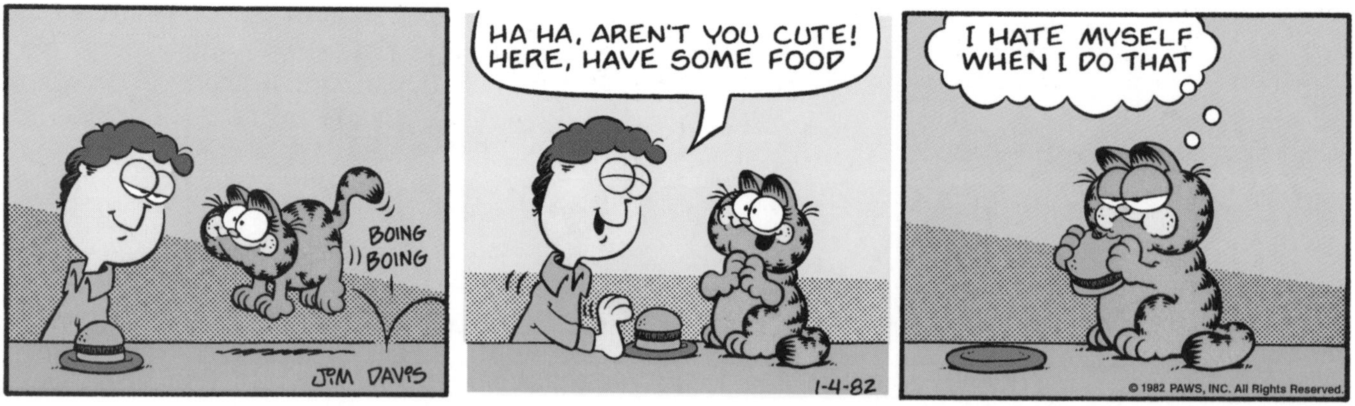
BOING
BOING
JIM DAVIS
HA HA, AREN'T YOU CUTE! HERE, HAVE SOME FOOD
1-4-82
I HATE MYSELF WHEN I DO THAT
© 1982 PAWS, INC. All Rights Reserved.

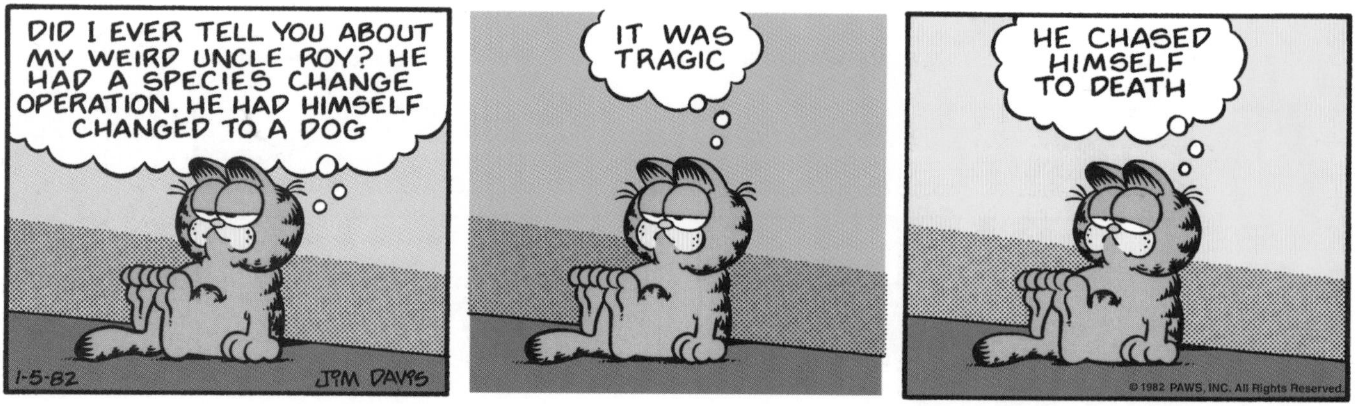
DID I EVER TELL YOU ABOUT MY WEIRD UNCLE ROY? HE HAD A SPECIES CHANGE OPERATION. HE HAD HIMSELF CHANGED TO A DOG
1-5-82
JIM DAVIS
IT WAS TRAGIC
HE CHASED HIMSELF TO DEATH
© 1982 PAWS, INC. All Rights Reserved.

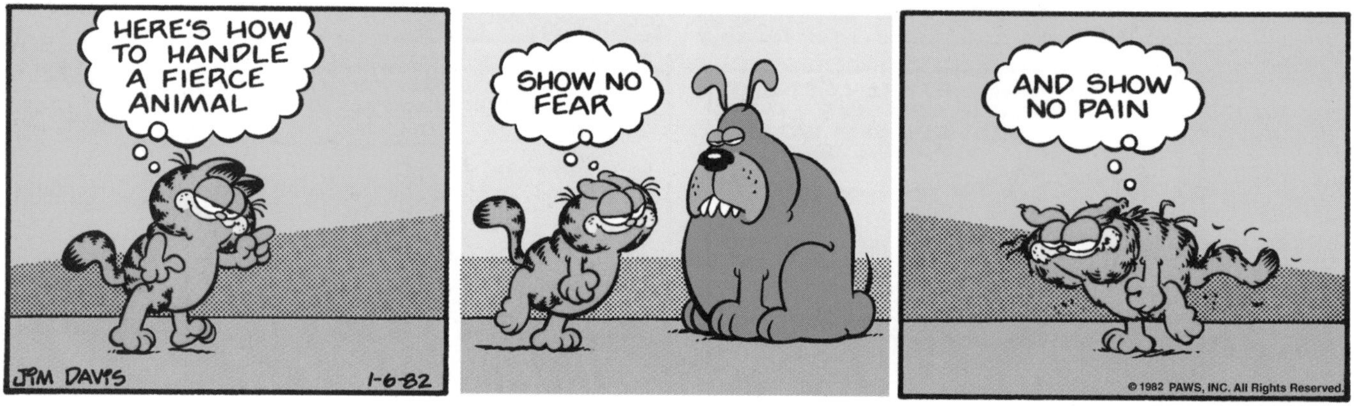
HERE'S HOW TO HANDLE A FIERCE ANIMAL
JIM DAVIS
1-6-82
SHOW NO FEAR
AND SHOW NO PAIN
© 1982 PAWS, INC. All Rights Reserved.

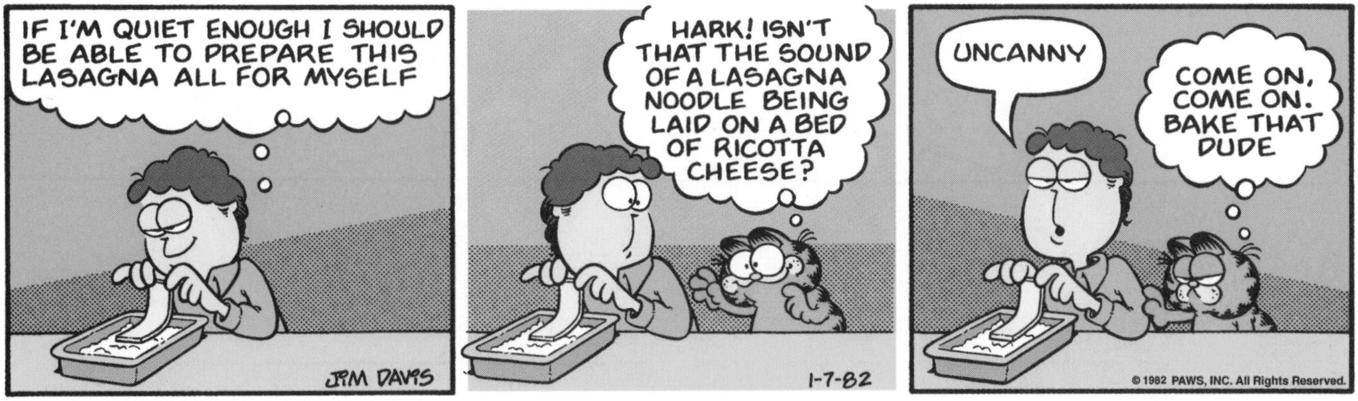
IF I'M QUIET ENOUGH I SHOULD BE ABLE TO PREPARE THIS LASAGNA ALL FOR MYSELF
JIM DAVIS
HARK! ISN'T THAT THE SOUND OF A LASAGNA NOODLE BEING LAID ON A BED OF RICOTTA CHEESE?
1-7-82
UNCANNY
COME ON, COME ON. BAKE THAT DUDE
© 1982 PAWS, INC. All Rights Reserved.

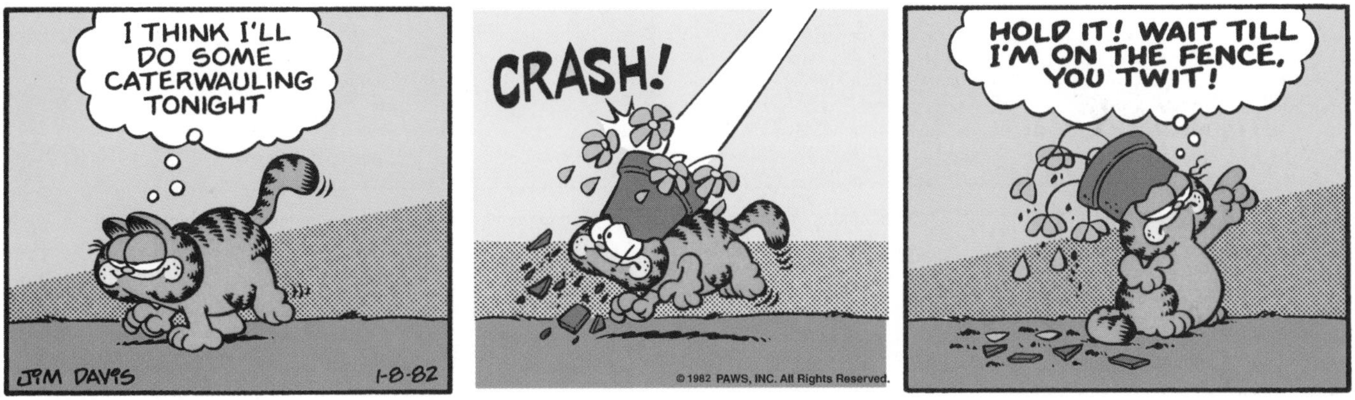
I THINK I'LL DO SOME CATERWAULING TONIGHT
JIM DAVIS
1-8-82
CRASH!
© 1982 PAWS, INC. All Rights Reserved.
HOLD IT! WAIT TILL I'M ON THE FENCE, YOU TWIT!

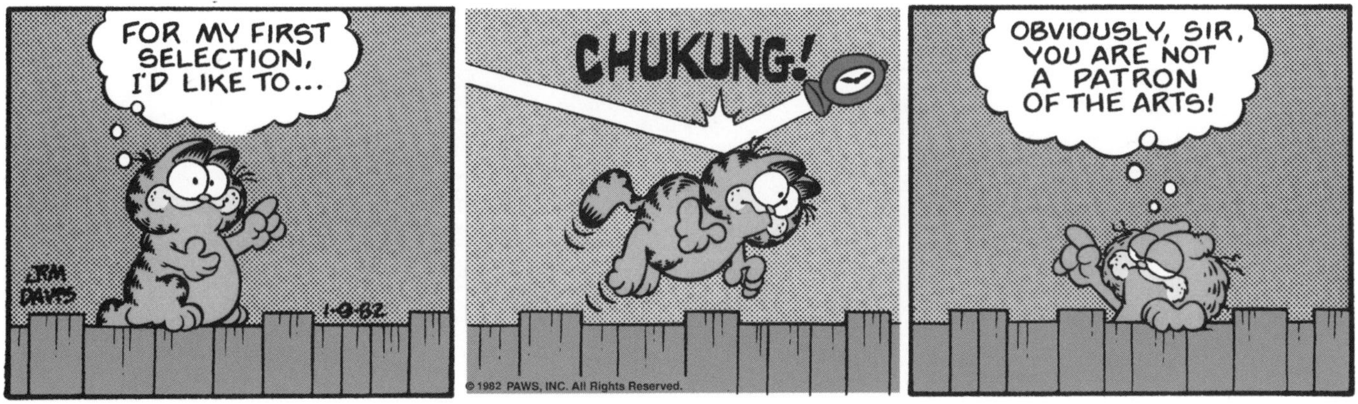
FOR MY FIRST SELECTION, I'D LIKE TO...
JIM DAVIS
1-9-82
CHUKUNG!
© 1982 PAWS, INC. All Rights Reserved.
OBVIOUSLY, SIR, YOU ARE NOT A PATRON OF THE ARTS!

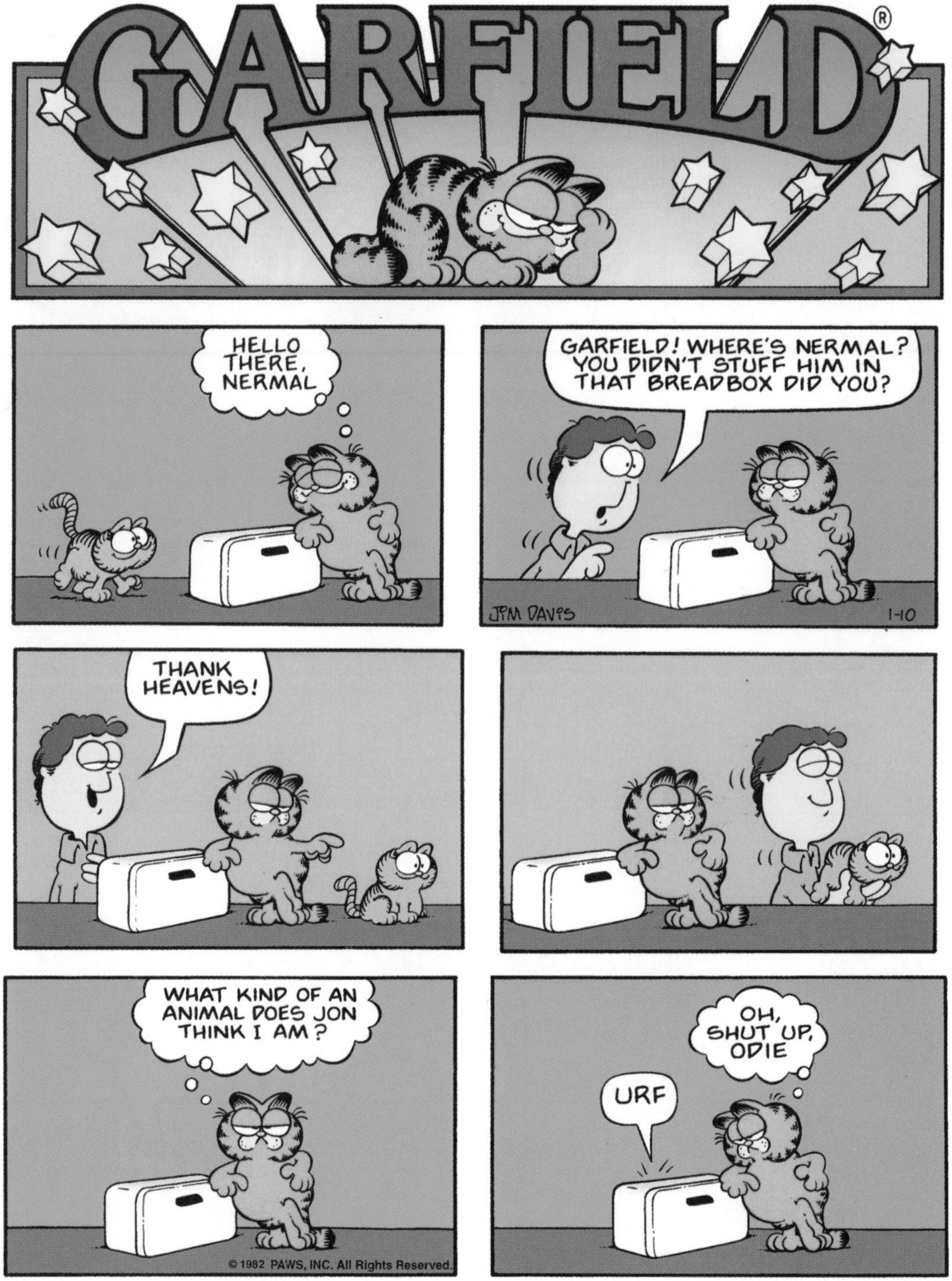
GARFIELD®
HELLO THERE, NERMAL
GARFIELD! WHERE'S NERMAL? YOU DIDN'T STUFF HIM IN THAT BREADBOX DID YOU?
JIM DAVIS
1-10
THANK HEAVENS!
WHAT KIND OF AN ANIMAL DOES JON THINK I AM?
URF
OH, SHUT UP, ODIE